Political Choice

Roland M. Czada,
Adrienne Windhoff-Héritier (Editors)

Political Choice

Institutions, Rules, and the Limits of Rationality

Campus Verlag · Frankfurt am Main
Westview Press · Boulder, Colorado

Copyright © 1991 by Campus Verlag, Frankfurt am Main

Published in 1991 in the United States by WESTVIEW PRESS
Frederick A. Praeger, Publisher
5500 Central Avenue
Boulder, Colorado 80301

Library of Congress Cataloging-in-Publication Data

Political choice : institutions, rules, and the limits of rationality
/ edited by Roland M. Czada and Adrienne Windhoff-Héritier.
   p. cm.
   ISBN 0-8133-1164-0
   1. Political science--Decision making. I. Czada, Roland M.
II. Windhoff-Héritier, Adrienne, 1944–
JA74.P623 1990
306.2--dc20   90-40917
                                                                    CIP

CIP-Titelaufnahme der Deutschen Bibliothek

Political choice : institutions, rules, and the limits of
rationality / Roland M. Czada ; Adrienne Windhoff-Héritier
(Ed.). – Frankfurt am Main : Campus Verlag ; Boulder, Colo. :
Westview Press, 1991
   ISBN 3-593-34342-8
NE: Czada, Roland M. [Hrsg.]

Contents

I don't think that the system of self-interest as it is professed in America is in all its parts self-evident, but it contains a great number of truths, so evident, that men, if they are only educated, can't fail to see them.

Alexis de Tocqueville, 1835

Preface

The idea of this book was born on the occasion of a birthday celebration that was held in Konstanz in honor of Gerhard Lehmbruch. Asked whether he would prefer an international conference or a publication as a present to his 60th birthday, Gerhard Lehmbruch did not hesitate to choose the conference. As it turned out, he has not been spared either one. A lively and fruitful academic discussion emerged at the conference, focusing on the interplay of institutions, collective action, and choices in politics. Contributions which explored recent major trends in theory-building have been included in this volume.

The authors proceed from different approaches: concepts of corporatism and network-analysis, organization theory, institutional economics, rational choice and game theory. Each of the chapters written by Gerhard Lehmbruch, Johan P. Olsen, Fritz W. Scharpf, Adrienne Windhoff-Héritier, Wolfgang Streeck, Marc Schneiberg and J. Rogers Hollingsworth, Franz Lehner, and Roland M. Czada represents at least one of these fields of research. All focus, however, on the question: Which particular rules, logics, or strategies of action can be found in the realm of politics? As such "political choice" and, generally, the institutionalization and mechanisms of governance and interest intermediation come to the fore.

Whereas structures and outcomes of interest intermediation in and between organized groups have been discussed in a large body of literature, the principles of political - in contrast to economic - choice have rarely been analyzed. From an institutionalist point of view, political choices aim at and are influenced by organizational structures, conventional procedures, legal-administrative rules, and organizational incentives. Relations of choice and structure compose the logics of political action. The authors discuss these in terms of "garbage can solutions", strategic dilemmas, association-building, and social networking, as well as constraints, rigidities, or even pathologies of institutional decision-making.

We are grateful to many people for their help. The "Deutsche Forschungsgemeinschaft" (German Research Foundation), the "Fritz-Thyssen-Stiftung" (Fritz-Thyssen-Foudation), and the "Freunde und Förderer der Universität Konstanz" (Sponsors of the University of Konstanz) generously supported our international conference. We also like to thank all paper-givers and discussants, who, with the authors included in this volume, contributed to the liveliness and yields of the debate: Hans Daalder, Wolfgang Fach, Peter Gerlich, Henry J. Jacek, Berndt Keller, Peter Knoepfel, Michael Kreile, Claus Offe, Victor Pestoff, Manfred G. Schmidt, and Phillipe C. Schmitter. In particular, we wish to thank Karin Tritt, Hans Dieterle, Anne Hodgson, Njunga M. Mulikita, and Janett McPherson for seeing the book through publication and proof-reading.

October 1990

Roland M. Czada
Adrienne Windhoff-Héritier

Contributors

Roland M. Czada, Assistant Professor, Faculty of Administrative Science, University of Konstanz

Rogers M. Hollingsworth, Professor of History, Sociology and Industrial Relations, University of Wisconsin, Madison

Gerhard Lehmbruch, Professor of Political Science, University of Konstanz

Franz Lehner, Professor of Political Science, Ruhr-University, Bochum, and President of the Institute for Work and Technology, Gelsenkirchen

Johan P. Olsen, Professor of Public Administration and Organisation Theory, Norwegian Research Center in Organization and Management, Bergen

Fritz W. Scharpf, Professor of Political Science, Director at the Max-Planck-Institute for Social Research, Köln

Marc Schneiberg, Lecturer at the Department of Sociology, University of Wisconsin, Madison

Wolfgang Streeck, Professor of Sociology and Industrial Relations, University of Wisconsin, Madison

Adrienne Windhoff-Héritier, Professor of Political Science, University of Bielefeld

I

INTRODUCTION

Adrienne Windhoff-Héritier
and Roland M. Czada

We use the concept of *political choice* to express the thrust of argument underlying the contributions to this volume. It implies that there is a difference between the formation of social choice and actors' political choices. Politics is a process based on relations of conflict and consensus among interdependent individual and corporate actors. It depends on actors' deliberate choices achieved within specific institutional settings and results in decisions or policies that are binding for individual and corporate actors within territorial (state, county, municipality) or social organizational boundaries (firm, association). A potential sanctioning power is added to the mandatory character of these decisions. As far as state politics is concerned, this includes the legitimate use of physical force. Political choices, however, are not necessarily located within the state's organizational domain. Contractual relationships, private corporate hierarchies, or social associations employ such choices as well - although their ultimate legitimation is usually derived from state laws and governmental direction.

Political choices aim at desired macro states and imply actors' aspirations to guide social processes through collective action or individual interaction. Contrary to the functioning of markets or any other processes of transitory coupling between individuals, politics is characterized by actors' attempts to manage *micro-macro links of action*. Therefore, the concept of political choice, in our view has to deal with efforts to coordinate mutually depent actors, organize collective action, and exercise social guidance in order to reach individually desired social states. Political choices attempt to overcome self-regulatory social processes.

Let us discuss the *"invisible hand mechanism"* of a migrational process and confront it with a scenario of political choice in order to illustrate our point. People moving from one place to another, simultaneously contribute to changes in the social structure of communities. Thus, as an unintended consequence of their moves, they influence the very conditions which have induced them (and other actors) to move. Individually, rational actors then become "victims" of a systemic process, in which seperate though interdependent individuals unintentionally influence macro-structures which in turn feed back on their future choices. This pattern of emerging social states is devoid of politics. Politics comes in when actors realize that their own interests can only be realized when mobility is controlled. As a consequence, they will try to change the self-regulatory character of the migrational process. They will no longer only move where they wish to, but will also try to shape the conditions under which people can move; for instance by enacting specific zoning laws. In brief, actors try to influence the social conditions of their individual lives and fortunes through political choices.

Social rules, administrative routines, institutions and traditional patterns of policy-making, as emphasized in Olsen's and Lehmbruch's contributions, are obviously also intended to shape social macro states. They can substitute actual policial choices and, therefore, lie within the scope of political inquiry. The same holds true for strategies of policy-making like bargaining or "problem-solving" (cf. Scharpf, this volume). Going beyond an institutional definition of politics, which is commonly bound to a state-centered view, one could say that political action seeks to convert the transitory linking of individual actions into patterns of joint, or consciously coordinated actions.

Non-political social choices can be viewed without the notion of an actor, since a systemic process occuring "behind the backs" of single actors translates their choices into social aggregates and, in this manner, determines the macro-level consequences of individual actions. Political science explains why, how, and to what ends men engage in public affairs in order to reach their individual goals, resisting to the fate of being entrapped by anonymous social processes.

Most of the contributions to this volume are based on the assumption that political action can be understood in terms of rationality. Corresponding to the above argument, this implies that political actors have a particular awareness of individual and collective goals, which they seek to make congruent. Viewing a set of alternatives, preferences can be conceived of as preference orders. One cannot postulate, however, that such preference orders are stable or exogeneously given. This follows from the processual character and dynamics of politics, which compel actors to cope with changing social ecologies. Additionally, nothing is said about the rational foundations of political choices. There are many faces to the rationality of political actors. They may follow time-tested "rules of appropriateness" and institutional guidance (cf. Olsen's contribution) or estimate the actual costs and benefits of their action. In a real world involving incomplete information and high costs of decision making, choices can also be called rational if they evolve from experience and are approved of in interaction. This is particularly true when interactional dilemmas or the public goods problem compel political actors to make and eventually test assumptions about the behavior of others.

Political choice, shaping mandatory policies for collectivities, is concerned with the provision of public goods. These are characterized by the jointness of supply and differing degrees of excludability with respect to consumption. Once provided to one member of a specific group, a public good cannot feasibly be withheld from any other member of that group. By contrast, the notion of social choice is not limited to the provision of public goods. Economists have traditionally studied the allocation of private goods through rationally motivated exchanges on markets. While the market process is based on individual actors' choices, its social outcome - the overall allocation of goods - can be conceived of as supra-individual social choice. Arrow (1963:1) distinguished "two methods by which social choices can be made: voting, typically used to make political decisions, and the market mechanism, typically used to make economic decisions".

The term *public choice* has been applied to the making of collective decisions based on individual preferences. Public choice theory deals with the economic study of nonmarket decision-making, i.e. the translation of individual preferences into public choices, either by voting or collective action. Unlike the course of practical politics, however, public choice theory conceives of this process as being purely aggregative. It neglects the integrative functions of interest associations, parties, and administrations. In reality, however, politics is bound to the *organization* of individuals. It is true that Mancur Olson's theory of collective action considers interest group formation and its effects on politics. In his theory, however, collective action is based on aggregative mechanisms as well. Political choices, however, should be viewed as being subjected to integrative forces of social institutions, organizations, and rule-systems. Strategies of political actors depend on historical paths of institutionalization as elucidated in Gerhard Lehmbruch's contribution. They may follow established rules of appropriateness, as stressed by Johan P. Olsen, or employ interactional strategies of bargaining and "problem-solving", as analyzed by Fritz W. Scharpf.

While public choice theory is oriented to the social outcomes of individual choices, game theory concentrates on problems of strategic interaction between two actors. It deals with actors' choices in specific interest constellations like "Prisoner's Dilemma", "Assurance Game", "Chicken Game", or "Battle of the Sexes". Game theory attempts to explain the stability of interactional strategies solely in terms of individual pay-offs, and, hence, disregards social outcomes. The authors of this volume, however, suggest various answers to the question of how actors' rational choices can be linked to institutional rules and social outcomes of decision-making.

Thus, from different viewpoints, the essays contribute to currently debated problems of a macro-micro theory of action. In politics, the value of institutions as macro-pillars protecting micro-actors, and thereby enabling them to choose between alternatives in a rational fashion, has been appreciated since millennia. It seems adequate to subsume the following chapters under the notion of political choice, since they deal with possible syntheses of concepts of rational choice and action with the idea of institutional embeddedness, constraints, and opportunities of policy-making processes.

The first part of the book, subtitled "political actors in institutional settings", addresses the main lines of reasoning of the new political institutionalism and rational choice theory. The situation of political science, being confronted with two explanatory paradigms, is discussed in Adrienne Windhoff-Héritier's contribution. In her view, both *rational choice theory* and the *new political institutionalism* offer central insights into political processes, and the elimination of one paradigm to the benefit of the other would entail a loss in the explanatory power of political science. Accordingly, the central question is not which analytical approach should be used, but rather how to link the analytical possibilities of a rational choice perspective to an institutionalist approach. In order to deal with this question, the contribution focuses on the concept of "constraints", since political institutions constitute a central element of the restrictions determining the actions of the individual agent.

A first analytical link of rational choice theory and institutionalism may be seen in the *"Two Filter Model"* (Elster 1979). In a first filter process structural constraints, such as political institutions, determine the realm of possible action alternatives of the individual: "the feasible set". A second filter process consists of an actor's choice of an alternative among the possible options, guided by individual rationality principles.

However, the analytical perspective also points in the opposite direction and shows that institutional structures flow in part from rational choices of political actors, as shown by constitutional economics. The development of self-binding constitutional principles which limit democratic majoritarian decisions may serve as a case in point. This does not mean that institutions can be reduced to individual rational decisions. For institutions expand so widely in space and time that "... they escape the control of every individual actor" (Giddens 1988:78).

Institutions do not only function as restrictions of individual action, they also offer opportunities for action, or even enable action, by making the environment of the individual calculable and reliable. Since institutions hardly ever determine actions completely, they still leave room for self-interested and strategic action. The possibilities of these strategic actions depend - according to an organizational resource dependence model - on an actor's specific resources within the context of a specific policy field.

Consequently, linking the analytical perspectives of rational choice and political institutionalism seems not only logically and empirically possible and necessary, but should also be supplemented by a third analytical view: the specific policy context within which it is embedded. The surrounding policy field implies a specific distribution of resources among the actors concerned which engage in rational and strategic decision-making processes within the enabling and restricting institutional environment.

Fritz W. Scharpf, in his essay, elaborates on the relationship between political institution, on the one hand, and the quality of policy choice, on the other. What are the institutional variables determining the opportunities of political actors and which policy results do they produce - as measured by the quality of interpersonal inclusiveness ("are the objectively affected interests considered in choice processes?"), their intertemporal quality ("are they able to stand the test of time?"), and finally, by their collective social welfare function? Boundary and decision rules - in Scharpf's view - are the most important institutional variables shaping policy outputs. As compared to markets and hierarchies, which are rather well understood by now, the frequency and importance of consensual and unanimous coordination has been underestimated. While unanimous decisions serve to defend existing patterns of distribution (under the condition that exit is only possible under high costs for all parties concerned), hierarchical and majoritarian decision rules offer the possibility of involuntary redistribution. Hierarchical rules also include the possibility of considering long-term policy concerns, while majoritarian decision rules tend to favor short-term benefits. Although policy consequences may be related to institutional rules in such rudimentary ways, Scharpf emphasizes the perplexing empirical findings that "similar institutions will work differently in different countries and at different times, and that similar policy choices may be produced within highly dissimilar institutional arrangements". He concludes that there must be additional factors affecting policy choices which may modify the influence of institutional arrangements and decision rules.

These factors may be viewed as different *"styles of decision-making"*, namely confrontation, bargaining and problem solving. Applying these decision-styles to various mixed-motive games, theoretical arrangements such as "Assurance", "Prisoner's Dilemma", "Chicken", and "Battle of the Sexes" may help to explain policy choices. "Battle of the Sexes", in particular, applies to a wide range of empirical political situations in which benefits are dependent upon the ability to cooperate, but cooperation is seriously threatened by conflict over the choice of one of two possible cooperative solutions.

However, in order to introduce the decision-styles as an additional explanatory factor, the game-theoretical assumptions need to be expanded to overcome the "motivational simplifications of microeconomics". Scharpf uses the concept of Kelley/Thibaut, who distinguish between the "given" and "effective payoff-matrix", the former being the objective payoff-matrix, the latter the one effectively determining the choices of the players. The difference between the two matrices are interpreted according to certain rules by the concerned parties. The rules are identical with the "decision styles" suggested by Scharpf. The most important rules are "the maximization of one's own gain," "the maximization of one's relative gain," and "the maximization of joint gains." The first rule of "own gain maximization" leaves the given matrix or objective matrix unchanged. It corresponds to the individualistic rational assumptions of micro-economics and conventional game theory claiming that actors are solely maximizing their own payoffs and coincides with the decision style of bargaining. Under conditions of "Battle of the Sexes", "relative gain maximization" implies the competitive transformation of the "objective matrix": the parties concerned are not interested in mutual advantageous compromises; the game is about losing or winning, and corresponds to the decision style of "confrontation". The third rule, finally, is identical with "problem solving", since the actors are interested in cooperation, seeking an alternative that achieves the highest joint outcome for both. Within the context of this rule the individualistic view, typical for micro-economics, is transcended. Thus, these three distinct social psychological mechanisms, and this is the central argument forwarded by Scharpf, imply a critique of political institutionalism as well as of the individualistic viewpoint of rational choice theory. The three decision styles of "bargaining", "confrontation", and "problem solving" will influence the likelihood of socially superior or inferior policy choices quite independently from the applicable formal rules of decision-making.

Johan P. Olsen, in his chapter concentrates on how administrative rules determine administrative action, and thus, substitute for consequential rational choices in politics and administration. He tackles this by assessing the mutual analytical benefits which political science and organization theory offer each other. His argument: integrating organization theory may help political science to develop a new political institutionalist theory that does not merely consist of a modification of a theory of choice, conceiving of decision-makers as rational, strategic self-interested actors, but offers an alternative theory which takes account of the weight of institutional structures, rules, and ideologies. He points to the need of focusing on models at the meso-level; models of institutions, rather than models of man. According to Olsen, institutional theory conceives of man as having a potential for manifold decision-making behaviors. They may act goal-oriented or follow institutionally defined rules and obligations, they may identify with a variety of smaller or larger collectives, such as organizations, professions, or client groups. A central task is to clarify how organizational contexts influence the potentials which are actually evoked. Organization theory draws attention to the role of political institutions, to the questions of how they are organized, what their causal impact is, and how they change.

Contrary, however, to the view that decision-making is a result of choices made by well informed, rational individuals, Olsen stresses that bounded rationality, conflict, and ambiguity are typical traits of organizational decision-making. Standard operating procedures, i.e. routinized, experience-based programs of action (as distinguished from formal, legal sets of rules), can predict behavior in relatively great detail. The logic of "appropriateness" means that individual action is guided by duties and obligations rather than by calculations of the returns expected from alternative choices. The "Garbage can model" of organizational decision processes suggest a temporal rather than a causal-instrumental order of behavior (cf. March and Olsen 1976). Organizational routines buffer organizational decision-making from environmental influence as well as from the self-interested behavior of organizational members.

Viewed in such a mode, politics does not only deal with "Who gets what" through analyzing the allocation of scarce resources, but is also a vehicle for educating citizens, improving cultural values, and testing individual and group preferences, rather than just aggregating them.

A critical point in assessing the power of an analytical approach is its capacity to explain institutional change. In the view of institutionalism, the possibilities for intentional institutional change are constrained by earlier choices and institutional history. "If institutions can be instantaneously and costlessly transformed to new optimality every time functional imperatives change there is no need for an institutionalist perspective." (p. 101) The institutional approach predicts infrequent changes, primarily in crisis-situations. "The solutions selected are, then frozen into structures which constrain future change" (p. 101) and entail relatively long periods of stability.

Due to their mere existence, which influence options for policy-making and institutional change, existing political institutions in Olsen's view are the main "building blocks of politics".

Picking up the institutionalist argument, Gerhard Lehmbruch's essay offers an explanation of how administrative rules of conduct emerged from historical political choices. He focuses on the contribution of national state traditions to the configuration of policy-networks between public administrations and organized groups of society. Corporatist theories, he argues, explain cross-sectoral variations of such networks from strategic choices and structural preconditions such as for instance the centralization and membership density of interest associations. Cross-national variations, however, might be better explained by administrative strategies towards organized interests. Linkages of governments and organized interests came into being during formative phases of national bureaucracies. They may then have become dissociated from the strategic choices of that formative phase and have survived as institutional residues of past organizational options. One can understand policy networks as the result of a process in which the developments of state structures and societal organizations interact in a sequential manner.

Lehmbruch emphazises that interactions of government bureaucracies with associations or other corporate economic actors constitute a link between the national macro level and sectoral meso levels of governance. Thus, despite the sectoral task contingencies of associations, administrative strategies towards associations can explain the apparent correlation between organizational properties of sectoral groups such as farmers associations and labor unions within nation states.

A comparison of French, Swiss, Austrian, and American historical experiences demonstrates the different strategic codes of national bureaucracies which are employed in their relationships with economic interests. To understand national policy-networks, Lehmbruch argues, is not simply to describe inter-organizational linkages, but includes the reconstruction of underlying rule-systems that support their institutionalization. Such rule-systems can be traced back to certain interpretational concepts of state and society that have been important during formative phases of national bureaucracies. Lehmbruch points to the Hegelian view of a unitary bureaucracy representing the general interest of society. With regard to Prussia this was the product of a situation in which the Prussian society lacked strong autonomous organizations. In such a state without religious, ethnic, legal and geographic unity, the civil service was the only integrating element and the driving force of social reform. Hegel's view of an autonomous administration continued to be effective in the later German national state, and still influenced Max Weber's notion of an instrumental civil service with its disinterested bureaucratic ethos.

The second part of the book focuses on "the politics of collective action". While the view of integrative institutions prevails, emphasis is placed on the formation and conditions of choice in interest-associations and structures of interest-intermediation. Wolfgang Streeck concentrates on how the capacity to organize interests is determined by their heterogeneity. He confronts Offe's and Wiesenthal's theory of "two logics of collective action" with a body of empirical data on sectoral associational systems of business and labor in nine countries. The results of his analysis show that the organizational patterns of the two classes differ strongly, but in the opposite direction of what the theory predicts. Streeck argues that the superior ability of labor to build encompassing organizations cannot be explained by a higher organizational capacity to manage interest heterogeneity. It is due to the absence of a range of interests from trade union concerns, namely interests concerned with "trade" or "production" in particular, which are more specific and divisive than labor market or "class" interests. Since the former type of interests are often shared with capital, trade unions in modern, "mature" industrial relations systems have been able to leave their pursuit to business associations, thereby protecting their own organizational unity. It is suggested that with the progressive "dematurity" of industrial relations under "Post-Fordist" economic and institutional conditions, trade unions should be less able than in the past to avoid organizational fragmentation by evading the domain of production-related interests. Streeck predicts a more decentralized organizational pattern of labor which is more similar to that of capital.

Marc Schneiberg and Rogers Hollingsworth discuss an explanation of trade associations that concentrates on their cost-saving properties in relation to transactions on markets. Assuming that institutions can be understood in terms of their capacity to regulate transactions in an efficient and economic manner, they use an approach that rejects technological, legal, and class-analytic explanations of organizational action. However, constructing an alternative theory of governance that dimensionalizes transactions, identifies mechanisms and institutional arrangements, which "harmonize the interfaces" between actors and uses a comparative assessment of the cost and performance attributes of these arrangements, cannot fully explain organization-building from rational choices of individual or corporate actors.

The analysis shows that Transaction Cost Economics cannot explain the initial emergence or the ongoing reproduction of economic associations. Actors create these associations for strategic and distributional purposes, that is, to enhance their power. In particular they try to shift the risks and burdens of adjustment onto their exchange partners. Moreover, firms choose an associative strategy in order to regulate relations in which they perceive themselves as vulnerable to the strategic behavior of others. They do that whether prior transfers of goods and services took place or not. Schneiberg and Hollingsworth emphasize that state policies toward associational action play a far more important role than competition and transaction-cost economizing. Nevertheless, they conclude that Transaction Cost Economics allow valuable insights within a more general theory of the factors, forces, motives, and contextual conditions underlying governance structures and their transformation. This is shown by the following chapter, in which systems of interest-intermediation, consociationalism and corporatism in particular, are being compared with respect of their cost-effectiveness and allocative effciency.

Franz Lehner, in his contribution, focuses on how special interest groups affect the authority and efficiency of governments in the field of economic policy-making. He, too, applies a politico-economic approach, emphazising the decision-costs and externalities associated with different institutional arrangements. Following

Buchanan and Tullock (1962), decision-making in institutions is characterized by an inverse relation of decision-costs and externalities. Lehner argues that the extent to which decision-costs reduce efficiency depends upon the internal structures of distributional coalitions and the types of policy. Comparing the Swiss consociational system of interest intermediation with Austrian and Swedish experiences, he states that in all three cases the costs of decision-making are high. However, complex coalition-building of small narrow interest groups in Switzerland restricts the externalization of agreement costs to the public sector, whereas highly centralized and powerful corporatist associations have led to considerable fiscal expansion in Austria and Sweden.

The analysis indicates that arrangements associated with high decision-costs do not restrict the capacities of economic policy-making, which are generally high in consociationalist and corporatist systems. They reduce externalities and allow for long-term structural policies. Corporatism, however, concentrates social power. This enables dominant organizational powers to externalize the costs of decisions in a cartel-like manner. Therefore, the outcomes of corporatist structures differ from the Swiss-type consociationalism. Moreover, Lehner argues that the nature of economic problems affects the appropriateness of certain institutional solutions as well.

Rationalities of interest intermediation, its action patterns and characteristic outcomes, are also at the center of Roland M. Czada's contribution. Whereas several chapters emphasized the positive effects of organization, namely the routinization of action, decreasing transaction-costs, and opportunities for strategic interaction, Czada raises the question whether and how rational actors respond to the growth, stickiness, and economic malfeasance of institutions.

Political actors interested in strenghtening their power position in the face of distributional conflict build coalitions with others and organize their political activities. Thus, problems of associational order and interorganizational relations arise. The social closure of interests, biases of political representation, and rigidities of income-distribution have been held responsible for declining economies by many economists and politicians. In reality, however, the flexibility and adaptibility of social and political institutions varies considerably across nations, and it is still an open question how economic markets and interest associations interact, and how economic welfare is affected by specific forms of governance. Czada, starting from Mancur Olson's "stagnation hypothesis", explains why social rigidities are much less ubiquitous in democratic systems than predicted.

Three principle mechanisms are identified as preventing social rigidities and economic decline. 1. Inefficient political redistributions cause "dead-weight" losses which eventually deteriorate the cost-benefit relation of beneficiaries and encourage the opposition of negatively affected narrow interest groups (cf. Becker 1986). 2. Scale-economies of associations favour encompassing organisations and "inclusive" social networks which can be viewed as joint ventures economizing the costs of interest-politics in fields where overlapping interests of narrowly defined groups are concerned. 3. Multiple individual preferences and overlapping membership being neglected in current theories of rational choice, imply intersecting group-boundaries and result in a rationally motivated openness of actors.

In general, these mechanisms support a relative social openness as well as the universalisation and efficiency of social order. However, their concrete operation depends on institutional and, probably, cultural prerequisites, and does not solve the manifold problems of economic governance in an equally efficient manner. Hence, their effectiveness varies across countries with different institutions, social cleavages, and economic problems.

Roland Czada concludes that in a democratic system with freedom of association, cost/benefit calculations of interest politics and the intersection of group-boundaries typically counteract the organization and pressure for singular ends of narrow interest groups. Therefore, in the context of economic rather than democratic theory, associational interest intermediation is likely to promote allocative efficiency and economic wealth.

References

Arrow, Kenneth, J. (1963) *Social Choice and Individual Values*, 2nd edn, New York: Wiley.

Becker, Gary, S. (1986) 'Public Policies, Pressure Groups and Dead Weight Costs', pp. 85-105 in George W. Stigler (ed.) *Chicago Studies in Political Economy*. Chicago: University of Chicago Press.

Giddens, Antony (1988) *Die Konstitution der Gesellschaft*. Frankfurt: Campus Verlag.

Elster, Jon (1979) *Ulysses and the Sirens*. Cambridge: Cambridge University Press.

March, James, G. (1978) 'Bounded Rationality, Ambiguity, and the Engineering of Choice'. *Bell Journal of Economics* 9:587-608.

March, James G. and Johan P. Olsen (1976) *Ambiguity and Choice in Organizations*. Bergen: Universitetsforlaget.

Olson, Mancur (1982) *The Rise and Decline of Nations. Economic Growth, Stagflation and Social Rigidities*. New Haven, London: Yale University Press.

Part one

Rational Actors in
Institutional Settings

II

Institutions, Interests and Political Choice

Adrienne Windhoff-Héritier

In the past years homo oeconomicus has invaded political sciences, rational choice explanations penetrating into all fields of research: Voters presumably vote with respect to their interests and legislators organize coalitions according to their intentions. Bureaucratic and associative behavior, even the development of constitutions - all enjoy the analytical attention of rational choice theorists. In their view political decisions result from a rational process which assesses the benefits and costs of a specific course of action in the light of defined targets.

Inspite of, or because of its fascinating simplicity, the model of rational man has provoked as much enthusiastic acceptance as vehement criticism from political scientists. It gave rise to a renewed controversy over alternative explanatory approaches in political sciences which may be reduced to the following question: Are political decisions and actions more adequately understood in terms of intentional action guided by individual preferences or as the outflow of institutional structures and procedures? New political institutionalism is the keyword in this controversy.

The new political institutionalism claims, that reducing political phenomena to economic explanations is tantamount to admitting that political institutions in themselves do not influence political be-

havior. Consequently, it is assumed that political sciences do not
have original explanatory power, that they lead a "second-hand life".

James G. March and Johan P. Olsen were the first to critically
point out the economy- and society-centeredness of political sciences.
Later Peter B. Evans, Dietrich Rueschemeyer, and Theda Skocpol
called for a revival of an institution-centered analysis of political behavior.

Political institutions in the view of these political scientists are not
merely the arenas in which political processes occur, and which are
moved by external economic and social factors. Rather, political institutions such as the distribution of political positions, procedural
rules, and standard operating procedures, have a weight of their
own. They determine political decision processes and their outcomes
to a considerable extent. "Political institutions are building blocks of
politics. They influcence available options for policy-making and for
institutional change. They also influence the choices made among
available options. Thus, an institutional perspective requires a careful delineation of the nature of particular institutional arrangements"
(Krasner 1987).

Both analytical approaches, the rational choice approach as well
as the institutionalist approach, are no doubt of theoretical and empirical relevance in explaining political decisions. Assuming this is
the case, it still remains unclear, however, whether or not they are
mutually exclusive. If not, how do they relate to each other, if both
are applied to the explanation of political decision-making in a specific policy field? It is the aim of this contribution to examine possibilities of linking the two analytical perspectives. More modestly,
their mutual relationship will be assessed under some selected aspects, since political sciences can only lose if one approach is used
exclusively.

To develop the argument, I will proceed in three steps: Firstly,
central assumptions of rational choice theory, and the critique waged
against it, as well as the ensuing modifications in theory will be
summarized roughly. Secondly, the contrasting institutionalist view
will be presented and criticized, thirdly, the possibilities of linking

the two analytical perspectives will be discussed on a theoretical level and illustrated by means of examples of empirical research.

Rational Choice and Political Decision-making

According to rational choice theory, all decisions can be explained by recurring to the rational self-interest of the individual agent. The latter pursues specific intentions, assesses alternative actions in terms of their benefits and costs, and thereby develops his preferences. It is assumed that he is well aware of his preferences, that he is able to compare them and bring them into a systematic order. All possible options of action, as well as their consequences, are known to him. Thus, agents are supposed to assess alternative courses of action in the light of the highest possible benefit or least possible cost (Stigler 1981:188), "...be it a real one (like profit) or a purely notional one (like the utility function representing preferences)" (Elster 1979:113). However, the agent acts within specific "constraints" which are assumed as given.

It is widely accepted that this decision model, intriguing as it may be in its simple elegance, far from adequately explains even trivial political everyday decisions. The criticism applied to it not only points out that political institutions and society in general are reduced to the "constraints" within which the agent is deciding; it also emphasizes that this simple model abstracts from the complexities of political reality, enhancing at best in the Weberian idealtypical sense that rational action and the disorderly reality of political life diverge to a large extent.

More precisely, critics stress that an individual is always acting in relation to other agents. The actor does not know with certainty what his preferences are, much less what those of the other agents are. Moreover, the assumption that the rational agent disposes of complete information about all possible courses of action seems questionable. This is especially the case, once you try to imagine how many costs it would create to provide complete information about all possible courses of action and their consequences. Therefore, through a decisionist short-cut, decision-makers recur to a mode of "satisficing" decision-making to economize information costs (Simon 1954:99f) since every decisional situation is characterized by uncertainty, information overload and ambiguity.

But ambiguity lies within the individual, too. Its preferences are manifold ("the multiple self" - Elster 1985) and are changing constantly. The agent may disapprove of his decision once he experiences its results ("complexities of the second guess"). His multiple preferences are not consistent, may be conflicting, and are non-transitive. They are lexikographic, which means that some preferences cannot be substituted by others, but by their very nature range above others. In short, preferences are not equivalent: Not everything has its price (Tietzel 1988:15). Rather, man has the capacity to reflect upon his preferences and to rank them (George 1987:94). Preferences which are of immediate relevance for action are derived from "higher" meta-preferences. Thus, the individual may be seen as managing his various preferences within his "egonomics" (Schelling 1984:5). The potential infinite regress in the derivation of preferences is short-cut by a decision to identify with a specific preference, or by explaining preferences by causal factors such as social norms or institutional structures (Elster 1979:115). In short, preferences cannot be assumed as given, instead are being shaped by the individual himself, by society, by cultural traditions, and by political institutions.

In many respects, rational choice theory has taken account in its further developments of the criticisms addressed to its explanatory approach. Thus, the "new institutionalist economics" explicitly claim that preferences are not to be viewed as static and external to economic analysis, but as a dynamic and integral part of economic theory (Sheffrin 1978:785). The individual agent is no longer seen in a parametric, constant environment, but in a changing environment. Thus, the concept of strategic rationality, developed in game theory, includes other agents as well who - to a large extent - constitute the environment of the agent, while the latter in his turn makes up the environment of the other actors.

Strategic rationality has still another implication for rational choice theory. It not only means that other actors are taken into account when the agent acts rationally. It also indicates that the agent may forego short-term benefits in order to realize long-term benefits, that collective actors may subordinate special interests to common interests, in short, that the agent is capable *"de reculer pour mieux sauter"* (Leibniz, cf. Elster 1979:10). In doing so the agent intentionally creates constraints which restrict the realm of his possible actions. If we relate the strategic concept of action to the above-mentioned concept of meta-preferences or multiple individual preferences, it may be expressed in the following terms: The immediately action-relevant preferences of the "doer", which are of a short-term character, are dismissed in favor of the long-term interests of the "planner" (Thaler/Shefin 1981:394).

Finally, public choice theorists, especially Mancur Olson, demonstrated that individual rationality may not be congruent with collective rationality. For, as the famous free-rider problem shows, from the viewpoint of the individual it is not rational to participate in the production of a collective good if he cannot be excluded from the consumption of this collective good.

The short outline of the basic assumptions of rational choice theory may have shown that in many respects this theoretical approach is inadequate to explain complex political behavior. Also depicted, however, is the modification of the theory as presented by the discussion about endogenous preferences. It integrates the development of preferences into economic explanations, as well as including other actors in game theory as part of the environment. Finally, the emphasis on metapreferences and strategic rationality offers important analytical viewpoints. These in turn lend themselves to the integration of rational choice theory and institutionalist analysis.

Before assessing some of the possibilities of tying rational choice and institutionalist analysis together, the main aspects of the institutionalist approach and its problems will be outlined.

New Institutionalism and
Political Decision-making

Given a second, more scrutinizing look, "new" political institutionalism is revealed to be an "old" institutionalism. Plato de-
scribes the pursuit of justice as one of the main tasks of the state.
Aristotle claims that the constitution enables a good and virtuous
life, and they both focus on the institutional conditions which
"render the citizen good through habitualisation" (Aristotle). Only
with the rise of the modern, mechanistic conception of the world did
human behavior and collective action come to be considered rational.
Perceived benefits and costs were weighed on the one hand, and
means and purposes on the other (Hobbes, Bentham).

Durkheim and Weber were the first to emphasize the influence of
social order and traditions on human behavior. Next to rational and
value-orientied behavior they constitute the third source of human
behavior. Traditional behavior is "...very often a matter of almost
automatic reaction to habitual stimuli which guide behavior in a
course which has been repeatedly followed. The great bulk of
everyday action to which people have become habitually
accustomed approaches this type."(Weber 1968:25). According to Weber, traditions represent individual conceptions of social order which
do not fully determine social behavior, but offer opportunities of
action which are observed by most actors in a society. An
institutionalist argument is presented by Weber as well in his
analysis of bureaucracy, when he emphasizes the perils of
bureaucracy as the *"Gehäuse der Hörigkeit"*, inevitably resulting from
the bureaucratic domain and endangering the individual autonomy
of man. This peril - in his view - can be domesticated only by
parliamentarian control.

In recent times institutionalist analysis has been revived by comparative policy and politics research. Without explicitly trying to
make an institutionalist argument, institutions are regarded as one
independent variable among others to explain policy decisions. This
research often furthered empirical evidence showing that political
institutions, to a significant extent, explain policy outcomes (von

Beyme 1987:58). This finding culminated in the - for political scientists reassuring - insight that "politics matter" (Newton/Sharpe 1984; Schmidt 1986).

However, it was James G. March and Johan P. Olsen who most emphatically advanced the new institutionalist approach as a systematic program of research: According to March and Olsen, political and policy decisions may in part be derived from political institutions as "irretrievable sources" of political action. The authors define institutions in a somewhat loose sense as a number of interconnected rules and routines which define the adequate action as a relationship between a role and a situation (March/Olsen 1989).

In their view, structures and rules influence decisions in their own right. For politics is only in part rational and consequence-oriented. It also is oriented to a considerable extent in the process itself: Decisional processes are just as concerned with the attribution of status, with the definition of truth and virtue, and the maintenance of loyalty and legitimacy (March/Olsen 1975:12). Thus, standard operating procedures "...affect the substantive outcomes of choices by regulating the access of participants, problems, and solutions to choices, and by affecting the participants' allocation of attention, their standards of evaluation, priorities, perceptions, identities, and resources" (Olsen, this volume, p. 93).

Along this line of argument, March and Olsen contrast the rule of *"appropriateness"* to the rule of *"consequentiality"* as principles of action. According to the rule of "appropriateness", actions are matched by choosing adequate rules and routines in specific situations. They conclude that the individual personality and will of political actors is less important than historical traditions, as they are embedded within rules, and that the calculus of political costs and benefits is less important than routines and norms as expressions of learning (March/Olsen 1989).

A similar argument is presented by Evans, Rueschemeyer and Skocpol (1985) in the recent discussion regarding the role of the state. They critically address the society-centeredness in the explanations of politics by theories of pluralism (under which they subsume methodological individualism), in general systems theory and marxist theories of the state. In their view these explanations neglect the autonomous weight of the state and the autonomy of state actors in conceiving and realizing policy objectives. As a consequence, the environment of political institutions is wrongly considered as a fluid surroundings "... in which a shift in resources and in incentives will quickly lead to a shift in behavior" (Krasner 1988:69). In contrast Evans et. al. emphasize the effects organizations of the state have on the contents of policies and the way policy processes function, using political and administrative structures, institutional change and inertia as major explanatory variables and a starting point of analysis.[1] Institutionalists, thus, hypothesize that political decision-making can be derived from rules, organizational structures, and role definitions on the one hand, and that these institutional structures persist over time. Early policy choices determine the policy options available at later points in time and constitute the path-dependency of policy developments (Krasner 1988:73).

State autonomy is investigated empirically by Nordlinger, who analyzes to what extent state actors initiate new policy measures finding that state officials develop their own policy preferences which diverge from the preferences of the rest of society. In a "strong state", Nordlinger assumes, state officials are able to realize these preferences against the will of powerful societal actors. As additional indicators of autonomous state power, he measures the endeavours of citizens to limit the encroachment of the state on society (Nordlinger 1988).

---

1   Kiser and Ostrom have developed a number of institutional rules in order to compare various institutionalist studies. At least seven different institutional rules structure every situation of action: 1. Positional rules describe the position taken by actors when they interact. 2. Boundary rules define the conditions which actors must fulfill in order to act in a position, such as entry and exit rules (for example in the position of an elector). 3. Authority rules determine which actions are allowed in which position. 4. Rules of scope prescribe which outcomes actors may aspire to in specific positions, which they must not, and which they should aspire to. 5. Aggregation rules specify how the actions of the single actors are aggregated into a joint result. 6. Information rules determine which ways of communication are to be used among individuals. 7. Pay-off rules, finally, define how costs and benefits of specific actions are devided up between actors. These various institutional rules are interlinked and materialize in specific configurations (Kiser/Ostrom 1987:20).

The institutionalist argument may be illustrated with examples of political behavior: Electoral behavior for instance, when interpreted from a rational choice viewpoint as an attempt to maximize individual benefits, is not really worth while. For one vote among millions of others does not make any difference as far as policy benefits are concerned. The institutionalist viewpoint offers a better explanation, suggesting that citizens vote out of a sense of duty and an inherent interest in the political process itself (Elster 1987:24).

Another example may illustrate the influence of institutional structures on policy outcomes: German tripartist bodies in technical norm production tend to produce only incremental and status quo-orientied policies. This is because redistributive innovative decisions regularly fail to reach the consent of employers' associations, since their members have to finance the investments. To put it more poignantly: Because of its representative structure, tripartist bodies cannot bring about redistributional policies (Windhoff-Héritier 1989:119 pp.). Or, as Scharpf points out referring to the Coase theorem: The potential for redistribution is reduced "as one moves from... hierarchical to unanimous decisions... Thus, contracts and unanimous decisions permit each party to defend the existing pattern of distribution while majoritarian and hierarchical decision rules create the possibility of involuntary redistribution" (Scharpf, this volume, p. 60).

In another context an empirical institutionalist argument is presented by Weir and Skocpol. They show that in Sweden a policy of social Keynesianism was realized in the late 1920s and early 30s because the Swedish administration had integrated economic experts into the governmental policy-making process at an early point in time, whereas in Great Britain the early existence of unemployment insurance prevented social Keynesianism from becoming an established governmental policy (Weir/Skocpol 1984:10 pp.).

Thus far, the institutionalist thrust of argument refered to the link between institutional structures and policy contents. However, institutionalism also aims at the question: How do policies themselves and political institutions influence the socio-political environment, such phenomena as political culture and interest group forma-

tion. Political effects also comprise the activation of political groups
by political processes (Olsen, this volume, p. 98). Along this vein of
argument, Graham K. Wilson shows, that there is a link between
institutional structures in Western democracies and the development
of neocorporatism in macroeconomic policies: Federalism and the
fragmented administrative and associative structures of the United
States are not propitious for the development of neocorporatist bodies. In contrast, the centralized administrative and associative structure in Sweden offers favorable conditions for such a development.
In a very general sense, so goes Olsen's argument in this volume,
parliamentary systems and competitive party systems offer more
opportunities for institutionalized opposition and public appeals,
while corporatist arrangements limit political competition and conflict (Olsen, this volume, p. 99).

Another empirical example of the so called Tocquevillian argument in institutionalism (Katznelson 1985) is as follows: State laws
concerning health and safety at work in Great Britain, Germany and
the United States not only brought about an improvement in protective measures for the health of workers; they also resulted in a
strengthening of the decisional position of the latter within the firm.
For the first time in Great Britain, the integration of a labor representative in the decision-making process was legally sanctioned. In the
United States, the Occupational Health and Safety Act is said to serve
unions as a leverage point by summoning OSHA inspections, putting companies under pressure and forcing them to accept unionization.

In summary, institutional structures and rules, by their very existence, influence policy decisions. The latter, in their turn, influence
socio-political structures. As plausible as this may be, however, the
new political institutionalism does not offer a systematic theoretical
framework as an analytical alternative to rational choice theory. The
various explanatory variables of political institutionalism, that is
political structures, rules, and the contents of laws, are not
sytematically related in an explanatory scheme. They all have a
relative autonomy in explaining political behavior; as single variables they are not systematically related and are not established in a

hierarchical order. Political institutionalism is therefore threatened by explanatory eclecticism (Smith 1988): A number of explanatory variables are produced in an ad-hoc manner. Often institutions and their effects are only described in detail (Kitschelt 1989:53 pp.). Moreover, the danger of tautology is just around the corner when institutionalists argue - such as Heclo does - that policy contents in social welfare policy are to be explained by the very existence of already established social welfare policy measures.[2]

What can we conclude after this short outline of the two contrasting explanatory approaches? On the one hand, we have the elegant model of a self-interested, rationally calculating agent. Notwithstanding its intriguingly simple elegance, it reduces drastically a complex political reality. On the other hand, we have the institutionalist approach, which takes account of the disorderliness of the political world by analyzing a multiplicity of institutional factors, while simultaneously failing to systematically interrelate these factors.

What can be done in this situation? The plausibility of our everyday political experience tells us that both approaches, the rational choice as well as the institutionalist approach - offer valuable insights into political actions. The relevant question is therefore: How can they be tied together in a useful analytical way? Such a combination can focus on the central concept of "constraints", those being the restrictions which delimit the individual rational calculation and of which political institutions constitute an important element.

Linking Rational Choice and Institutionalist Explanations

Political science lacks a consistent theory of political institutions (Göhler 1988:14). Sociological theories of institutions such as those developed in general systems theory (Parsons 1968; Luhmann 1984)

---

2   This analytical trap may be avoided by a clear conceptualization of institutional variables, in such a mode as to seperate the institutional variables considered the causes of policies clearly from the policies to be explained. Preferably, the independent institutional variables should have existed a long time before the policies to be explained were developed (Kitschelt1989:54).

and in symbolic interactionism (Berger/Luckmann 1971; Mead 1973; Lau 1978) or in cultural anthropology (Malinowski 1975; Gehlen 1978) are being used in political science, but there have been no systematic endeavours to determine the specifically political elements of these societal institutions. Nor are systematic explanations offered as to why political institutions develop, what their effects are, and how they vanish again (Göhler 1988:14). Since such a political theory of institutions is not at hand to help to overcome institutional eclecticism, I will focus on one central aspect which constitutes a link between institutional structures and the single rational agent: Constraints, that is political institutions restricting the realm of action of the individual. For our analytical purposes, we define the political institution as a system of rules to produce and implement binding decisions (Göhler 1988:14) as well as organizational structures. The rules are made and performed by actors on whom the formal power to decide and implement has been purveyed (Levi 1988).

The Two Filter-Model

With his two-filter model, Jon Elster offers an analytical tool of linking rational choice theory and institutionalist analysis. According to his model, every human action, such as political action, can be understood in terms of two successive filtering processes: In the first process structural constraints, such as institutional arrangements, rules, physical and technological conditions, as well as value systems of a society or group (Kiser/Ostrom 1987:3) reduce the universe of possible decision alternatives open to an agent to a relatively small subset of possibilities. This is referred to as the *"feasible set"*. The constraints effective in this first filtering process are cultural norms, economic and technological conditions, and political institutions. Only the latter are of concern to us.

In the second filtering process, the individual agent chooses one alternative from the "feasible set" of alternatives[3] (Elster 1979:113,5;

---

3   The selection process of an alternative of action among the options of the "feasible set" may be based on a nonrational process, as well, such as imitation or habit.

Franz 1986:3). Thus, by means of the two-filter-model, it can be shown that state activities and structures can determine elements of rationality for the single agent. That is, institutions influence the interests of an individual. An example is offered by Rothstein who shows that in Sweden the enactment of a specific form of unemployment benefits (the Ghent fonds) administered by unions, gave them important new functions regarding the control of the labor supply ("How is unemployment defined?", "Do workers on strike receive unemployment benefits?" etc.). Thus, the individual worker, by institutional design, got an incentive to enter unions (Rothstein 1989:30).

The Choice-Genesis of Institutions

However useful the two-filter model may be in emphasizing the institutional determination of individual and collective choice processes, it does not make clear that political actors themselves create the institutions which in turn constitute political constraints. In other words, it would be a mistake to consider the relationship between institutions and choice as a one-way street.

On the contrary, a further analytical link between rational choice theory and institutionalism is to be seen in the fact that institutions originate in the individual choices of man. Analytically, this means that the choice origins of institutions should, if possible, be revealed, and the change of institutions should be reconstructed and interpreted in terms of the history of individual and collective choices. One famous argument made for the choice genesis of institutions is put forward by Brennan and Buchanan. They show that according to the contract tradition in state theory, institutions develop from the very self-interest of actors and the ensuing conflicts. Institutions are founded in order to regulate and contain these conflicts (Brennan/Buchanan 1985).

The creation of institutional rules to constrain individuals may be understood as a process of self-binding (Elster 1979). In its most famous form, we encounter it in the shape of constitutions. Constitutions provide decision rules and principles which may not be altered at all, or may be modified only under highly restrictive conditions. Only the constituant assembly is able to pursue a "politique politisante". Elster refers to this as the paradox of democracy, since all following generations are obliged to pursue a "politique politisée" within the frame of rules provided by the constituant assembly (Elster 1979:94). Rational choices, in short, can initiate institutional change, formalizing them into rules. They in turn again constitute constraints for the individual choices of later generations. In this sense, rules are always introduced because of the consequences they produce for society, making them, too, "consequential". This viewpoint has been elaborated particularly by the "New Institutional Economics" as developed by Williamson, showing that transaction and information costs may be saved by introducing rules and structures into market exchange processes, whereby hierarchies are created and attention is drawn to organizational boundaries (Williamson 1975).

The fact, however, that institutions are created and changed by rational individual and collective decisions does not imply that institutions may be reduced to individual rational decisions. For, as Giddens remarks, institutions expand so widely in space and time that they "...escape the control of every individual actor" (Giddens 1988:78). Analytically, this may be conceived of as non-intended effects of institutions.

More importantly, it would be fundamentally wrong to think of political institutions solely as constraints in the literal sense. By reducing the uncertainty of the individual in a complex environment, they offer the very possibility of action. In other words, institutions have a double function. They set restrictions, but at the same time they offer opportunities. They relieve the agent of the burden of deciding case by case, over and over again in similar situations by formulating rules, guaranteeing reliability and fulfilling the "Entlastungsfunktion" (relief function) described by Gehlen. Paradoxically, therefore, uncertainty constitutes the most important source of rules. This is because the latter specify social action in recurrent situations in such a way that they are acknowledged as valid by the environment. In short, institutional structures constrain and constitute actions (Krasner 1988:69).

Institution as Restriction and Opportunity

Institutions have two faces. They restrict alternatives of action, but by doing so, they make political action calculable to a certain extent and unfold opportunities of action. The latter originate in two aspects. On the one hand, the authoritative aspect (Zwangsaspekt) of institutions, reaching from sheer force to more subtle forms of inducing obedience, creates power for specific actors. This constitutes the enabling aspect of institutions, since this power offers the possibility of producing intended consequences of action (Giddens 1988:227). All different forms of coercion, therefore, at the same time constitute in various modes forms of enablement. As much as they serve to restrict or negate specific alternatives of action, they simultaneously disclose others (Giddens 1988:22).

On the other hand, institutional structures and rules are rarely ever deterministic, in the sense that they shape behavior fully. Instead they convey general orientations for action, they open "Gestaltungskorridore", leaving room for self-interest and strategic decisions. Rules always have to be interpreted in a situational context. Moreover, several rules of action may be pertinent in a specific situation, and the decision which rule to apply may be derived from the principle of consequentialism (March/Olsen1989). "Non-routinized situations and open organizational structures give few rules regulating the access of decision-makers, problems, and solutions to choice opportunities, and few rules regulating how they can be attached to each other and handled" (Olsen, this volume, p. 91).

Thus, many laws create only a general framework of action, which may serve as an example of the multi-valence of rules. They only offer a base for bargaining processes of non-parliamentary actors, be they administrative actors or private actors.

A case in point is the German Health and Safety at Work Act. The process of "wheeling and dealing" over the precise rules of the act started to set only in after the law had been enacted. Only then, was it decided how high the costs would be, costs which employers would be requested to pay to protect the lives and health of the workers.

The less precisely, however, institutional rules and powers are defined, the more important the resources available to the individual actor are in obtaining bargaining advantages in filling out rules. These rules, though more precise, are open to interpretation in a specific situational context (March/Olsen 1989). In short, political institutions have to fulfill a double task. They have to select actions by prescribing rules, thereby stabilizing political interaction. On the other hand, they keep possibilities of actions open in their "optionality". This is particularly true for political decision bodies (Vollrath 1987:208).

The above mentioned fact that individual actors can have an influence on institutional structures and rules, and that this influence depends on the resources actors command, points to a further aspect: The policy contingency of interaction between individuals and institutions. The following example may illustrate this.

Western democracies with a neocorporatist structure more easily managed the economic crisis of the 70s than did states without such decisional constellations. But this was only the case, as long as the policy objective of those states was a Keynesian full-employment policy, a policy requiring that unions be integrated into an anti-inflationary wage policy scheme. As soon as governments switched to a monetaristic, supply-side oriented policy, the need for unions and business associations to cooperate no longer existed. Consequently, neocorporatist institutions lost their importance as an explanatory factor for policy outcomes as well (Scharpf 1985:168/9).

Methodologically, we may draw the following conclusion from the policy contingency of the interaction between institutions and individuals: Only the careful reconstruction of political institutions within a specific policy context may reveal whether or not institutions exert an enabling or restricting influence on the actions of specific rational actors (Scharpf 1985:168/9).

Linking Rational Choice and Institutional Factors: Normative and Empirical Developments in Political Decision-making

Two examples of institutional developments may illustrate the inter-dependence of institutional structures and individual preferences of actors: The first example sheds some light on the normative demo-cratic definition of institutions. The second example, illustrates an empirical development of political decision processes under the con-ditions of a highly differentiated and complex society. That is, the transformation of formal institutional rules into informal bargaining processes. This in turn, represents a deviation from the postulated democratic norms.

Under normative aspects every political institution is based on the consensus of the individuals carrying the institution (Durkheim). A process of change in institutional rules and structures may be ini-tiated if institutions do not correspond to the preferences of those on whose democratic support they depend. Conflicts may arise which lead to institutional changes, unless the institution has developed a degree of autonomy which makes it "self-sufficient", meaning de-pendent on the preferences of a small circle of organizational mem-bers, rather than of a larger constituency. If the institutional philoso-phy is derived from an *"Idée directrice"* (Hauriou) oriented toward democratic principles, institutional reality may be in conflict with this idea and the preferences of the members of the institution or its constituency. In other words, every political institution is always in search of a fragile equilibrium between a generalized support and trust (Luhmann) of its members and of an "inductive trust" (Waschkuhn 1987:90). This equilibrium has to be found again and again under changing conditions, the latter being defined by indi-vidual participation and empirical individual preferences which feed new targets and objectives into the institutional decision process, providing for its ongoing dynamics.

Let us relate the interaction between institutional rules and indi-vidual actors to the above-mentioned concept of metapreferences or the "multiple self" (Elster 1985); then the question arises, as Offe points out: How do democratic institutional structures enhance or restrict the capacities of the individual to deal in a self-reflective way with his/her intra-individual preferences? Institutions, accordingly, should not only be indifferent to specific group interests, e.g. should not be advancing the interests of one group more than the interests of another group. Above that, they should also be assessed as to whether or not they offer a basis for the critical self-evaluation of preferences of the individual actor. These preferences span the field from "local" to "global rationality", from "self to other-regardingness", as well as from short-term to long-term orientations (Offe 1988:63; Scharpf, this volume) and should be brought into an equilibrium. Critical self-evaluation by the individual actor is furthered by institutional structures which favor critical reasoning and arguing and are open for learning (Offe 1988:63).

If we confront the above democratic postulate with an empirical development in the interaction of institutional rules and preferences, a two-fold divergence emerges:

Firstly, central democratic institutions such as elections and majority decisions/plebiscites (Guggenberger/Offe 1984) offer only the possibilities of a "yes" or "no" decision and do not include the opportunities of a critical evaluation of multiple individual preferences based on argumentation and discourse. Such a situation is conceived in a fictional sense by Rawls (1971), as well, if decisions occur behind "the veil of ignorance". Individuals may emphasize "other-regarding", "future-regarding" and "fact-regarding" interests (Offe 1988) if they make decisions under conditions in which they are not aware of their future interests and of the way they will be affected by the decision at hand in the future (Kirchgäßner 1989:8).

Secondly, decisional situations in a highly complex environment, the consequences of which cannot be foreseen, abound (Luhmann 1983:304f). Therefore, rules of procedural character are used which allow for permanent self-correction (Ladeur 1983:473 pp.; Teubner and Willke 1980:17). Legislative decisions, in practice, are being transformed into negotiating processes in closed circles subject to the special influences of powerful individual and collective actors. As much as this makes sense in a highly differentiated society, it leaves also ample discretion for the implementing agencies and for private actors to shape public policies. The decreasing specificity of rules renders democratic control of parliamentarians questionable. This is especially true for planning and welfare activities which offer many possibilities for rational strategic actions of concerned private actors.

Thus, the German "Bundesbaugesetz" explicitly leaves it to the performing administration, "die öffentlichen und privaten Belange gegeneinander und untereinander gerecht abzuwägen", that is, to weigh public and private interests against and among each other (Par.1 Abs.7 BBauG.). In environmental policy, as well as in health and safety policy, general regulatory clauses , such as the observing of "accepted technical rules" ("die anerkannten Regeln der Technik", Par.3, 6, Bundesimmissionsschutzgesetz) and the loose mandate given to administration to weigh different interests against each other, actually amount to the fact, that legal acts are not specifically prescribing actions, but are distributing negotiating positions between the affected parties (Knoepfel/Weidner 1980:82ff).

Scharpf described the transformation of legally mandated, formally hierarchical decision processes into bargaining processes among a limited number of state and private actors as "Politikverflechtung" (Scharpf 1988:69). It occurs between central government and sub-states, between state, business associations and unions, and is pertinent for the field of implementation as well. Hierarchal rules between state and private actors - although formally shaped as such - represent the exception rather than the typical case (Mayntz 1980:89), the typical pattern being the corporatist networking of organizations. "Implementation coalitions" entering the scene determine the rules to be put into effect (Ladeur 1982:76). These consensual bargaining processes define the costs and benefits of the political measures to be performed. As a consequence, not only the link to the will of the democratic legislator is loosened, but also established positions of social power are being reproduced in these bargaining processes (Maus 1987:145).

Since state actors often and to a large extent depend on the resources of powerful private actors for the performance of public policies, as a consequence they may even cede decisional powers to private actors in these bargaining processes in order to reach, in turn, policy concessions by the private actors (Scharpf 1988:70).

Thus linking the normative postulate of democracy and factual developments, we face a dilemma: On the one hand, the policy problems to be solved require the softening and loosening of decision-making processes and their procedural and regulatory openness; on the other hand, however, this openness is occupied by powerful private actors and used to their specific advantages to the detriment of less powerful societal groups, thereby jeopardizing the democratic character of the political decision-making processes.

To improve the opportunities of less powerful groups to put forward their preferences in the ever more expanding bargaining processes which are made possible by soft rules - and this constitutes the dilemma - new, and more precise institutional rules may be needed again. Alternatively, strategies of strengthening the resources of less powerful groups are being discussed which may be helpful in emphasizing the interests of weaker participants, such as the advocacy models being practiced in the policy for the handicapped and other public policy fields.

But this model, as well, implies political decisions or rules which favor a redistribution of material and decisional resources. Accordingly, the behavior aspired to cannot be expected to result solely from individual preferences and incentives since these require a moral process of self-binding which in turn may be favored by specific institutional arrangements (Offe 1989:761). The crucial question , however, is to what extent these preferences of inclusiveness, intertemporality, and social welfare (Scharpf, this volume) may be intentionally produced by institutional arrangements.

In conclusion, the discussion of normative and empirical problems of democratic political decision processes may have shown that the systematic linking of both analytical perspectives, of rational choice theory and institutionalism, is imperative in any case . Linking the two perspectives displays the tension between the normative democratic philosophy of institutions and the individual aspirations of actors in institutions. They may, at best, be held in ever so delicate a balance.

References

Berger, Peter L. and Thomas Luckmann (1971) *Die gesellschaftliche Konstruktion der Wirklichkeit*. Frankfurt/Main: S. Fischer.

Brennan, Geoffrey and James M. Buchanan (1985) *The Reason of Rules*. Cambridge: Cambridge University Press.

Durkheim, Emile (1977) *Über die Teilung der sozialen Arbeit*. Frankfurt/M.: Suhrkamp Verlag.

Elster, Jon (1979) *Ulysses and the Sirens*. Cambridge: Cambridge University Press.

Elster, Jon (ed.) (1985) *The Multiple Self*. Cambridge, Mass.: Cambridge University Press.

Evans, Peter, Dietrich Rueschemeyer and Theda Skocpol (eds.) (1984) *Bringing the State Back In*. Cambridge: Cambridge University Press.

Franz, Peter (1986) 'Der "Constrained Choice"-Ansatz als gemeinsamer Nenner individualistischer Ansätze in der Soziologie', *Kölner Zeitschrift für Soziologie und Sozialpsychologie*, 38: 32-54.

Gehlen, Arnold (1971) *Der Mensch. Seine Natur und Stellung zur Welt*. 9th edition. Frankfurt/M.: Athaenum-Verlag.

Giddens, Antony (1988) *Die Konstitution der Gesellschaft*. Frankfurt: Campus Verlag.

Göhler, Gerhard (1987) 'Institutionenlehre und Institutionentheorie in der deutschen Politikwissenschaft nach 1945', pp. 15-47 in Gerhard Göhler (ed.) *Grundfragen der Theorie politischer Institutionen*. Opladen: Westdeutscher Verlag.

Göhler, Gerhard (1988) 'Soziale Institutionen - politische Institutionen. Das Problem der Institutionentheorie in der neueren deutschen Politikwissenschaft', pp. 12-28 in Wolfgang Luthard and Arno Waschkuhn (eds.) *Politik und Repräsentation, Beiträge zur Theorie und zum Wandel politischer und sozialer Institutionen*. Marburg: ST Verlag Nobert Schüren.

Göhler, Gerhard (ed.) (1987) *Grundfragen der Theorie politischer Institutionen.* Opladen: Westdeutscher Verlag.

Habermas, Jürgen (1987) 'Wie ist die Legitimität durch Legalität möglich?', *Kritische Justiz* 20: 1-16.

Heiner, Ronald A. (1983) 'The Origin of Predictable Behavior', *The American Economic Review*, 73: 560-595.

Katznelson, Ira (1985) 'Working Class Formation and the State: Nineteenth-Century England in American Perspective', pp. 257-284 in Peter B. Evans, Dietrich Rueschemeyer and Theda Skocpol (eds.) *Bringing the State Back In.* Cambridge: Cambridge University Press.

Kaufmann, Franz-Xaver (1988) 'Steuerung wohlfahrtsstaatlicher Abläufe durch Recht', pp. 65-108 in Dieter Grimm und Werner Maihofer (eds.) *Gesetzgebungstheorie und Rechtspolitik, Jahrbuch für Rechtssoziologie und Rechtstheorie 13.* Opladen: Westdeutscher Verlag.

Kirchgäßner, Gerhard (1989) *Homo Oeconomicus. Das ökonomische Modell individuellen Verhaltens und seine Anwendung in den Wirtschafts- und Sozialwissenschaften.* Osnabrück, Zürich, ms.

Kiser, Larry L. and Eleonor Ostrom (1987) *Reflections on the Elements of Institutional Analysis.* Workshop in Political Theory & Policy Analysis, Indiana University, Bloomington.

Kitschelt, Herbert (1989) *Explaining Technology Policies, Competing Theories and Comparative Evidence,* Center for Interdisciplinary Research, Bielefeld.

Knoepfel, Peter and Helmut Weidner (1980) 'Normbildung und Implementation: Interessenberücksichtigungspotential in Programmstrukturen von Luftreinhaltepolitiken', pp. 82-104 in Renate Mayntz (ed.) *Implementation politischer Programme.* Königstein/Taunus: Hain Verlag.

Krasner, Stephen D. (1984) 'Approaches to the State, Alternative Conceptions and Historical Dynamics', *Comparative Politics* 16: 224-246.

Krasner, Stephen D. (1988) 'Sovereignity - An Institutional Perspective', *Comparative Political Studies* 21: 66-94.

Ladeur, Karl-Heinz (1982) 'Verrechtlichung der Ökonomie - Ökonomisierung des Rechts?', pp. 74-92 in V. Gessner and G. Winter (eds.) *Rechtsformen der Verflechtung von Staat und Wirtschaft. Jahrbuch für Rechtssoziologie und Rechtstheorie, Band 8.* Opladen: Westdeutscher Verlag.

Lau, Ephrem Else (1978) *Interaktion und Institution.* Berlin: Duncker & Humblodt.

Levi, Margaret (1988) *A Logic of Institutional Change*, Paper, International Political Science Association Meetings: August 27-31. Washington D.C.

Luhmann, Niklas (1983) *Rechtssoziologie.* Opladen: Westdeutscher Verlag.

Luhmann, Niklas (1984) *Soziale Systeme.* Frankfurt/M.: Suhrkamp

Malinowski, Bronislaw (1975) *Eine wissenschaftliche Theorie der Kultur.* Fankfurt/M.: Suhrkamp Verlag.

March, James G. and Johan P. Olsen (1975) 'The Uncertainty of the Past: Organizational Learning Under Ambiguity', *European Journal of Political Research*, 3:147-171.

March, James G. and Johan P. Olsen(1989) *Rediscovering Institutions*, New York: The Free Press.

Maus, Ingeborg (1987) 'Verrechtlichung, Entrechtlichung und der Funktionswandel von Institutionen', pp. 132-172 in G. Göhler (ed.) *Grundfragen der Theorie politischer Institutionen.* Opladen: Westdeutscher Verlag.

Mayntz, Renate (1980) 'Einleitung', pp. 1-9 in Renate Mayntz (ed.) *Implementation politischer Programme.* Königstein/Taunus: Hain Verlag.

Mead, George H. (1973) *Geist, Identität und Gesellschaft.* Frankfurt/Main: Suhrkamp Verlag.

Nordlinger, Erich A. (1988) 'The Return to the State: Critiques', *American Political Science Review* 82: 875-885.

Offe, Claus (1984) 'Politische Legitimation durch Mehrheitsentscheidung', pp. 150-183 in Bernd Guggenberger and Claus Offe (eds.) *An den Grenzen der Mehrheitsdemokratie.* Opladen: Westdeutscher Verlag.

Offe, Claus (1988) *Endogenous Preferences and Institutional Choice.* unpublished manuscript, Univ. of Bielefeld.

Offe, Claus (1989) 'Bindung, Fessel, Bremse. Die Unübersichtlichkeit von Selbstbeschränkungsformen', pp. 739-775 in Axel Honneth, Thomas McCarthy, Claus Offe, and Albrecht Wellmer (eds.) *Zwischenbetrachtungen - Im Prozeß der Aufklärung.* Frankfurt: Campus.

Olson, Mancur (1965) *The Logic of Collective Action.* Cambridge, Mass: Harvard University Press.

Parsons, Talcott (1968) *The Structure of Social Action.* New York: The Free Press of Glencoe.

Rawls, John (1971) *A Theory of Justice.* Oxford: Clarendon Press.

Rothstein, Bo (1989) *Marxism and Institutional Analysis*, Paper presented at the European Consortium for Political Research, Joint Session of Workshops. Paris.

Scharpf, Fritz W. (1988) 'Verhandlungssysteme, Verteilungskonflikte und Pathologien der politischen Steuerung', pp. 61-68 in M. G. Schmidt (ed.) *Staatstätigkeit, Politische Vierteljahresschrift, Sonderheft 19.* Opladen: Westdeutscher Verlag.

Scharpf, Fritz W. (1985) 'Die Politikverflechtungs-Falle: Europäische Integration und deutscher Föderalismus im Vergleich', *Politische Vierteljahresschrift* 26: 323-356.

Scharpf, Fritz W. (1987) *Sozialdemokratische Krisenpolitik in Europa.* Frankfurt: Campus.

Schelling, Thomas C. (1984) 'Self-Command in Practice, in Policy, and in a Theory of Rational Choice', *American Economic Review* 74/2: 1-11.

Schelling, Thomas C. (1984) *Choice and Consequence*. Cambridge Mass.: Cambridge University Press.

Schmidt, Manfred G. (1986) 'Politische Bedingungen erfolgreicher Wirtschaftspolitik. Eine vergleichende Analyse westlicher Industrieländer', *Journal für Sozialforschung* 26/3: 251-273.

Sharpe, Laurence J. and Ken Newton (1984) *Does Politics Matter? - The Determinants of Public Policy*. Oxford: Clarendon Press.

Sheffrin, Steven (1978) 'Habermas, Depoliticization, and Consumer Theory, *Journal of Economic Issues* 12:785-797.

Simon, Herbert (1954) 'A Behavioral Theory of Rational Choice', *Quarterly Journal of Economics* 96: 99-118.

Smith, Rogers (1988) 'Political Jurisprudence, the "New Institutionalism" and the Future of Public Law', *American Political Science Review* 82/1: 89-108.

Stigler, George J. (1981) Economies or Ethics. *The Tanner Lectures on Human Values Vol. II:* 145-191. Cambridge.

Teubner, Günther and Willke, Helmut (1980) 'Dezentrale Kontext-steuerung im Recht intermediärer Verbände', pp. 46-62 in Rüdiger. Voigt (ed.) *Verrechtlichung*. Königstein/Taunus: Hain Verlag.

Thaler, Richard H. and H. M. Shefin (1981) 'An Economic Theory of Self-Control', *Journal of Political Economy* 89/2: 392-406.

Tietzel, Manfred (1987) *Zur Theorie der Präferenzen*. Manuscript, Witten-Herdecke.

Vollrath, E. (1987) 'Handlungshermeneutik als Alternative zur sys-temtheoretischen Interpretation', pp. 204-212 in G. Göhler (ed.) *Grundfragen der Theorie politischer Institutionen*. Opladen: Westdeutscher Verlag.

von Beyme, Klaus (1987) 'Institutionentheorie in der neueren Politikwissenschaft', pp. 48-60 in G. Göhler (ed.) *Grundfragen der Theorie politischer Institutionen*. Opladen: Westdeutscher Verlag.

Waschkuhn, Arno (1987) 'Allgemeine Institutionentheorie als Rahmen für die Theorie politischer Institutionen', pp. 71-97 in G. Göhler (ed.) *Grundfragen der Theorie politischer Institutionen.* Opladen: Westdeutscher Verlag.

Weber, Max (1968) *Economy and Society. An Outline of Interpretive Sociology.* Berkeley, Los Angeles: Univ. of California Press.

Weir, Margaret and Theda Skocpol, (1987) 'State Structures and the Possibilities for "Keynesian" Responses to the Great Depression in Sweden, Britain, and the United States', pp. 71-97 in Peter B. Evans, Dietrich Rueschemeyer and Theda Skocpol (eds.) *Bringing the State Back In.* Cambridge: Cambridge University Press.

Wiesenthal, Helmut (1987) 'Rational Choice, Ein Überblick über Grundlinien, Theoriefelder und neuere Themenakquisition eines sozialwissenschaftlichen Paradigmas', *Zeitschrift für Soziologie* 16/6: 434-449.

Williamson, Oliver E. (1979) 'Transaction-Cost Economics: The Governance of Contractual Relations', *Journal of Law and Economics* 22/2: 233-261.

Wilson, Graham K. (1985) *The Politics of Safety and Health, Occupational Safety and Health in the United States and Britain.* Oxford: Clarendon Press.

Windhoff-Héritier, Adrienne (1989) 'Institutionelle Interessenvermittlung im Sozialsektor', *Leviathan* 1: 108-126.

III

Political Institutions, Decision Styles, and Policy Choices[*]

Fritz W. Scharpf

Introduction

Policy research is a multi-disciplinary enterprise attempting to explain the success or failure of political systems in guiding the evolution, and solving the problems, of their societies. The enterprise is based on two central assumptions: On the one hand, it must be presumed that some degree of political guidance is possible because societal developments are affected in a predictable fashion by the policy resources (primarily physical force, law and money) available to the political system. On the other hand, however, political guidance is perceived as inherently problematic for two reasons: First, societal developments are neither random nor entirely plastic or malleable but tend to share the characteristics of open systems whose autonomous (stabilizing or de-stabilizing) dynamics may be resistant to certain kinds of political intervention (Mayntz/Nedelmann 1987). These questions need to be addressed in substantive policy analyses which, on the basis of an explicit understanding of the internal dynamics of specific "target" systems (economic, education, health, etc.) must try to explain and predict their response or resistance to certain kinds of political intervention.

---

[*] With minor revisions, this is the paper presented at the conference in honor of Gerhard Lehmbruch at Konstanz University, April 20-21, 1988. An expanded version has since been accepted for publication by the Journal of Theoretical Politics.

Equally problematic, however, is the guidance capacity of the
political system itself, i.e. its ability to adopt and carry out precisely
those interventions which substantive policy analyses have shown to
be effective in influencing societal dynamics. The problem could not
exist if the political system were the monolithic actor engaged in the
single-minded and omniscient pursuit of a unified concept of the
public weal as it is often conceptualized in substantive policy analyses. In reality, however, the political system is composed of a plural-
ity of actors with competing notions of what is good for society,
competing perceptions of reality, competing hypotheses about what
effects different policy interventions are likely to have, and different
notions of their own institutional self-interest. Effective policy, furthermore, is not the simple aggregate of individual choices but the
outcome of strategic interactions which are patterned by widely differing institutional arrangements. In multi-disciplinary policy research, these questions fall into the domain of political scientists with
a general interest in the political feasibility of policy options and a
special concern for the influence of political institutions on effective
policy choices (as distinguished from policy outcomes).

We know that this cannot be a simple one-on-one relationship.
Given institutional conditions cannot fully determine policy choices
but will, at most, define a set of constraints limiting the set of feasible
choices. Within these constraints, choice is exercised by political actors according to their own normative goals, cognitive world views
and egoistic interests. These normative, subjective and potentially
idiosyncratic elements of policy choice create a problem for theory-
oriented policy research in general, and for political science research
in particular. Which problems should we treat as relevant, whose
goals and which constraints should we consider, and from whose
means-end-hypotheses should our analyses proceed?

Faced with this problem, substantive-policy analysts whose primary goal is recommendation or evaluation, tend to assume responsibility for the "scientific" definition of objective constraints and of
means-end hypotheses - which forces them to cope somehow with
the ubiquitous disagreement among competing schools of policy-oriented scientific theory (such as between Keynesians and Monetarists

in macro-economic policy). With regard to the choice of goals, however, they often tend to adopt a "client-centered" perspective, which tries to focus upon the empirical goals of a single policy maker. In this they are often frustrated by the ambiguity and volatility of subjective decision premises and even more by the limited practical relevance of single-actor perspectives in the context of what are inherently processes of collective choice. Alternatively, many policy analyses (especially those undertaken by economists), tend to adopt an explicitly normative perspective - defined by reference to some kind of postulated social welfare function - only to be disappointed by the lack of political support for high-minded and technically impeccable recommendations that in one way or another violate the self-interest of the political actors who would have to adopt and implement them (Wiesenthal 1988).

Political scientists, on the other hand, with a "structuralist" interest in establishing empirical connections between institutional constraints and policy choices, cannot hope to neutralize the empirical variance of political preferences and perceptions in quite the same fashion. In order to explain effective policy choices, we can neither adopt a single-actor perspective nor base our analyses on normative postulates that may have been empirically irrelevant for the set of actors involved in collective policy processes. When we are aware of these difficulties, we often try to avoid them by focusing empirical research on severe and obvious policy problems - in the implicit hope that these "single exit" conditions (Latsis 1972; Zintl 1987) might have "wonderfully focussed the minds" of political actors upon convergent goals and hypotheses. Alternatively, or additionally, we may explicitly limit our analyses to subsets of policy makers with common ideological orientations, and, presumably, shared goals and perceptions. When that assumption is approximately correct, it becomes much more plausible that differences in policy choices might in fact be explained by differences in institutional constraints.

We must realize that these are limited solutions. Single-exit assumptions often founder on the realities of ideological conflict and historical change, and if the search for ideologically homogeneous preferences and perceptions should be successful, we often end up with so few cases that the tools of statistical analysis, with which we would have liked to test our hypotheses, become inapplicable. Nevertheless, many of us have pursued these research strategies in the hope of using "obvious" cases for discovering instances of universal regularities which might then be applied, as inductively validated laws, in empirical analyses of the more muddled and confused situations which are the stuff of ordinary politics. In my view, we have every reason to continue with this work. But given the inherent limitations of its empirical base, we also need to supplement the inductive development of "grounded theory" (Glaser/Strauss 1967) with an investment in the development of more abstract models (John 1980) representing the possible relationships of political institutions on the one hand and the quality of policy choices on the other hand. This is what I intend to do here.

In more abstract models, however, the highly concrete dependent variables of empirical research (specific policy choices evaluated by the goals of empirical policy makers) must also be replaced by more abstract descriptors of the quality of policy choices. At the most general level, policies might be compared along an inter-personal, an inter-temporal and a substantive social-welfare dimension. The first refers to the criterion of interpersonal inclusiveness: To what extent will different institutional arrangements assure that interests that are objectively affected by a policy choice are in fact taken into account in choice processes? In the intertemporal dimension, the criterion might be stability: To what extent are institutional conditions conducive to policy choices that are able to stand the test of time - in the sense that they will reflect not momentary impulses but - in the words of one of the great justices of the United States Supreme Court - "the sober second thought" of the community (Stone 1936: 25; Bickel 1962: 23-28)? In the substantive dimension, finally, one might refer to collective welfare criteria: To what extent will institutions affect allocative efficiency by favoring policy choices that will exploit available opportunities for increasing total social welfare production?

The Influence of Institutions on Policy

How could institutional arrangements affect the interpersonal, intertemporal and substantive quality of policy choices? Institutions may be conceptualized as sets of rules, or as normative constraints structuring the interaction of participants in policy processes. Of the great variety of types of rules that one may usefully distinguish (Ostrom 1986), there are two which appear to be particularly powerful predictors of policy choices: boundary rules defining the units of effective collective action, and decision rules governing the transformation of individual preferences into effective policy choices within and between such units.

To begin with what I consider the most fundamental feature: Boundary rules define collective identities. Even within the strictest confines of methodological individualism, one must surely recognize that the reference system of individual action may be defined at various levels of identification - my family, my firm, my union, my party, my local community, my country -- all these units and many more may at one time or another become the focus of one's "we-identity" (Elias 1987) and hence the collective referent for the development and evaluation of policy options. To the extent that this is true, individual action can only be explained by reference to a collective utility function. In addition, collective units are often capable of coordinating the actions of their members through collectively binding decisions and they may be held collectively accountable for these decisions. For some purposes, therefore, the collective unit may be treated as a ("corporate") actor in its own right (Coleman 1974).

Thus institutionalized boundary rules separate and unite. They unite individuals who share a common identity or collective utility function. They separate them from others whose (collective) identity is recognized as being distinct. More important for our purposes, institutional boundaries unite those individuals whose actions may be coordinated by some form of collectively binding choice mechanism (hierarchy, majority rule, or even unanimous assent) and they separate them from others with whom coordination is only possible in the forms of unilateral adaptation, coercion or voluntary agreement.

Institutional boundaries, in other words, define the difference between intra-unit "governance" and inter-unit "bargaining".

But while the difference is obviously important, it is not as clearly
dichotomous as it might seem. One theoretical bridge between the
extremes is provided by the famous "Coase Theorem" (Coase 1960)
which demonstrates that in the absence of transaction costs all coor-
dinative and regulatory functions of government could also be
achieved by voluntary contract - but with different distributive consequences. The theorem has given rise to the development of
transaction cost economics which at first have tended to emphasize
the comparative advantages of "hierarchical" over "market" forms of
coordination (Williamson 1975). In the meantime, however, lawyers
and sociologists have (re)discovered a variety of more stable and
elaborate forms of "relational" or "hierarchical" contract relations
(Macneil 1978, 1983; Dore 1983; Stinchcombe 1985; Powell 1987)
which are far removed from the "spot contracts" among perfect
strangers that presumably are characteristic of the "market" end of
the dichotomy. As a consequence, transaction cost economics have
also come to recognize types of coordination that fall between the
extreme forms of pure markets and pure hierarchies (Williamson
1979, 1985).

Thus, the categorical difference between "markets" and "hierarchies" or, more generally, between inter-unit "bargaining" and intra-unit "governance", tends to become a matter of degree when relational and hierarchical contracts are included on the one side,[2] and
governance by unanimous agreement is allowed on the other side.
Nor is governance by unanimous agreement the exotic and rare exception as it would appear if only formal decision rules are considered. Gerhard Lehmbruch was the first to direct our attention to the
importance of de facto unanimity in "consociational democracies"
that are, of course, formally governed by majority decisions

---

2   In the literature, a further distinction is introduced between "classical con-
     tracts" conforming to our description of "spot" contracts and "neoclassical con-
     tracts" refering to longer-term relationships with provisions for adjusting to
     uncertain future events which are, however, less elaborate than those associ-
     ated with "relational contracts" (Williamson1979). This only emphasizes the
     continuity among various forms of coordination.

(Lehmbruch 1967, 1968, 1979; Lijphart 1969). Similarly, Philippe Schmitter's (1979, 1981) neo-corporatist patterns of interest intermediation also imply the consensual settlement of issues which are formally subject to the exercise of hierarchical government authority. In the same vein, Renate Mayntz has shown that hierarchical relationships between the ministerial bureaucracy and its political leaders should often be interpreted as a "dialogue model" (Mayntz/Scharpf, 1975). She also found negotiated settlements to be characteristic features within the formally hierarchical relationship between administrative agencies and private firms in the implementation of environmental regulations (Mayntz et al. 1978). In our own studies of federal-state relations in Germany, we also observed a practice of unanimous agreement even in policy areas where majority decisions or even unilateral decisions by the federal government are formally prescribed (Scharpf et al. 1976; Garlichs 1980). In a similar vein, the precepts of "participative management" or "Japanese-style management" as well as the imperatives of "just-in-time" production and of "flexible specialization" emphasize the need for consensus within the firm and between the firm and its environment of suppliers and customers (Piore/Sabel 1984; Sabel 1987).

In short, recent developments in the private as well as in the public sector seem to emphasize the practical importance of coordination mechanisms that occupy a middle ground between the theoretical extremes of markets and hierarchies. Unfortunately, the policy implications of consensual negotiating systems with "the properties of a minisociety" (Williamson 1979:238) are theoretically less well understood than either pure markets or clearcut hierarchical or majoritarian decision systems. Leaving pure markets aside, however, it may nevertheless be possible to derive some hypotheses about the policy implications of negotiating systems as compared to the properties of majoritarian and hierarchical forms of coordination.[3]

---

3   In a sense, the theory of coordination forms is now finally catching up with the practice of international law, where the distinctions between multilateral treaties, international organizations, supranational organizations, and confederate states have always been difficult to define with precision.

With reference to interpersonal inclusiveness, the first of the three criteria introduced above, all systems will favor the interests of their members over those of outsiders. This once more emphasizes the importance of boundary rules. Whether decision rules will make any difference in this regard is quite uncertain. Conceivably, however, high transaction costs may further reduce the likelihood of generosity in systems operating under the unanimity rule. With regard to internal distribution, on the other hand, the implications seem more certain: As was recognized in the Coase Theorem itself, the potential for redistribution is reduced as one moves from "government" to "contract" and from "hierarchical" to "unanimous" decisions. While hierarchical authorities or hegemonic powers are free to disregard any interests and to choose any distributive rule, and while majoritarian decisions may at least disregard minority , the unanimity rule eliminates the possibility of involuntary redistribution. That does not, of course, exclude highly unequal contractual exchanges. These are, however, derived from a pre-existing inequality of bargaining positions (i.e. of the availability of alternative options when the bargain is not concluded), rather than from the decision process itself (Nash 1950, 1953; Bacharach/Lawler 1981). Thus, contracts and unanimous decisions permit each party to defend the existing pattern of distribution, while majoritarian and hierarchical decision rules create the possibility of involuntary redistribution (which may, of course, increase as well as decrease existing inequality).

With regard to the second criterion, the intertemporal stability of policy choices, hierarchical decision systems have perhaps the greatest freedom to consider long-term as well as short-term concerns, and majoritarian systems may tend to maximize short-term benefits when elections are frequent and pluralities uncertain. By comparison, the implications of the unanimity rule seem more uncertain: Freed from (some of) the pressure of party competition and secure in their expectations of continuing participation, decision-makers are not forced to maximize short-term advantages. But given the high transaction costs associated with the unanimity rule, effective policy choices will often depend on complexity-reducing and conflict-avoiding redefinitions of the problem at hand (Scharpf et al 1976) -

and limiting discussion to incremental changes and their short-term consequences is perhaps the most common technique for reducing complexity (Braybrooke/Lindblom 1963).

Finally, with regard to the substantive criteria of allocative efficiency, the unanimity rule is strongly favored in public-choice theory (Buchanan/Tullock 1962:85-96). Precisely because the rule excludes involuntary redistribution, agreement can only be obtained for policy choices which are Pareto superior to the status quo, so that the trend of decisions is likely to approach the frontier of Pareto optimality. From this perspective, unanimity is clearly the ideal decision rule,[4] compared to which majority decisions are likely to be substantively inferior - even though they may become a practical necesssity when decision costs are considered.

As I have tried to show elsewhere (Scharpf 1986/1988), the normative attractiveness of unanimity is critically dependent upon what Elinor Ostrom (1986a) has called the "default condition" or "reversion rule" that specifies the consequences of non-agreement. In single-shot negotiations among independent parties, non-agreement leaves everybody free to pursue their alternative options individually. Under such conditions, unanimity is indeed likely to increase allocative efficiency. In ongoing decision systems, by contrast, from which exit is impossible or very expensive, non-agreement is more likely to imply the continuation of earlier policy choices.[5] Where that is the case, the unanimity rule protects vested interests in existing regulations and government services regardless of changes in external conditions or political preferences that would preclude contemporary agreement on these same measures. In ongoing decision systems, there is thus no reason to associate either efficiency or libertarian

---

4   Dennis Mueller (1979:207-226) has shown that authors arguing for the normative superiority of majority decision presuppose zero-sum choices, while arguments favoring the unanimity rule proceed from assumption of positive-sum games.

5   Dennis Mueller (1979:214) comes close to recognizing the problem when he mentions that the unanimous adoption of one proposal on the Pareto frontier will henceforth prevent the adoption of all other proposals from the Pareto-efficient set. What is added here is the possibility that the earlier choice is moved away from the frontier by changes in circumstances or preferences.

values with the unanimity rule or with contractarian institutions: They will prevent deregulation and privatization along with all other policy changes that do not provide for the full compensation of the losers, and - given the inherent difficulties of full compensation - they are likely to produce (or maintain) policy choices that are inferior to those that might have been produced under hierarchical or majority decision rules.

This is about as far as it is possible to analyze the policy consequences of the unanimity rule and of negotiation systems in the abstract. Yet we know that similar institutions will work differently in different countries and at different times, and that similar policy choices may be produced within highly dissimilar institutional arrangements. Thus there are surely additional factors affecting policy choices which may modify or override the influence of institutional arrangements and decision rules. But is it possible to say anything about these additional influences without moving to a much lower level of abstraction in studies of greater historical and substantive specificity? I think, yes.

Styles of Decision-making

Interacting with formal rules of decision, there is another set of cognitive and normative factors, which specify the way in which interests may be defined, and issues framed and resolved under the applicable rules. To characterize this second set of factors, I have used the term "styles of decision-making" in an earlier paper (Scharpf 1986/1988). In spite of considerable differences in terminology, I have also found a high degree of substantive convergence on three distinct categories in the literature. Where Mary Parker Follet (1941) had talked about the resolution of industrial conflict through "domination," "compromise," or "integration", Amitai Etzioni (1961) had distinguished between "coercive," "utilitarian," and "normative" commitments and controls in organizations, while Thomas Bonoma (1976) had described differences between "unilateral", "mixed" and "bilateral" power systems and Russell Hardin (1982) had identified "conflict", "contract" and "coordination" as forms of collective action. Taking my terminological cues from March and Simon (1958) and

Johan Olsen and colleagues (1982), I have used "confrontation", "bargaining," and "problem solving" for my own classification of styles of decision-making. "Confrontation" refers to interactions in which winning, or the defeat of the other side, has become the paramount goal, and which are often decided by superior force. In a "bargaining" relationship, by contrast, participants are exclusively motivated by their own, egotistic self-interest and the typical outcome is a compromise. Problem solving, finally, implies the pursuit of common goals and the common search for an optimal solution. In all three instances, the intended meanings may be intuitively obvious, but their further clarification will profit from the application of game theoretic analyses. However, this necessitates a brief look at some of the fundamentals.

When theorizing about the normative patterns that may affect the definition of interests and the framing of issues, one must necessarily presuppose a certain degree of loose coupling between objective reality and the perception of interests. This departure from parsimonious rational-choice assumptions would not be useful, or even plausible, if real-world decision problems were often of the kind presumed by the conventional dichotomy of either "symbiotic" or "competitive" relationships between the interests at stake. In both cases, misperceptions or redefinitions of the "objective" game situation (pure zero-sum or pure coordination) by rational actors would be too idiosyncratic and infrequent to justify much theoretical or practical interest.

But in the real world, purely symbiotic or purely competitive interest constellations are extremely rare, and probably unstable,[6] compared to "mixed-motive" constellations in which the parties have common as well as competitive interests. It is their objective am-

---

6   The game of pure coordination will turn into the mixed-motive "Assurance Game" if there is any uncertainty about the other party's understanding of the interest constellation; it may be transformed into a "Prisoners' Dilemma" if there is suspicion of free-riding; or it may assume the character of "Battle of the Sexes" if the distribution of the costs and benefits of joint action becomes an issue. Conversely, pure competition will be transformed into the mixed-motive game of "Chicken" if the common interest in avoiding mutual destruction is realized by the participants.

bivalence, pulling participants toward cooperation and toward conflict at the same time, which also creates room for the redefinition of the interests and issues at stake.

In the game-theoretical literature, most attention is focussed on four prototypical mixed-motive games, "Assurance", "Prisoner's Dilemma", "Chicken", and "Battle of the Sexes" (Figure I). In each of these constellations, the application of conventional game-theoretical assumptions and solution concepts will lead either to stable solutions which are clearly suboptimal for both parties or to outcomes which are unstable.[7] This surely explains the enormous attention which mixed-motive constellations have received in analytical and experimental game-theretical research.

Most of this work, however, is concentrated on the study of non-cooperative games which are defined by the absence of communication between the parties and by the impossibility of binding agreements. When we are dealing with the governance of political systems or organizations or with stable, long-term negotiation systems, these assumptions are, of course, unrealistic. But when they are relaxed, the choice of a cooperative solution becomes a trivial problem in three of the four prototypical mixed-motive games. In the "Assurance Game", as well as in the "Prisoner's Dilemma" and in "Chicken", it is obvious that voluntary agreement could never be obtained for those outcomes in which the "cooperation" of one party is exploited by the "defection" of the other one (D/C or C/D). Once the possibility of exploitation is eliminated, there is no doubt that both parties will prefer the outcome obtained by mutual cooperation (C/C) over that which is expected in the case of mutual defection (D/D). In each of these three cases, therefore, agreement is entirely unproblematical if binding agreements are possible.

The same is not true, however, in the game known as "Battle of the Sexes" (the name reflects the problems of a couple who would like to spend an evening going out together, but she would prefer

---

7   In the "Assurance Game " and in "Prisoner's Dilemma", the suboptimal equilibrium (D/D) is obtained if both parties apply the minimax rule. In "Chicken", the minimax rule would produce a cooperative outcome (C/C) which, however, is not a game-theoretical equilibrium. In "Battle", minimax strategies would lead to a suboptimal outcome (O/B) which is also unstable.

Figure I:

Payoff Matrices of Four Mixed-Motive Games *

	C	D
C	4 4	3 1
D	1 3	2 2

Assurance

	C	D
C	3 3	4 1
D	1 4	2 2

Prisoner's Dilemma

	C	D
C	3 3	4 2
D	2 4	1 1

Chicken

	O	B
O	3 4	2 2
B	1 1	4 3

Battle of Sexes

* Payoffs ranked from 1 (worst) to 4 (best); C = Cooperate, D = Defect, O = Going to the Opera, B = Going to the Ball Game

the opera and he a ball game). While it is clear that both would prefer one of the coordinated outcomes (O/O or B/B) over the possibility of each going his/her own way (O/B), that is by no means the end of their difficulties because now they have to choose between two solutions whose distributional characteristics are significantly different from each other.

Before we go further, it is perhaps important to note that the characteristics of "Battle" apply to an extremely wide range of real-life constellations. Not only intimate partners, but also business firms engaged in joint ventures, unions and management in collective bargaining, bureaucrats in the process of interministerial coordination, political parties in a coalition (Tsebelis 1988) and presumably most other joint undertakings are all confronted with the same problem: While important benefits are dependent upon the ability to co-operate, cooperation is seriously threatened by conflict over the

choice of one of the cooperative solutions (or over the distribution of
the costs and benefits of cooperation).

In spite of its enormous practical significance, however, "Battle of
the Sexes" has found much less attention in the game-theoretical
literature than the "Prisoner's Dilemma" or "Chicken" games
(Luce/Raiffa 1957:90-94; Hamburger 1979:128-130; Snidal 1985:931-
32). That is clearly related to the fact that, as a non-cooperative game,
"Battle" does not have a unique and stable solution, if conventional
solution concepts are applied.[8] As a consequence, interest has shifted
from the positive analysis of expected outcomes to the discussion of
"fair" solutions in the context of normative theories of negotiation
(Raiffa 1982). From the vantage point of empirical political science,
that is perhaps not the most promising theoretical development to
pursue. Instead it now seems useful to turn to some findings of
experimental game research which have challenged conventional assumptions of game-theoretical analysis, and which are directly pertinent to our interest in operational definitions of different styles of
decision-making.

Game theory started as a branch of economics (von Neu-
mann/Morgenstern 1944), and it has always maintained the motivational assumptions of micro-economic theory. Foremost among these
is an individualistic "live-and-let-live" definition of the utility which
players are supposed to seek: All of them are single-mindedly maximizing their own expected payoffs, with no concern for the payoffs
received by other players (except as far as is necessary to anticipate
their moves). But that is, surely, not the full range of potential human
motivations. Actors may be engaged in strategic interaction not only
as strictly self-interested individuals, but also as competitors or even
as mortal enemies, as partners in a common enterprise or even as
participants in an altruistic helper-client relationship.

Social scientists and psychologists have, of course, long objected
on similar grounds to the motivational simplifications of micro-eco-

---

8   Applying the minimax rule, the players would converge upon a suboptimal
    outcome (O/B) which (by contrast to the Prisoner's Dilemma) is not a game-
    theoretic equilibrium. Both players would like to leave that cell - but in differ-
    ent directions.

nomics. What is new and promising is a conceptualization of such objections which facilitates, rather than precludes, application of the analytical tools of game-theoretic and, more generally, rational-choice analyses. The conceptual innvovation was achieved when Harold Kelley and John Thibaut (1978:14-17) summarized a series of experimental findings by distinguishing between the "given matrix" of objectively defined payoffs and an "effective matrix" which in fact determines the strategy choices of the players.

The distinction rests on the recognition that actors' choices in a game situation depend on their interpretation of payoffs in the light of perceived relationships to the other parties, rather than on the "objectively" given payoffs as such. By itself, that would hardly be news. What is exciting is the promise that these subjective interpretations might be captured by a limited number of easily identifiable "transformation rules" which convert a given matrix into a variety of different effective matrices. For empirical social scientists this implies the hope that we might finally be able to profit from the analytical power of the rational-choice apparatus without having to ignore most of what we know about the variance and contingency of human motives.

Of the transformation rules suggested by experimental work in social psychology, three are of particular importance for the empirical analysis of political interactions: The maximization of one's "own gain", the maximization of one's "relative gain" compared to another party, and the maximization of "joint gains" of all parties (Messick/Thorngate 1967; McClintock 1972; Kelley/ Thibaut 1978:140-150).[9]

---

9 McClintock as well as Kelley/Thibaut also discuss an "altruistic" (maximize other's gain) transformation which they consider to be of little practical significance. This ignores the importance of "trust" in the altruism of professional helpers (Barber1983). In addition, Kelley/Thibaut(1978:145) also mention the possibility of an "egalitarian" transformation (minimize differences) which might be relevant in socialist communities. But that does not seem to exhaust the potential range of human motives: Ethnic and religious conflict often seems to imply a "punitive" transformation (minimize other's gain), and some choices may even be motivated by a desire for "self punishment" (minimize own gain).

Thus, a more complete typology might include the following potential rules of transformation :

Figure II:

Competitive and Cooperative Transformations of Battle of the Sexes

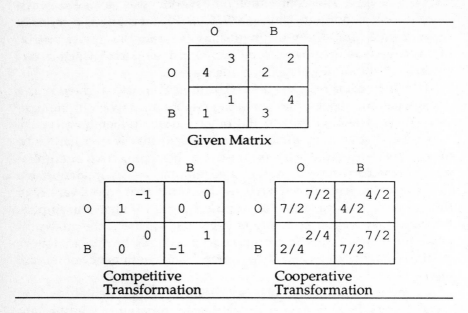

Given Matrix

Competitive
Transformation

Cooperative
Transformation

The first of these rules, "own gain maximization", leaves the "given matrix" unchanged. It thus corresponds to the "individualistic" assumptions of micro-economics and conventional game theory according to which actors are guided only by a concern for their own payoffs. Thus, the rule provides a precise operational definition of the attitudes and behavioral tendencies associated with the "bargaining" style of decision-making. Under the conditions of "Battle of the Sexes", players will be interested in an evening together, but each

- maximize/minimize own gain,
- maximize/minimize joint gains,
- maximize/minimize differences,
- maximize/minimize other's gain.

Additional and more complex "social orientations" have been identified by Schulz and May (1989) will also try for her/his best outcome, and so they are likely to disagree endlessly over choice of a meeting place.

The second rule, "relative gain maximization", suggests a competitive transformation of the "given matrix" with an emphasis on winning or losing in comparison to others (Figure II). It has excellent credentials in sociological and psychological theories of reference groups and of relative deprivation (Stouffer et al. 1949; Merton 1957; Runciman 1966; Pettigrew 1967). It also corresponds well with the emphasis on competition in the socialization of individuals in Western culture (Deutsch 1979). Examples that come to mind are competitive sports, party competition, or the arms race. Among our three styles of decision-making, the rule corresponds to the one we have labeled "confrontation". Where it applies, the parties are not interested in mutually advantageous compromises; the game is about winning or losing. Under the conditions of "Battle", each player will thus prefer to spend the evening alone, rather than submitting to the other's preferences.

The third rule, finally, implies a "cooperative" or "solidaristic" transformation of the "given matrix", so that "an actor seeks those alternatives that afford both himself and the other the highest joint outcome" (McClintock 1972:447). If both parties apply the rule, the difference between their individual payoffs will become irrelevant, and they are both free to engage in a search for the optimal common outcome which corresponds directly to our definition of the "problem solving" style of decision-making. Examples may be found among happy marriages, winning sports teams, "solidaristic" unions, or government coalitions in their honeymoon. Applied to "Battle", the parties will be happy to spend the evening together regardless of which site is chosen.

What is important for our purposes is that both the "competitive" and the "cooperative" rules will transform "Battle of the Sexes" from a game without solution into one with stable solutions - which differ, however, in their "objective" properties as these had been defined in the "given matrix". If the parties revert to an "individualistic" view of the world (as they are likely to do every once in a while), they will discover that the outcomes achieved through "problem solving" are objectively superior for either of them, even if one is ahead of the other one.

Thus, if preferences or attitudes could be chosen at will, the parties would clearly be better off with a cooperative or problem-solving view of the world. Yet the continuing conflict over distribution would probably frustrate any purely instrumental adoption of "as-if" attitudes. What is psychologically more likely instead is an oscillation between competition and cooperation, or perhaps the kind of cyclical changes of attitudes which have been observed in long iterations of the "Prisoner's Dilemma" (Kelley/Thibaut1978:231). In the case of "Battle" one might thus expect that parties finding their search for advantageous solutions obstructed by disagreement under "bargaining" conditions might then turn to "problem solving" - whose unequal outcomes may, eventually, be so resented by the disadvantaged party that it will ultimately prefer the mutual misery of "confrontation" to the feeling of being unilaterally exploited.

The Importance of Distributional Justice

But where does this leave us in our search for institutional explanations of policy choices? The first conclusion that should be drawn is that the constellation of interests which is represented by "Battle of the Sexes" is particularly difficult to cope with under conditions of unanimous decision-making - much more difficult in fact than the games of "Chicken" and the "Prisoner's Dilemma" which have received so much more attention in game-theoretical research. However, "Battle" is also a game constellation that occurs very frequently in real-world policy processes.

Secondly, the difficulties encountered in "Battle"-type constellations must be particularly acute under conditions of unanimous decision-making when the bargaining positions of the parties are nearly equal. Clearly, neither hierarchical nor majority decision systems would have any problem here: Under both rules, the dominant party would choose the one outcome which it most prefers for itself - leaving the other side with its second-best payoff which, however, is objectively still more desirable than would be the outcome of a deadlock between more nearly balanced bargainers. Similar results may be expected even under the unanimity rule if one of the parties enjoys a clearly superior bargaining position - defined by either more attractive exit options or by a greater threat potential (Nash 1950, 1953; Bacharach/Lawler 1981). This may be the analytical explanation behind Manfred Schmidt's (1986) discovery that both labor-dominated and capital-dominated political economies have dones better economically during the crises of the 1970s and early 1980s than countries in which the economic and political weights of capital and labor are more evenly balanced. The distributional characteristics were of course quite dissimilar, but total welfare production may indeed have been greater in either type of hegemonic system.

Finally, we have been able to identify three distinct social-psychological orientations, corresponding to the decision styles of "bargaining", "confrontation", and "problem solving". These will influence the likelihood of socially superior or inferior policy choices quite independently from the applicable rules of decision. Unfortunately, however, the most common and in many ways psychologically most robust "bargaining" style is likely to generate endless disagreement, blockades and socially suboptimal outcomes when the interest constellation resembles "Battle of the Sexes"[10] (while "bargaining" would be a socially satisfactory decision style under conditions resembling the "Prisoner's Dilemma"). "Problem solving" on the other hand, which clearly would be the socially most desirable decision style under the circumstances, seems always threatened by an erosion of the underlying "cooperative" definition of the mutual interests involved. It is explained by the constant irri-

---

10 The famous "Nash solution" of normative bargaining theory (Nash 1950, 1953) eliminates the crucial element of "Battle" - i.e. the need to choose between distinct and distributively different solutions - by assuming that outcomes are continuously variable (or can be made through side payments or package deals). Where that is the case, it is indeed plausible that the parties ought to "split the difference", and that outcomes will represent the respective bargaining or threat positions of the participants. That point may be hard to identify in practice, and it may depend much on the strategies and tactics of negotiation (Bacharach/Lawler1981; Fisher/Ury1983), but there is no reason to assume that the collective optimum will be systematically violated - as it is likely to be when "Battle of the Sexes" is played with distinct and "lumpy" outcomes.

tation which the unequal distribution of outcomes must imply for the disadvantaged party.

Thus what is special about "Battle of the Sexes" is the fact that the coexistence of cooperative and competitive motives continues even when binding agreements are possible and when both parties are genuinely interested in reaching an agreement. If that is so, cooperation would be clearly facilitated by arrangements permitting the separate settlement of distributive conflict.[11] There are hints of this in the game theoretic literature: When solutions to "Battle of the Sexes" are discussed at all, reference is usually made to the simple expedient of turn-taking - which of course presupposes an ongoing, "iterated" relationship (Kelley/Thibaut 1978:101-102). Indeed, if the couple is able to agree that they should follow her preferences one week and his the next, they could enjoy each other's company without one or the other submitting to an exploitative relationship. Unfortunately, real-world choice situations are not often so standardized and repetitive as to make simple turn-taking a plausible option - even though rotating prime-ministerships in the coalition governments of Israel or Italy and the rotating chairs of the European Community or of university departments suggests that such solutions are not entirely uncommon in practice. At any rate, the underlying logic seems sound. By agreement on rules of procedure, temporal hierarchies are created which permit deadlocks to be broken without permanently favoring the distributive interests of one party over all others. In a somewhat attenuated sense, the same logic also legitimates the quasi-dictatorial powers of parliamentary majorities which may be displaced in regular and fair elections.

The question is whether functionally equivalent solutions are available in decision situations where the unanimity rule cannot be relaxed through resort to temporal hierarchies. This includes most of the negotiating systems that have grown up informally in institu-

---

11 That is different from the confidence-building strategies often advocated to improve the chances of cooperation in the "Prisoner's Dilemma". In "Battle", the problem is not the mutual fear of defection, but the reality of exploitation, and what is required for an effective solution is not mutual trust, but distributional fairness.

tions that are formally governed by hierarchical or majority rule.[12] The most promising solution seems to suggest a procedural separation between the settlement of distributive conflict and negotiations over substantive issues. If agreement on *general* rules of distributive justice or fairness can be reached, it may then be possible to neutralize distributive conflict in the *individual* game and, thus, to facilitate cooperative "problem solving" in the search for productive solutions.

In the real world, this separation of production from distribution seems to be practiced quite frequently: Organizations settle the conflict over the proper inducements/contributions balance of their employees in negotiations over wages and hours of work which are separate from the coordination problems encountered in their daily work (Barnard 1947; Simon 1957:110-122). Similarly in the economy, reference to market prices helps to reduce distributive conflict between buyers and sellers, and the same effect is achieved for the relation between clients and professional helpers (which is particularly vulnerable to suspicions of exploitation) by the public regulation of professional standards and fees (Barber 1983). At another level, it can be shown that economically rational collective bargaining in Sweden was greatly facilitated, from the late 1960s to the mid 1970s, by an agreement of employers and competing unions on the so-called EFO-Formula, which defined the permissible scope for wage settlements in the domestic sector by reference to economically acceptable wage increases in the export sector (Scharpf 1987). The same function is served by the ubiquitous and rigid distributional rules governing federal-state policy-making in West Germany (Scharpf et al. 1976). Carrying the idea one step further, it was recently proposed that the European Community should try to facilitate agreement over substantive policy choices by fixing in advance the levels of net contributions to the Community budget for each member country. Thus countries that profit less than average from the incidence of specific Community programs could expect a budgetary rebate while others

---

12 One disadvantage of informal rules is that they cannot be relaxed without undercutting their binding force altogether. This seems to be a fear associated with the de-facto changes introduced by Margaret Thatcher in Britain's unwritten constitution.

would have to pay a surcharge over and above their regular budget contribution (Padoa-Schioppa 1988:104-108, 150-161).

But although the logic of such solutions is impeccable, *general resolutions* of distributive conflicts tend to have their own difficulties as well. Many of them arise from the fact that real-world decision situations tend to have unique characteristics about which the parties care enough to rule out generalized settlements that are unrelated to the merits of the specific case. Even more fundamental difficulties arise from the fact that generalized solutions often force parties to explicate their criteria of justice - and hence to confront their *bona fide* disagreement about them.

Social psychologists have been able to empirically identify at least three competing concepts of distributive justice - "equality", "equity", and "need" (Deutsch 1975, 1979, 1985), which also find support in normative treatments of justice in philosophy and law (Rawls 1972; Noll 1983). While it may be true that competition among these criteria is limited by the fact that each is most appropriate for specific domains, these plural "spheres of justice" (Walzer 1983) are bound to overlap, or to invade each other, and their underlying "institutional logics" are often in conflict (Alford/Friedland 1985) Even when research is restricted to the criterion of "equity" (Berkowitz/Walster 1976; Greenberg/Cohen 1982), the underlying norm of proportionality is full of ambiguities and its interpretation crammed with furious disputes, as George Homans (1976, 1982) had occasion to remind his fellow equity researchers. The same is obviously true for the competing standards of "need" and "equality" as well. In short: Distributive conflict is not necessarily resolved more easily by shifting the frame of reference from agreement in the individual case to agreement on a general rule of distributive justice.

Nevertheless, this seems to be the most promising institutional strategy for policy-making systems struggling under de-facto unanimity conditions. At least if we disregard the possibility of a sweeping reassertion of hierarchical authority, the best chance that systems with very high consensus requirements might maintain or regain their capacity for productive policy innovation seems to depend on their ability to achieve or maintain agreement on issues of distributive justice. Hierarchical and majoritarian systems, by contrast, are much less constrained in their capability for political innovation by the virulence of unresolved distributive conflict.

This is about as far as the present line of speculative theorizing ought to be pushed. From here on, we need to return to our empirical and comparative work in order to further develop and differentiate these hypotheses and, above all, to specify their empirical referents as well as the contextual conditions under which they are likely to be - in the words of Jim Coleman - "sometimes true theories" (Coleman 1964:516-519; McGuire 1983).

Fortunately for our purposes, political systems in Western Europe seem to provide sufficient empirical variance along both of the dimensions whose theoretical significance I have discussed. While Britain Great seems to have the most hierarchical and majoritarian policy processes of any Western European country, Switzerland may have the most consensual ones. But the need for de-facto unanimity among different political camps and competing economic interests seems to be almost as great in Austria, in the Federal Republic and, perhaps, in Sweden. Distributive justice, on the other hand, has been a highly salient political issue in Sweden, and to a lesser degree also in Britain, throughout the postwar period. In Switzerland, Austria, and West Germany, by contrast, distributive issues have been almost completely absent from public political discussion during the same period. Yet the presence or absence of explicit public discussion may not be a very good indicator of the virulence of distributive conflict in each of these countries. It is at least conceivable that Sweden, Switzerland and perhaps Austria may be more similar to each other in their degree of consensus over issues of distributive justice, while Britain and West Germany may each have to cope with considerable distributive conflict which, however, is more explicit in one country than in the other.

These are questions, not hypotheses. What will be important is to devise empirical indicators that would permit us to answer them one way or another in order to get on with our common business of theoretically oriented comparative policy studies.

References

Alford, Robert R. and Roger Friedland (1985) *Powers of Theory. Capitalism, the State and Democracy.*Cambridge: Cambridge University Press.

Bacharach, Samuel B. and Edward J. Lawler (1981) *Bargaining. Power, Tactics, and Outcomes.* San Francisco: Jossey-Bass.

Barber, Bernard (1983) *The Logic and Limits of Trust.* New Brunswick: Rutgers University Press.

Barnard, Chester I. (1947) *The Functions of the Executive.* Cambridge, MA: Harvard University Press

Berkowitz, Leonard and Elaine Walster (eds.) (1976) *Equity Theory: Towards a General Theory of Social Interaction,.* (Advances in Experimental Social Psychology 9), New York: Academic Press

Bickel, Alexander M. (1962) *The Least Dangerous Branch. The Supreme Court at the Bar of Politics.* Indianapolis: Bobbs-Merrill.

Blalock, Hubert M. (1961) *Causal Inferences in Nonexperimental Research.* Chapel Hill: University of North Carolina Press.

Bonoma, Thomas V. (1976) 'Conflict, Cooperation and Trust in Three Power Systems', *Behavioral Science* 21: 499-513.

Braybrooke, David and Charles E. Lindblom (1963) *A Strategy of Decision. Policy Evaluation as a Social Process.* New York: Free Press.

Buchanan, James M. and Gordon Tullock (1962) *The Calculus of Consent. Logical Foundations of Constitutional Democracy.* Ann Arbor: University of Michigan Press.

Coase, Ronald (1960) 'The Problem of Social Cost', *Journal of Law and Economics* 3: 1-44.

Coleman, James S. (1964) *Introduction to Mathematical Sociology.* New York: Free Press.

Coleman, James S. (1974) *Power and the Structure of Society*. New York: W.W. Norton Co.

Collard, David (1978) *Altruism and Economy. A Study in Non-Selfish Economics*. New York: Oxford University Press.

Dahl, Robert A. and Charles E. Lindblom (1953) *Politics, Economics, and Welfare. Planning and Politico-Economic Systems Resolved into Basic Social Processes*. New York: Harper & Row.

Deutsch, Morton (1985) *Distributive Justice: A Social Psychological Perspective*. New Haven: Yale University Press.

Dore, Ronald (1983) 'Goodwill and the Spirit of Market Capitalism', *British Journal of Sociology* XXXIV: 459-482.

Douglas, Mary (1986) *How Institutions Think*. Syracuse: Syracuse University Press.

Douglas, Mary and Aaron Wildavsky (1983) *Risk and Culture*. Berkeley: University of California Press.

Elias, Norbert (1987) 'Wandlungen der Wir-Ich-Balance', pp. 207-315 in: Norbert Elias, *Die Gesellschaft der Individuen*. Frankfurt: Suhrkamp.

Etzioni, Amitai (1961) *A Comparative Analysis of Complex Organizations*. New York: Free Press.

Feick, Jürgen and Werner Jann (1988) ' "Nations Matter" - Vom Eklektizismus zur Integration in der vergleichenden Policyforschung? ', *Politische Vierteljahreschrift*, Sonderheft 19.

Fisher, Roger and William Ury (1983) *Getting to Yes. Negotiating Agreement Without Giving In*. Harmondsworth: Penguin.

Garlichs, Dietrich (1980) *Grenzen staatlicher Infrastrukturpolitik. Bund/Länder-Kooperation in der Fernstraßenplanung*. Königstein/Ts.: Anton Hain.

Glaser, Barney G. and Anselm L. Strauss (1967) *The Discovery of Grounded Theory. Strategies for Qualitative Research*. Chicago: Aldine Atherton.

Greenberg, Gerald and Ronald L. Cohen (eds.) (1982) *Equity and Justice in Social Behavior*, New York: Academic Press

Greenwald, Anthony, Anthony A. Pratkanis, Michael R. Leippe and Michael H. Baumgardner (1986) 'Under What Conditions Does Theory Obstruct Research Progress?', *Psychological Review* 93: 216-229.

Hamburger, Henry (1979) *Games as Models of Social Phenomena*. San Francisco: Freeman.

Hardin, Russell (1982) *Collective Action*. Baltimore: Johns Hopkins University Press.

Harsanyi, John C. (1980) 'Rule Utilitarianism, Rights, Obligations and the Theory of Rational Behavior', *Theory and Decision* 12: 115-133.

Hirschman, Albert O. (1977) *The Passions and the Interests. Political Arguments for Capitalism before its Triumph*. Princeton: Princeton University Press.

Homans, George C. (1976) 'Commentary', pp. 231-244 in Berkowitz, Leonard and Elaine Walster (eds.) *Equity Theory: Towards a General Theory of Social Interaction*, New York: Academic Press

Homans, George C. (1976) 'Foreword', pp. XI-XVIII in Greenberg, G. and R.L. Cohen (eds.) *Equity and Justice in Social Behavior*, New York: Academic Press

John, Robert (1980) 'Theory Construction in Sociology: The Competing Approaches' *Mid-American Review of Sociology* 5: 15-36.

Jönsson, Christer (1983) 'A Cognitive Approach to International Negotiation', *European Journal of Political Research* 11: 139-50.

Kahneman, Daniel and Amos Tversky (1984) 'Choices, Values, and Frames', *American Psychologist* 39: 341-350

Kaufmann, Franz-Xaver, Giandomenico Majone and Vincent Ostrom (eds.) (1986) *Guidance, Control, and Evaluation in the Public Sector*. The Bielefeld Interdisciplinary Project. Berlin: de Gruyter.

Kelley, Harold H. and John W. Thibaut (1978) *Interpersonal Relations. A Theory of Interdependence*. New York: John Wiley

Kennett, David A (1980) 'Altruism and Economic Behavior, I: Developments in the Theory of Public and Private Redistribution', *American Journal of Economics and Sociology* 39: 183-198.

Kennett, David A. (1980a) 'Altruism and Economic Behavior: II. Private Charity and Public Policy' *American Journal of Economics and Sociology* 39: 337-354.

Kolm, Serge-Christophe (1983) 'Altruism and Efficiency' *Ethics* 94: 18 - 65.

Latsis, Spiros (1972) 'Situational Determinism in Economics' *British Journal for the Philosophy of Science* 23: 207-245.

Layder, Derek (1982) 'Grounded Theory: A Constructive Critique' *Journal for the Theory of Social Behavior* 12: 103-123.

Lehmbruch, Gerhard (1967) *Proporzdemokratie. Politisches System und politische Kultur in der Schweiz und Österreich.* Tübingen: Mohr.

Lehmbruch, Gerhard (1968) 'Konkordanzdemokratie im politischen System der Schweiz' *Politische Vierteljahresschrift* 9: 443-459.

Lehmbruch, Gerhard (1976) *Parteienwettbewerb im Bundesstaat.* Stuttgart: Kohlhammer.

Lehmbruch, Gerhard (1979) 'Consociational Democracy, Class Conflict and the New Corporatism', pp. 53-62 in Philippe C. Schmitter and Gerhard Lehmbruch (eds.) *Trends Towards Corporatist Intermediation.* London: Sage.

Lijphart, Arendt (1969) 'Consociational Democracy' *World Politics* 21: 207-225.

Lowi, Theodore (1964) 'American Business, Public Policy, Case Studies and Political Theory' *World Politics* 16: 677-715.

Luce, R. Duncan and Howard Raiffa (1957) *Games and Decisions. Introduction and Critical Survey.* New York: John Wiley.

Macneil, Ian R. (1978) 'Contracts: Adjustment of Long-term Economic Relations Under Classical, Neoclassical, and Relational Contract Law' *Northwestern University Law Review* 72: 854-905.

Macneil, Ian R. (1983) 'Values in Contract: Internal and External' *Northwestern University Law Review* 78: 340-418.

Macneil, Ian R. (1987) *Political Exchange as Relational Contract*. Ms. Florence: European University Institute.

March, James G. and Herbert A. Simon (1958) *Organizations*. New York: John Wiley.

Margolis, Howard (1982) *Selfishness, Altruism, and Rationality. A Theory of Social Choice*. Cambridge: Cambridge University Press.

Mayntz, Renate and Birgitta Nedelmann (1987) 'Eigendynamische soziale Prozesse. Anmerkungen zu einem analytischen Paradigma' *Kölner Zeitschrift für Soziologie und Sozialpsychologie* 39: 648-668.

Mayntz, Renate and Fritz W. Scharpf (1975) *Policy-Making in the German Federal Bureaucracy*. Amsterdam: Elsevier.

Mayntz, Renate, H.-U. Derlien, E. Bohne, B. Hesse, J. Hucke and A. Müller (1978) *Vollzugsprobleme der Umweltpolitik - Empirische Untersuchung der Implementation von Gesetzen im Bereich der Luftreinhaltung und des Gewässerschutzes*. Materialien zur Umweltforschung, ed. by "Rat von Sachverständigen für Umweltfragen". Stuttgart: Kohlhammer

McClintock, Charles G. (1972) 'Social Motivation - A set of Propositions' *Behavioral Science* 17: 438-454

McGuire, William J. (1983) 'A Contextualist Theory of Knowledge: Its Implications for Innovation and Reform in Psychological Research', pp. 1-47 in Leonard Berkowitz (ed.) *Advances in Experimental Social Psychology vol 16*. Orlando, FL: Academic Press.

Merton, Robert K. and Alice S. Rossi (1957) 'Contributions to the Theory of Reference Group Behavior', pp. 279-334 in Robert K. Merton (ed.) *Social Theory and Social Structure*. Glencoe, IL: Free Press (Rev. ed)

Messick, David M. and Warren B. Thorngate (1967) 'Relative Gain Maximization in Experimental Games',*Journal of Experimental Social Psychology* 3: 85-101

Michels, Roberto (1915/1962) *Political Parties.* New York: Collier Books.

Midgaard, Knut (1983) 'Rules and Strategy in Negotiations: Notes on an Institutionalist and Intentionalist Approach' *European Journal for Political Research* 11: 151-66.

Mueller, Dennis C. (1979) *Public Choice.* Cambridge: Cambridge University Press.

Nash, John F. (1950) 'The Bargaining Problem', *Econometrica* 18: 155-162.

Nash, John F. (1953) 'Two-Person Cooperative Games', *Econometrica* 21: 128-140.

Nisbett, Richard and Lee Ross (1980) *Human Inference: Strategies and Shortcomings of Social Judgment.* Englewood Cliffs: Prentice-Hall.

Noll, Peter (1983) *Diktate über Sterben und Tod*, Zürich: Pendo

Olsen, Johan, Paul Roness and Harald Sætren (1982) 'Norway: Still Peaceful Coexistence and Revolution in Slow Motion?'. pp. 47-79 in Jeremy Richardson (ed.) *Policy Styles in Western Europe.* London: George Allen & Unwin.

Olson, Mancur (1982) *The Rise and Decline of Nations. Economic Growth, Stagflation, and Social Rigidities.* New Haven: Yale University Press.

Ostrom, Elinor (1986) 'A Method of Institutional Analysis', pp. 459-475 in Franz-Xaver Kaufmann, Giandomenico Majone and Vincent Ostrom (eds.) *Guidance, Control, and Evaluation in the Public Sector.* The Bielefeld Interdisciplinary Project. Berlin: de Gruyter.

Ostrom, Elinor (1986a) 'An Agenda for the Study of Institutions', *Public Choice* 48: 3-25.

Ostrom, Elinor (1988) *The Commons and Collective Action*. Ms. Workshop in Political Theory and Policy Analysis. Indiana University.

Ouchi, William G. (1980) 'Markets, Bureaucracies and Clans', *Administrative Science Quarterly* 25: 129-41.

Ouchi, William G. (1984) *The M-Form Society. How American Teamwork Can Recapture the Competitive Edge*. Reading, Mass: Addison-Wesley.

Padoa-Schioppa, Tommaso et. al. (1988) *Efficiency, Stability, and Equity: A Strategy for the Evolution of the Economic System of the European Community*, Oxford: Oxford University Press.

Parker Follett, Mary (1941) 'Constructive Conflict', pp. 30-49 in Henry C. Metcalf and L. Urwick (eds.) *Dynamic Administration. The Collected Papers of Mary Parker Follett*. New York: Harper.

Pettigrew, Thomas E. (1967) 'Social Evaluation Theory: Convergences and Applications', pp. 241-315 in David Levine (ed.) *Nebraska Symposium on Motivation 1967*. Lincoln: University of Nebraska Press.

Piore, Michael J. and Charles F. Sabel (1984) *The Second Industrial Divide. Possibilities for Prosperity*. New York: Basic Books.

Posse, Achim Ulrich (1986) *Föderative Politikverflechtung in der Umweltpolitik*. München: Minerva-Publikation (Innenpolitik in Theorie und Praxis 16).

Powell, Walter W. (1987) *Neither Market Nor Hierarchy: The Limits of Organization*. MS Stanford: CASBS, June 1987

Pruitt, Dean G. and Steven A. Lewis (1975) 'Development of Integrative Solutions in Bilateral Negotiation', *Journal of Personality and Social Psychology* 31: 621-33.

Przeworski, Adam and Henry Teune (1970) *The Logic of Comparative Social Inquiry*. New York: John Wiley.

Raiffa, Howard (1982) *The Art and Science of Negotiation*. Cambridge: Harvard University Press.

Reh, Werner (1986) *Politikverflechtung im Fernstraßenbau der Bundesrepublik Deutschland und im Nationalstraßenbau der Schweiz: Eine vergleichende Untersuchung zur Effizienz und Legitimation des bürokratischen Föderalismus*. PhD-Dissertation. University of Mannheim.

Runciman, W.G. (1966) *Relative Deprivation and Social Justice. A Study of Attitudes to Social Inequality in Twentieth-Century England*. Berkely: University of Californian Press.

Sabatier, Paul A. (1987) 'Knowledge, Policy-Oriented Learning, and Policy Change', *Knowledge: Creation, Diffusion, Utilization* 8: 649-692.

Sabel, Charles F. (1987) *The Reemergence of Regional Economies: Changes in the Scale of Production*. Ms: Cambridge, MA: Massachusetts Institute of Technology.

Scharpf, Fritz W. (1972) 'Komplexität als Schranke der politischen Planung', *Politische Vierteljahresschrift* 13, Sonderheft 4: 168-192.

Scharpf, Fritz W. (1986) 'Die Politikverflechtungs-Falle: Europäische Integration und deutscher Föderalismus im Vergleich', *Politische Vierteljahresschrift* 26: 323-356. Translated: 'The Joint Decision Trap', (Forthcoming).

Scharpf, Fritz W. (1987) *Sozialdemokratische Krisenpolitik in Europa*. Frankfurt: Campus (English translation forthcoming)

Scharpf, Fritz W. (1988) 'A Game-Theoretical Interpretation of Inflation and Unemployment in Western Europe', *Journal of Public Policy* 7: 227-257.

Scharpf, Fritz W. (1988a) 'Verhandlungssysteme, Verteilungskonflikte und Pathologien der politischen Steuerung', *Politische Vierteljahresschrift*, Sonderheft 19:61-87.

Scharpf, Fritz W., Bernd Reissert and Fritz Schnabel (1978) 'Policy Effectiveness and Conflict Avoidance in Intergovernmental Policy Formation', pp. 57-112 in Kenneth Hanf and Fritz W. Scharpf (eds.) *Interorganizational Policy-making. Limits to Coordination and Central Control*. London: Sage.

84 Fritz W. Scharpf

Schmidt, Manfred G. (1986) 'Politische Bedingungen erfolgreicher Wirtschaftspolitik - eine vergleichende Analyse westlicher Industrieländer', *Journal für Sozialforschung* 26: 251-273.

Schmidt, Manfred G. (1987) 'The Politics of Labour Market Policy: Structural and political determinants of full employment and mass unemployment in mixed economies', pp. 4-63 in Francis G. Castles, Franz Lehner and Manfred G. Schmidt (eds.) *Managing Mixed Economies*. Berlin: De Gruyter.

Schmitter, Philippe C. (1979) 'Still the Century of Corporatism?', pp. 7-52 in Philippe C. Schmitter and Gerhard Lehmbruch (eds.) *Trends Toward Corporatist Intermediation*. London: Sage.

Schmitter, Philippe C. (1981) 'Interest Intermediation and Regime Governability in Contemporary Western Europe and North America', pp. 285-327 in Suzanne Berger (ed.) *Organizing Interests in Western Europe: Pluralism, Corporatism, and the Transformation of Politics*. Cambridge: Cambridge University Press.

Schulz, Ulrich and Theo May (1989) 'The Recording of Social Orientations with Ranking and Pair Comparison Procedures', *European Journal of Social Psychology* 19: 41-59.

Sen, Amartya K. (1977) 'Rational Fools: A Critique of the Bahavioral Foundations', *Philosophy and Public Affairs* 6: 317-344.

Shepsle, Kenneth A. and Barry R. Weingast (1981) 'Political Preferences for the Pork Barrel: A Generalization', *American Journal of Political Science* 25: 96-111.

Simon, Herbert A. (1957) *Administrative Behavior. A Study of Decision-Making Processes in Administrative Organization*. Second Edition. New York: Free Press.

Snidal, Duncan (1985) 'Coordination versus Prisoner's Dilemma: Implications for International Cooperation and Regimes', *American Political Science Review* 79: 923-942.

Stinchcombe, Arthur L. (1985) 'Contracts as Hierarchical Documents', pp. 121-171 in Arthur L. Stinchcombe and Carol A. Heimer (eds.) *Organization Theory and Project Management. Administering Uncertainty in Norwegian Offshore Oil.* Oslo: Norwegian University Press.

Stone, Harlan Fisk (1936) 'The Common Law in the United States', *Harvard Law Review* 50: 4-26.

Stouffer, Samuel A., et al. (1949) *The American Soldier, I: Adjustment During Army Life.* Princeton: Princeton University Press.

Thompson, James D. (1970) 'Comment: Power as Energy or Power as a Reflection of Things', pp. 90-92 in Mayer N. Zald (ed.) *Power in Organizations.* Nashville: Vanderbilt University Press.

Tsebelis, George (1988) 'Nested Games: The Cohesion of French Electoral Coalitions', *British Journal of Political Science* 18: 145-170.

Vayda, Andrew P. (1983) 'Progressive Contextualization: Methods for Research in Human Ecology', *Human Ecology* 11: 265-281

von Neumann, John and Oskar Morgenstern (1944) *Theory of Games and Economic Behavior.* Princeton: Princeton University Press.

Walton, Richard E. and Robert B. McKersie (1965) *A Behavioral Theory of Labor Negotiations. An Analysis of a Social Interaction System.* New York: McGraw-Hill

Walzer, Michael (1983) *Spheres of Justice. A Defense of Pluralism and Equality.* New York: Basic Books.

Weingast, Barry R. (1979) 'A Rational Choice Perspective on Congressional Norms', *American Journal of Political Science* 23: 245-263.

Wiesenthal, Helmut (1987) *Akteurrationalität. Überlegungen zur Steuerungsfähigkeit politischer Akteure in der Beschäftigungskrise.* MS Universität Bielefeld: Fakultät für Soziologie.

Willer, David (1978) 'What is Exact Theory?', in Robert Smith and Bo Anderson (eds.) *Theory Development.* New York: Halstedt Press.

Williamson, Oliver E. (1975) *Markets and Hierarchies. Analysis and Antitrust Implications.* New York: Free Press.

Williamson, Oliver E. (1979) 'Transaction-Cost Economics: The Governance of Contractual Relations', *Journal of Law and Economics* 22: 233-261.

Williamson, Oliver E. (1985) *The Economic Institutions of Capitalism. Firms, Markets, Relational Contracting.* New York: Free Press.

Zintl, Reinhard (1987) *Der homo oeconomicus als Generalist oder als Spezialist? Über die Verwendung rationalistischer Rekonstruktionen der Mikroebene.* Ms. München: Universität der Bundeswehr.

IV

Political Science and Organization Theory Parallel Agendas but Mutual Disregard[*]

Johan P. Olsen

Organization Theory and Political Research

The question: What can students of politics hope to learn by paying more attention to organization theory, has in the post-war period received a pessimistic answer most of the time. Political scientists have tended not to regard organization theory as particularly relevant, interesting, or important. There have been some significant instances of cross-fertilization, but most reviewers conclude that organization theory and political science have been in a state of mutual disregard for years.[2]

---

[*] Earlier drafts of this paper were presented at Konstanz University, Sozialwissenschaftliche Fakultät: "Politische Institutionen und Interessenvermittlung", Internationale Fachtagung zum 60. Geburtstag von Gerhard Lehmbruch, 20. und 21. April 1988, and at The Scandinavian Symposium for Organizational Research, "Models of Decision-making and Change in Organizations, and Contemporary Processes of Change and Reforms in the Nordic Countries", Hemsedal, Norway, June 13.-15. 1988. I want to thank participants in the two seminars and in particular Tore Grønlie, Per Lægreid, Richard Matland, Audun Offerdal, Per Selle, and Majla Solheim for advice and help.

2   Waldo 1961, 1978; Palumbo1975; Rainey 1983; Hall/Quinn 1983; Hardy 1987.

Political scientists have been sceptical to the usefulness of theorizing about formal organizations "as such", i.e. generic models assumed to be applicable across all formal organizations. In addition to complaints about harmful overgeneralization, political scientists have argued that students of formal organizations have neglected the major governmental agencies, and they have provided an inadequate analysis of the specific influences of the political environment upon organizations, public as well as private (Rainey 1983).

The state of mutual disregard (Hardy 1987) is surprising because there are important parallels between the questions raised in political science and in organization theory (Kaufman 1964). Students of politics have always been interested in how the political organization of a society contributes to the well-being of citizens. Political institutions have (most of the time) been seen as preconditions for a civilized society (Wolin 1960). Key questions have been how political institutions affect who-gets-what and the achievement of values such as justice and equality; how political institutions affect definitions of the good life and contribute to the education and socialization of citizens; and how political institutions develop and change, in particular what is the role of intention, reflection, choice and design in the transformation of political institutions (March/Olsen 1983, 1989).

The transfer of the professional basis of organization theory to business schools and lately also to private consulting firms has probably contributed to the alienation of political scientists from organization theory. Yet the relationship between the two fields has recently attracted some renewed attention. It has been suggested that there may be a convergence, or at least a reduced divergence, between organization theory and political research (Hall/Quinn 1983; Rainey 1983).

The great diversity of meanings ascribed to "political science" and "organization theory" makes it difficult to discuss the relationship between the two fields. Political science has shown great tolerance for theoretical pluralism or lack of an intellectual identity in terms of a shared theoretical core. Organization theory can no longer be seen as a subfield of public administration which, in turn, is seen as a subfield of political science. Presently organization theory is an inter-disciplinary cluster of more or less identifiable research ideas.[3]

Thus, no attempt is made here to attend to the possible usefulness of the various schools of organization theory to political research. Attention is concentrated on some possible contributions of a specific branch of organizational research: theoretically oriented and empirically based studies of organizational decision-making. Since making collective choices in organizational contexts is at the core of political life, this delimitation is not unreasonable. It will be argued that some recent developments in this branch of organizational research may help advance our understanding of political life, in particular our understanding of the role of political institutions - how they are organized, what impact they cause, and how they change.

Organizational Decision-Making: Contemporary Agenda

The predominant doctrine of organizational decision-making is rational choice. Organizational behavior is understood as the result of choices made by a rational, well-informed, unitary and value-maximizing decision-maker. Organizations are seen as instruments for making and implementing such choices. Often it is also assumed that organizations are acting in a perfectly competitive environment. They adapt to the contingencies of their environment, or they disappear.

Observations made by empirical students of organizational decision-making suggest several modifications of the model of rational choice. Since the major criticisms are discussed elsewhere (March 1981a, 1988), they are here treated in a summary fashion.

Bounded rationality, conflict, and ambiguity. Most decision-makers are most of the time not completely, or even well, informed. Time and attention are scarce resources, and the human brain has a limited capacity for information processing. Decision-makers can not attend

---

3   March 1965. Not everybody agrees with this description; see, e.g. Donaldson(1985) and the "symposium in print", in Organization Studies, 1988, (9), no.1.

to all goals, alternatives, or consequences at once. As a result, the allocation of attention is a critical process in organizations.

Most organizations most of the time do not function as unitary actors. Not all participants in an organization share the same goals. Conflict among them can not readily be managed through some prior contract, or through the decision of a sovereign leader. Organizations live with tensions and disagreements, and decision-makers have to convince, or bargain with, affected interests in order to achieve their support.

Most organizations most of the time do not function as rational decision-making machines. They survive (and thrive) with enduring ambiguity about preferences, causal linkages, and history. Decision-makers find themselves in a world where the past, present and future are ambiguous and call for interpretation (March/Olsen 1975). In modern organizations, developing meaning and socializing individuals into these interpretations are processes of equal importance to making choices. Often processes of interpretation are surrounded by myths, symbols, ceremonies, and rituals.

Standard operating procedures and garbage cans. Organizations cope with bounded rationality, conflict, and ambiguity by developing standard operating procedures. Most behavior in formal organizations is governed by routinized, experience-based programs of action. If we are familiar with an organization's programs of action, that is, actual routines, not a formal, legal set of rules, we can predict its behavior in relatively great detail. Simple stimuli trigger complex, standardized patterns of action without much analysis, problem-solving, or use of discretionary power. People do what they are accustomed to doing and can do well. Programs may be related to contents or procedures. They may determine the contents of decisions or the procedures for dealing with issues. Organizations have repertoires of programs and they use relatively simple rules to select programs (March/Simon 1958).

One implication is that organizational behavior is driven by available solutions as well as by problems (Cyert/March 1963). A second implications is that organizations most of the time function on the basis of a logic of appropriateness. Following rules and practices, that is, the normatively appropriate behavior in terms of the duties and obligations of specific roles, is more important than calculating the return expected from alternative choices. Tradition and trust, i.e., belief in the integrity and competence of other participants, is more important than rational analysis of issues. A third implication is that organizational repertoires might combine different "logics" and principles of coordination. "Appropriate behavior" is defined differently for different parts of the organization and for different situations.

Intelligence is embodied in routines. When organizational routines are evaluated on the basis of a specific and often deviant case, an organization may look "bureaucratic", rule bound, insensitive, and stupid. Still, organizational decision-makers may have good reasons for enacting routines rather than calculating consequences of alternative choices in each specific case. Most of the time standard operating procedures are reasonable approximations of average choices and average situations. Routines make it possible to coordinate many individuals to perform concerted tasks in an efficient way. Routines also embody organizational identities, interests, values, and causal theories. Standard operating procedures help organizations avoid some destructive conflicts. They also provide codes of meaning which facilitate the interpretation of an ambiguous world.

Not all organizational behavior is governed by pre-established programs, and studies of organizational decision-making in non-routinized situations throw some light on the significance of standard operating procedures. Non-routinized situations and open organizational structures give few rules regulating the access of decision-makers, problems, and solutions to choice opportunities, and few rules regulating how they can be attached to each other and handled. The absence of rules, however, does not neccessarily make rational choice models more useful.

Open structures tend to create complex ecologies of participants, problems, and solutions. Garbage can models of organizational choice suggest a temporal order rather than a causal instrumental order. Things are connected by their simultaneous presence or arrival more than by assessments of their importance[4] (Cohen/March/Olsen 1972; March/Olsen 1976; 1986a). Organizations attempt to avoid the unpredictability created by open structures and garbage can processes by establishing rules for the access of participants, problems, and solutions to choice opportunities.

Garbage can processes call attention to the significance of interorganizational links and relations. The problem of one organization is the solution of another. An entry in one choice is an exit somewhere else. Contemporary organizations face environments very different from those suggested by models of a perfectly competitive market or a perfect state hierarchy. Organizations are embedded in complex networks of interdependent and interacting organizations. Many standard operating procedures have an inter- rather than an intraorganizational character. In such situations the distinction between an organization and its environment is problematic, and models of single organizations responding to an environment might not be very useful.

The causal impact of organizations. Most organizational choices are most of the time affected but not dictated by functional neccessities. Choices are not instantaneous and unique adaptations to the objective environment and exogenously given preferences. Organizational routines buffer organizational decision-making from environmental influence as well as from the self-interested behavior of organizational members. In order to predict organizational behavior and decision outcomes it is neccessary to understand the processes that translate environmental conditions and individual preferences into organizational action (March 1981b; Simon 1985).

Behavioral theories of organizational decision-making try to specify how organizational structures and processes facilitate some behavior and constrain others. Standard operating precedures

---

4   The garbage can model assumes that problems, solutions, decision-makers, and choice opportunities are independent, exogenous streams flowing through a system. Solutions are linked to problems primarily by their simultaneity, relatively few problems are solved, and choices are made for the most part either before any problems are connected to them (oversight), or after the problems have abandoned one choice to associate themselves with another (flight) (Cohen/March/Olsen 1972).

(SOPs) affect the substantive outcomes of choices by regulating the access of participants, problems, and solutions to choices, and by affecting the participants' allocation of attention, their standards of evaluation, priorities, perceptions, identities, and resources. Open structures tend to make the creation of meaning, including the testing of values and visions, the allocation of honor and blame, and changes in self-identity and group-belonging, as important as the effects upon the substantive choice (March/Olsen 1976).

SOPs have special significance because of their effects on the division of labor and influence between policy specialists and non-specialists. Organizations (and sub-units) are often created in order to pay special attention to a specific problem, an aspect of a problem, or the concerns of specific individuals. Policy-specialists develop relatively stable values and assumptions linked to the tasks and decisions they are responsible for. Standard operating procedures define what is normal, acceptable, and reasonable. For long periods the specialists are allowed to act in a quasi-autonomous way. At the same time few issues fall exclusively within the domain of a single organization. Open structures allow non-specialists to challenge specialists. For instance, non-specialists may redefine who the legitimate participants, or what the legitimate problems, solutions, and rules of the game are. Such redefinitions tend to (temporarily) create garbage can processes which might have an impact upon the future division of labor between specialists and non-specialists as well as upon the outcome of the choice in focus.

Structural change and performance crisis. Organizations change routinely in an incremental way. The results and inferences of past experience are stored in standard operating procedures, professional rules, and practical rules of thumb. This does not imply that organizations adapt perfectly to changes in the environment or to arbitrary intervention by organizational leaders (March 1981b). Neither does it imply that organizations are neccessarily selected out if they do not adapt immediately. Extensive adjustment periods may be required in which diverse, conflicting, and inefficient solutions survive (North 1981:9). Organizations develop an institutional character which discourages arbitrary structural adaptions (Selznick 1957), and sometimes organizations change their environments rather than adapting to them (Nystrom/Starbuck 1981). Thus, it is neccessary to study the historical time paths to equilibria (March/Olsen 1984).

Changes in organizational identity and in repertoires of standard operating procedures are usually the result of a performance crisis, that is, a gap between the level of aspiration and the level of performance. Conflicts often function as triggers for search and change. Organizations devote more attention to activities that are failing to meet targets than to activities that are meeting targets (Cyert/March 1963). In order to change routines embedded in interorganizational networks there has to be a performance crisis which attracts widespread attention and deviates from the expectations of large proportions of the participants and the on-lookers. A performance crisis may result from a sudden raise in aspirations as well as from a decline in performance (Olsen 1988b).

Models of institutions and models of man. Empirical students of organizational decision-making have often written in the spirit of specifying constraints on rational choice models. As the list of such constraints has grown, indicating the limited cases where a rational choice model is a reasonably good approximation of empirical reality, it has become clear that there is a need for a different theory of organizational decision-making rather than a modification of a theory of choice which sees decision-makers as rational, strategic, self-interested actors continuously in competition with one another.

In particular, there is a need to focus on models at the mesolevel, models of institutions, rather than models of man which start out by specifying a priori characteristics of humans. Models of institutions see humans as having a potential for a great variety of decision-making behaviors. They may do good or evil; act goal-oriented or follow institutionally defined rules and obligations; pursue self-chosen goals or act strategically to achieve institutionally defined ends; and they may identify with a variety of smaller or larger collectives: organizations, professions, or client groups. A central task for organization theory is to clarify how properties of organizational contexts influence which of these potentials are actually evoked.

Today there is no well-developed theoretical alternative to rational choice models. The observations made by empirical students of organizational decision-making are, however, familiar to students of political institutions. The observations suggest a shared research agenda - one which has many similarities with some old themes and an old theoretical style in the study of political life. As such it may become part of a search for a new theoretical perspective - a new institutionalism - and thus contribute to a reorientation of the way we look upon the organization of political institutions, their causal effects, and how they change.

Political Research and the New Institutionalism

The new institutionalism refers to a heterogenous group of writers who challenge the research style and the basic vision that has characterized theories of politics since about 1950.[5] An institutional perspective assumes that the organization of political life makes a difference. Political institutions are the building blocks of political life. They influence available options for policy-making and for institutional change. They also influence the choices made among available options. Thus, an institutional perspective requires a careful delineation of the nature of particular institutional arrangements (Krasner 1988; March/Olsen 1989).

---

5   The style which has dominated political science in the past 30 years can be seen as (March/Olsen 1984):

(a) contextual, inclined to see politics as an integral part of society, less inclined to differentiate the polity from the rest of society;

(b) reductionist, inclined to see political phenomena as the aggregate consequences of individual behavior, less inclined to ascribe the outcomes of politics to organizational structures and rules of appropriate behavior;

(c) utilitarian, inclined to see action as the product of calculated self-interest, less inclined to see political actors as responding to obligations and duties;

(d) functionalist, inclined to see history as an efficient mechanism for reaching uniquely appropriate equilibria, less concerned with the possibilities for maladaptation and non-uniqueness in historical development; and

(e) instrumentalist, inclined to define decision-making and the allocation of resources as the central concerns of political life, less attentive to the ways in which political life is organized around the development of meaning through symbols, rituals, and ceremonies.

The organization of political institutions: mixed orders. Large scale, formal organizations which impose limited roles upon individuals increasingly dominate political, economic, and social life. It is possible that the real world of organizations is changing so rapidly that the development of our concepts has not kept pace. The growth of the public sector has occurred simultanously with, and in interaction with, the development of more complex patterns of organization. For instance, para-governmental organizations have become common in the delivery of public services (Hood/Schuppert 1988). The interdependence and penetration of the public and the private sector and of levels and sectors of government has increased. A result has been the emergence of structures which defy simple generalization and typologization (Bozeman 1987). Contemporary formal organizations are not easily captured by distinctions between a private and a public sphere, between state hierarchies and markets, or by distinctions based on the legal status of organizations.

Government is often described, not as Weberian bureaucracies, but as a conglomerate of semi-feudal, loosely allied organizations, each with a substantial life of its own, interacting with one another and interacting separately with civil groups. Government leaders can veto and disturb, but not substantially control, the behavior of organized coalitions of policy-experts (Allison 1971:67, Suleiman 1987). A growing public sector has not neccessarily meant increased political control.

From Plato, Aristotle, and Polybius down to Montesquieu, "mixed" orders and constitutions have been praised. By combining different principles of organization and coordination, "mixed orders" have been seen as helping to balance various interests and values and thus contributing to the good society. Yet, recent theoretical debates focus on a limited set of pure forms rather than trying to make sense of the hybrid forms and the uneasy equilibria between competing principles of coordination observed in everyday-life. Practical reformers have also most of the time tried to eliminate rather than to understand organizational hybrids. For instance, contemporary programs for reforming the public sector in Western countries emphasize the need for organizational forms which provide clear divisions of labor, authority, and responsibility[6] (Olsen 1988a).

In the search for simplification and clarity contemporary reformers often ignore the fact, that the political sphere has traditionally dealt with issues characterized by uncertainty, conflict, and ambiguity (Offerdal 1988). Political institutions are supposed to make decisions in the absence of agreement on objectives and with competing views of what the problems are and how they should be solved. The democratic state is distinguished by tensions and dilemmas. For instance, the wish for coherent, consistent, and efficient action has traditionally been weighted against the fear of the coercive potential of the state. As a result the state is intentionally adversarial. Political opposition is institutionalized and partly inconsistent principles of coordination and governance are built into the system. Clearly, our theoretical understanding and empirical descriptions of mixed orders and composite institutional regimes are still inadequate. Why do these organizations exist? What are their effects? A focus upon pure types like state hierarchies and markets may contribute to keeping hybrids and mixed forms off the research agenda.

The causal position of political institutions. In the short run established programs provide the menu of possible political actions. Institutions regulate the use of authority and power and provide actors with resources, legitimacy, standards of evaluation, perceptions, identities, and a sense of meaning. They provide a set of rules, compliance procedures, and moral and ethical behavioral norms which buffer environmental influence, modify individual motives, regulate

---

6 Practical reform programs often recognize the complexity of the present situation. For instance, in an OECD-publication (1987:119) it is argued that "One result of the differentiation in public organisations is that public services are increasingly delivered by "networks" of organizations involving different levels and sectors of government, para-statal bodies, private and charitable organizations and private enterprises. A main challenge will be learning how to manage these networks and ensure clear lines of accountability and consistent control systems. Networks incorporating bodies outside of "regular" central administration create additional pressure on the centre to accomodate the demands of network members as clients". Still, most of the debate is cast in a market - state hierarchy framework.

self-interested behavior, and create order and meaning
(March/Olsen 1984; Jepperson 1987; Krasner 1987).

Historically, theories of political institutions portrayed decision-
making as a process for developing a sense of purpose, commitment,
identity, and belonging. A spirit of citizenship implied to think and
act, not simply as self-interested individuals, or as members of particular interest groups, but as members of the community as a whole
(Arblaster 1987:77). Politics was seen as a vehicle for educating citizens, improving cultural values, and testing individual and group
preferences, rather than just aggregating them (March/Olsen 1984,
1986b; Olsen 1985: Wildavsky 1987). Students of politics need to go
beyond policy effects in terms of the allocation of scarce resources
and who-gets-what and return to an enlarged concept of "political effects".

An institutional perspective assumes that the actors and their endowments are not unilaterally determined by the individuals' position in social structure (e.g. class, religion, geography, or sex) and
that meaning and morality are not determined exclusively by social
institutions (e.g. church and family). Rather, political effects include
the constitution or activation of political groups by political processes. Political effects also include impacts upon the common aspiration of a people, upon the meaning given to concepts like
democracy, justice, liberty, and equality; upon the attitudes towards
the proper role of political institutions; upon the beliefs in the ability
of institutions to achieve common purposes; and upon the level and
types of conflict in society.

For instance, the ideological struggle over people's minds is an
important aspect of recent attempts to reorganize the public sector in
many OECD-countries. Attempts to introduce "more managerial
thinking and marketing mentality" (OECD 1987:117) are often presented as questions of efficiency. In reality they are closely linked to
fundamental political questions like the proper scope and role of the
public sector. It may well turn out that the effects of the reorganization efforts upon peoples' beliefs in the relative merit of public and
private solutions to pressing problems, and the effects in terms of
their trust, scepticism, or cynicism towards politics, will be of greater

significance than the immediate changes in organizational structures. In the longer run, Downs and Larkey (1986:23,163) argue, the creation of what they see as an unjustifiable romantic picture of the private sector and an unjustifiable cynical one of the public sector, and the attempts to displace the role of politics by an exclusive reliance on the criterion of economic efficiency, may threaten to undermine the role of political institutions.[7]

An important feature of organizational forms is the degree to which they create monopolies or allow political openness. This includes competition, conflict, public debate, and accountability. As for instance the parliamentary system and competitive party systems institutionalize opposition and public appeals, corporatist arrangements reduce political competition and conflict. Bargaining takes place behind closed doors. Deliberations are kept informal and secretive in an effort to insulate them as much as possible from outside pressures or from dissidents within the associational ranks (Streeck and Schmitter 1985:13). A result is that the actors, their endowments, and the definition of the issues tend to be taken as given. Political and moral questions are turned into questions of bargaining and efficiency (Olsen 1981).

A possible implication is that majority government might be strengthened by building competing norms and principles, together with opportunities for public appeal, into more institutions. Such an organizational arrangement is likely to create a political order with little differentiation between institutions and with bargaining among organized interests as the most typical process of coordination. An alternative mixed order is one with partly autonomous institutional spheres based on different norms and principles of coordination. This solution builds on the assumption that many political institutions, in the same way as courts of law, science, religion, and art, have a *raison d'être* and functional imperatives which should govern their decisions. Accordingly, the immediate, direct influence of ma-

---

7 Downs and Larkey (1986:227), for instance, argue that the American Grace Commission had no real interest in understanding how government works and why. They believed in a model of clear and well articulated goals, of centralized authority and complete information. To the extent that government is not like this, that is the government's problem.

jority government is limited to creating institutions and policing that their decisions are consistent with the institution's *raison d'être*.

Egeberg and Stigen (1985) argued that mixed organizational forms based on competing norms and decision principles create flexibility because they allow an organization to attach different importance to principles like hierarchy, professional selfgovernment, and bargaining among represented interests, in different choice situations. In comparison, a mixed order based on institutional differentiation of norms and principles of coordination may offer less flexibility and more predictability.

Variations in the interplay between autonomous, functional subsystems and more open political processes, focussed on influencing the policy specialists are likely to have important powerimplications. Departmentalization and functional differentiation tend to reduce attention problems, conflicts and ambiguity. Policy specialists become highly attentive to the special interests they are responsible for, depend on, and interact with. Often these interests are well organized with large, professional and well-financed staffs.

The relative importance of political power based on *numbers* compared to organizational-, staff-, and financial resources is likely to increase when specialized structures are challenged. When an issue reaches the public and national agenda, it is important to justify decisions in terms of publicly legitimate standards. The public's insight into and impact upon policy-making might increase. Open structures, however, do not guarantee representative decisions. They benefit those with *individual* resources and sometimes create more biased patterns of participation than the routinized forms of representation (Olsen/Sætren 1980).

Since the opening of specialized structures takes place in an atmosphere of crisis - the crisis that allowed them to rise to the top of the national agenda - the issues will usually be decided with no time to provide an adequate foundation of knowledge and analysis (Simon 1987:353). Sometimes such situations provide a new chance to old solutions, which are stored in archives or in the minds of participants, a new chance (Feldman 1983; Kingdon 1984). In general, the break-down of specialized structures, and the introduction of new participants, problems, and solutions, makes it more difficult to predict what will happen. Garbage can situations open for unusual outcomes.

Institutional change. Democratic ideology assumes that developing political institutions of self-governance is a first order political process, and that the struggle to modify existing institutions is at the heart of politics. In political theory the role of reflection and choice in the development of institutions has been a central issue. The heritage is ambiguous. Students of political development have been inclined to accept the optimistic idea of progress provided by nineteenth century liberals and radicals: a more or less inexorable historical movement toward some more "advanced" level. At the same time, political histories have often emphasized the unique significance of a particular sequence of events or choice (March/Olsen 1984). There has been a vision of political science as an architectonic discipline (Wheeler 1968), but it has also been argued that intention and choice play a modest role in the development of political institutions (Sait 1938). It has turned out to be problematic to specify a stable set of conditions under which explicit design is a major process in the development of political institutions (March/Olsen 1983).

Obviously, institutions do change. Routinely they modify processes and structures without changing their institutional identity. An institutional perspective suggests that the possibilities for arbitrary institutional change are constrained by earlier choices and institutional history. Decision-makers can change institutions and make history, but seldom under circumstances of their own choosing (Marx 1963). If institutions can be instantaneously and costlessly transformed to new optimality every time functional imperatives change there is no need for an institutional perspective. An institutional perspective predicts infrequent changes, primarily in crisis-situations, and followed by long periods of relatively stasis (Krasner 1988). The image is one of historical junctures which open for major change. The solutions selected are, then, frozen into structures which constrain future change.

Problems of attention, reluctance to create conflicts, and the ambiguity of meaning tend to insulate standard operating procedures at the institutional core from major reforms. In addition, attempts at comprehensive reforms are often detracked. Most of the time comprehensive reforms take place within open structures with few precise rules controlling the access of participants, problems, and solutions. As it is difficult to obtain the continued attention of top elected officials, major reorganizations tend to attract numerous unoccupied participants and unresolved issues. Often reorganizations become garbage cans - highly contextual combinations of participants and issues. Under such conditions the reorganization process may primarily function as civic education. The discovery, clarification, and elaboration of meaning become more important than the actual changes in institutional structures (March/Olsen 1983).

The likelihood of institutional change depends on the institution's robustness and its ability to change the environment, and on the nature of change attempted. Reformers are more likely to succeed if they understand the characteristics and historical development of an institution; if they use "natural" processes in an institution; and if they try to achieve changes consistent with an institution's identity. Major change in institutional identity is less likely the stronger the internal control with recruitment and socialization is, and the more the endowments and identity of individuals depend on the organization. Major change is also less likely the more an institution is integrated into a larger political order so that changes in one institution require changes in several other institutions (Krasner 1988).

Institutions tend to be more robust if there are what Merton (1957:318) has called institutionalized evasions. For instance, citizens' initiatives and civil disobedience might function as an institutional evasion of the normative prescription of representative democracy, making representative democracy more robust against change. Likewise, slack resources buffer inconsistencies and may reduce the felt need for change (Cyert/March 1963). As a corollary, in contemporary democracies which combine institutional interdependence and autonomy for policy-specialists, reduced slack may create performance crises and demands for change.

An Example: Political Institutions and the Challenge of Oil

The parallel agendas indicate that organization theory raises questions of interest to students of politics. Are, then, the theoretical ideas and answers suggested useful for empirical political research? An analysis of the encounter between Norwegian representative democracy and the oil age comprises a limited but particularly demanding test of an institutional approach. In 1962, Phillips Petroleum submitted its oil concession application - to the great surprise of Norwegian government - and the Ekofisk discovery in December 1969 made it clear that Norway soon might become an oil exporting country. Petroleum policy was a new field with an apparent lack of routines, and there was a demand for rational decision-making and majority rule in order to protect national interests.[8]

For Norway it was unclear how to define the situation, what opportunities and problems the country faced, and what interests should be taken into consideration. It was also unclear how decisions on oil issues would be made, what institutions would handle different decisions and who were the legitimate participants in various processes. Representative government was subjected to a difficult test. On the one hand, it was argued, oil gave Norway an historic chance to choose its future. On the other hand, the history of oil-exporting countries showed that large petroleum revenues have not guaranteed the well being of every oil-endowed country. Oil discoveries have created new power and dependency relationships, social distortions, cost pressures, inflation, migration, and de-industrialization. This is so, despite the desire expressed by the authorities to avoid such developments.[9]

State autonomy and functional neccessities. Small countries with open economies are often assumed to have very little latitude in es-

---

8   This part of the paper builds on Olsen (1988b), which again summarizes a research project on Norwegian representative democracy in the age of oil. The project is a collective effort of several of my colleagues and graduate students in Bergen.

9   Tugwell 1975; Coronel 1983; Jenkins 1986; Karl 1986.

tablishing economic policy. First, they are vulnerable to shifts in the international economy. Second, they depend on privately generated resources. It is beyond the state's capacity to organize the accumulation process (Lindblom 1977; Offe 1984). The petroleum industry also has its own dynamics which make political control difficult. When a country becomes "petrolized", oil and the money that accompany it change its expectations, political institutions, political processes and power relationships - regardless of decisions by political authorities (Karl 1987).

Despite these trends and predictions, Parliament (Storting) very early declared that the state was to be involved in the petroleum industry at all appropriate levels, including production. At the same time, the state would help coordinate Norwegian interests in the industry and build up an integrated Norwegian oil production system. The state's autonomy is illustrated by several decisions with significant consequences for the structure of the industry. A state oil company (Statoil) was established and given a dominant position on the Norwegian continental shelf.[10] The state expanded its ownership in Norsk Hydro (a company involving itself in the oil industry very early) to 51%. The state refused to give any of the newly created "peoples' joint-stock companies" any role in the industry. The state was active in coordinating private Norwegian interests and establishing the privately owned company Saga; and the state diversified the dependence on foreign oil companies by inviting companies from several countries and not allowing any of them to achieve a dominant position.

Rational choice and SOPs. Were these decisions in particular, and Norwegian oil-policies more generally, the results of the state acting as a unitary actor making rational calculations and choices? Is it useful to our understanding of the situation to analyse decisions in terms of economic planning models where a centralized governing body acts to utilize a non-renewable resource in a way that it maxi-

---

10 The establishing of a Norwegian state oil company is consistent with a more general world trend. In seventy-four countries governments have become entrepreneurs in the oil industry rather than leaving the business to the private sector (Klapp 1987).

mizes the net present value of investments (Aarrestad 1984; Rees 1985)? The Norwegian government formulated many goals but never established a clear and stable preference function which economic planning models assume. The policy-makers seldom considered several choice alternatives or examined their various consequences in any great detail. Rather, the government followed a few simple, experience based rules and standard operating procedures.

The prospects of an oil-age triggered off institutionally differentiated responses. The level of activity was determined by whether oil discoveries could directly influence the values and interests of a particular institution or group. Oil issues were interpreted and dealt with in the light of established routines. The response of the Maritime Directorate, responsible for safety on floating oil-riggs, is typical. The directorate did not have much experience with oil riggs, but when a rigg was viewed as a somewhat peculiar ship, the experts in the Directorate felt confident. They knew as much about safety on board of ships as anyone else in the world (Sangolt 1984). In general, the various state agencies wanted to use existing rules and routines rather than develop special rules. Important decisions thus appeared obvious, natural, and reasonable.

The Ministry of Industry was no exception. The ministry followed the standard operating procedures which have dominated Norwegian industrial policy-making in the post-war period. While the ownership of oil was a new situation, dependence on foreign capital and expertise was not. For instance, from the very start of the oil-age, images of the state's struggles with international companies over the ownership and use of Norwegian waterfalls in the first part of the century, and the concession-policies then developed, provided policy-makers a frame of reference.

Intervention in the industrial structure followed routines based on institutionalized norms and beliefs which can be traced back to the economic problems of the 1920s and 1930s. These included a strong faith in the value of developing an industrial society and the belief that the state has an important role to play in industrial development - that free markets will not produce desirable levels of employment, stability, and economic growth, and that the state is able

to perform tasks the private sector can not. A key idea has been to
create national champions, a small number of big firms which can
compete internationally. To do this the government has to be willing
to use state capital, to activate and coordinate private Norwegian
capital, and, if neccessary, to attract foreign capital (Grønlie 1977,
1988). Decisions in the petroleum sector was "business as usual"
more than innovations developed to fit the specific functional neccessities of the oil sector.

The role of corporatist arrangements. The Norwegian state has not
relied much upon corporatist arrangements in the oil sector. Neither
sectorial corporatism nor corporatist concertation (Lehmbruch
1984:61-2) have been used to the same degree as in other parts of industrial and economic policy-making (Leivestad 1986). This observation is interesting because most students of comparative politics
describe Norway as a political system with strong corporatist features; and because the oil sector could be expected to create the international economic pressure which should force the state, employers and trade unions to cooperate at home[11] (Katzenstein 1984, 1985).
Why, then, are corporatists arrangements so little used?

The state's high aspirations have led to extensive delegation of
discretionary power to the civil service and to Statoil (Lægreid 1988).
Government has, consistent with Norwegian traditions (Olsen 1983),
expressed a desire for a style of peaceful cooperation. Through the
concession system, in particular, the state has also established bargaining relations with the oil companies. What is missing (to a large
extent) is the routinized cooperation with the traditional partners in
corporatist bargaining in the industrial sector - The Federation of
Trade Unions (LO), The Employers' Federation, and The Confederation of Industries.

Some of the reasons for this pattern are obvious. The oil companies are important and powerful enough to bargain directly with
government officials. They do not need the peak organizations to get

---

11 One student of corporatism suggests that the international dependency has
   created a small country mentality - a widely shared understanding and consensus that continued prosperity depends on cooperation in order to be able to
   remain internationally competitive (Milner 1987:248).

access. Thus, in the oil sector the employers' associations have not been able to establish the strong position they have in other parts of Norwegian industry and industrial policy-making . For LO the situation is the same. A majority of the oil workers have seen little gain from the solidarity emphasis LO's wage policy promotes. A common complaint is that LO has not done a good job in the North Sea (Andersen 1988). Union "wars", strikes, and state compulsary arbitration have been much more common in the oil sector than in other sectors of Norwegian industry.

The pattern supports Lehmbruch's conclusion (1984:60) that corporatism is contingent rather than a secular trend reflecting functional prerequisites of advanced capitalism, or small, open economies. The observations also support the conclusion that the state bureaucracy prefers to interact and compromise with those groups which can seriously affect the goal achievements of the state (Rokkan 1966). Compromising with powerful groups is a more basic policy routine than the specific corporatist arrangements observed in other parts of Norwegian political life. The peak organizations are absent because they do not have the same leverage in the oil sector as in other parts of Norwegian economic life. The actual organizational pattern is a complex network of public, quasi-public, and private organizations. It is a network depending on, and responding to, both international markets and national politics, and in particular to performance crises and conflicts.

Conflict and change. Oil policy-making provides an uneasy balance between unity and conflict. On the one hand, external dependencies and threats generate appeals for national unity and for downplaying the traditional conflicts in Norwegian politics. On the other hand, oil policy-making directly affects the most important cleavages in Norwegian politics, including the role of the state in economic development. The changing emphasis upon unity and conflict and upon different cleavages have had important consequences for the changing demands for structural reforms. Here three potential cleavages are discussed: between political parties, between the state, unions, and companies, and between oil policy-specialists and others.

The Storting is a "working parliament" which endeavours to produce political compromises (Olsen 1983). At the same time, the political parties need to profile themselves. In oil policy-making coping with this dilemma creates an interesting pattern. All decisions of great national concern have been made unanimously or with large majorities. At the same time, Otterå (1985:146), who studied all the proposals on oil policies from the Storting committees up to 1985, observes that 64% of the proposals coming out of committees were split, nearly always along party lines. In comparison, the average for all policy areas was 23%. State ownership, state intervention, questions related to what kind of industrial structure should be developed, and defence of existing small and medium businesses can easily be related to cleavages which are reflected in the party system. This happens frequently, in particular in connection with industrial scandals and other performance crises. Usually attention has concentrated on the issue of controlling the state oil company. The subsequent demands for major reorganizations have so far ended in political compromises (Otterå 1985; Krogh 1987).

In many countries it has proven difficult to create peaceful coexistence between two worlds that are as different as politics and the oil business (Coronel 1983:283). These problems grow when the state moves from passive roles such as auctioneer, property owner and tax collector to the role of regulating the petroleum business and becoming an active participant in it, as has been the case in Norway. From the start the oil companies, too, organized themselves in the way they were accustomed to doing in other places, especially the Gulf of Mexico. This resulted in the introduction of forms of organization and management that clearly deviated from postwar traditions in the Norwegian labor market - something that gradually resulted in conflicts.

At first, Norwegian authorities just assumed that Norwegian traditions would be followed in the North Sea. Fairly soon it became obvious that this was not the case and the cultural conflicts between Norwegian industrial practice and "good oil field practice" became more intense as more Norwegians were employed. The state made several efforts to "normalize" the situation. In issues like the workers' right to organize, safety, and work environment the state supported the workers' demands for changes. With some success the state also requested the oil companies to follow Norwegian custom and join the Federation of employers. The latter appeal was closely linked to state efforts to control wages in the oil industry and to prevent "wage-contamination" to other sectors. The major trend has been towards more emphasis on Norwegian custom and traditions. The available data, however, make it difficult to isolate the impact of state policies compared to the fact that Norwegian companies and workers have achieved a more central role on the continental shelf.

The division of labor between oil policy-specialists and non-specialists, as well as their relative influence, has varied over time. Periods of great autonomy for the specialists have been succeeded by the mobilization of participants, problems and solutions external to the oil-policy network. During the 1960s most potential participants remained passive. They ignored the opportunities and problems that oil might bring, and left the decisions to the specialists. During the 1970s the oil sector became more vulnerable to the influence of non-specialists. With relative suddenness, many people began talking about the indirect effects of the oil industry. There were major changes in the interpretations of the economic effects of oil and the importance that should be attached to economic efficiency and growth, compared with other values. On the basis of a new international ecological awareness, there was a re-evaluation and questioning of the connections between economic growth and well-being. This helped legitimize a broad spectrum of considerations as being relevant to oil policy (Bratbak 1980). This tendency was reinforced by the political battle in Norway over membership in the European Community. Negative attitudes toward rapid economic transformation and changes were strong. In Parliament, members who did not work with oil matters on a daily basis were unusually active in questioning and making demands upon petroleum policy (Blichner/Olsen 1986).

During the 1980s, the petroleum sector has again become more closed. The number of participants and the number of considerations regarded as relevant have been reduced. Sector specialists and internal sectoral concerns have assumed a more dominant role. This time the process has taken place on the basis of the sector's importance and power and an understanding that in an economically difficult situation Norway must lower its expectations regarding the petroleum sector. Petroleum seems to be in the process of finding a niche in the political-administrative division of labor and governing system. Viewed from the standpoint of the oil sector, what has oc-cured is a political neutralization and de-ideologization, with an em-phasis on pragmatic solutions. A reduction in slack has lead to a concentration on the "primary" goal of economic efficiency. There has been a greater political acceptance for running the oil industry according to "petroleum policy, operational and business-related premises". Oil has, because of the 1986 drop in prices, become just another raw material. The oil industry is in the process of becoming like any traditional industry, without large profits. This leaves less room for maneuvering in Norwegian politics (Dæhlin 1986). Again the argument is that the economic situation is putting politics to a difficult test that requires a national sense of responsibility and a willingness to work together. There is no room for political tactics in such a serious situation.[12]

There is no reason to believe that the system of governance has found a stable equilibrium. The petroleum sector seems to have a hard time finding a balance between different interests and concerns. Cleavages compete for attention (Schattschneider 1960), and the out-comes have both policy implications and organizational implications. For instance, when the focus is on Norway-versus-the-multinational-companies, the solution is to build up Norwegian expertise and a state oil company. When tensions between the oil sector and the rest of society come in focus, political attention moves from problems of Norwegianization and creation of institutions and staffs with the neccessary expertise to problems in controlling the staffs themselves. Yesterday's solutions become today's problems. As sector-external

12 A key argument has been that readjustments problems in Norwegian industry and economy were concealed as long as export revenues from the oil sector could offset the deficit in the rest of the merchandise trade balance. The drop in oil prices and the falling U.S. dollar - the currency in which oil sales take place - revealed the underlying problems of the growing oil sector in Norway.

problems and criteria are evoked, the definition of expertise and the relevant participants also change.

Oil policy-making illustrates the importance of processes of interpretation in decision-making and institutional change. The answers to questions like, how different is the oil industry from other industries, how different is oil-drilling in the North Sea from drilling elsewhere, what are the criteria of success against which oil policy-making should be evaluated, are ambiguous. Finding the answers is part of a political process and the outcome of these processes influences both policy content and the direction of structural changes. At the same time, solutions chosen in one period make possible and constrain future changes. In the 1960s, when few participants were active, major parts of the organizational structure of oil policy-making were decided or defined.

Organization Theory - A New Paradigm of Political Research?

At the core of democratic theory is the idea that citizens are competent to make adequately enlightened judgments either about public issues themselves, or about the terms on which they may safely delegate to others the authority to make decisions (Dahl 1987:203). An institutional approach does not eliminate intelligent choice from politics. It is consistent with the view that human decision-makers are capable of making political choices based on reasonable judgments (Held 1987:180). In a world of scarce attention, conflict, and ambiguity, organizational choices are often made in an intelligent way, but differently from that suggested by models of rational choice.

An institutional approach shifts the focus from the specific decision-making process and *who* governs to the conditions for, and the implications of, vesting intelligence, morals, interests, and authority in institutional principles, procedures, and structures. The new institutionalism observes that it is problematic to change institutions in an arbitrary way. Still, the quality of a representative democracy may depend more on citizens' ability to influence the development of appropriate institutions than on their ability to analyze and influence single issues or the selection of individual representatives.

It is not unreasonable to argue that progression and retrogression of societies depends heavily on successes and failures in human organization (North 1981:59). Representative democratic government poses fundamental organizational questions and the study of politics needs good organization theories. In particular, most Western countries have entered a period of intense discussions about the appropriate scope and the institutional forms of the state. Possibly, the coalition supporting an interventionist welfare state is breaking down and there may be major institutional realignments. In a short time the idea that an interventionist, planning state is a suitable means to promote the welfare of citizens, have been replaced by neoliberal ideas of the contemporary state as an overgrown, expanding, intrusive, and unwieldly Leviathan. Privatization, together with the introduction of competition and market-like arrangements in the public sector, are offered as the best way out of present problems. This change creates fundamentally new questions concerning political organization and the roles to be entrusted to elected representatives, experts, bureaucrats, and citizens.

It is by no means clear what the net gain will be if students of politics pay more attention to organization theory. Today, organization theory cannot provide a ready paradigm for political research. Empirical studies of decision-making in formal organizations do, however, offer some observations and theoretical ideas which may be useful to students of politics. Hopefully, a new institutionalism will also move the study of politics closer to political theory, history, and law - without returning to the old tradition of a historical-descriptive, legalistic institutionalism.

Increased attention from students of politics is also likely to change organization theory. More attention may be given to the organizational characteristics of parliaments, public bureaucracies, political parties, interest organizations, and citizens initiatives, as well as to themes like conflict, power, justice, and equality and the development of norms, preferences, and meaning. The present concern for (economic) efficiency may be supplemented with a concern for values and criteria derived from political theory. In particular, organizational theory may have to take seriously the implications of democratic principles for the organization of state and society.

References

Aarrestad, Jostein (1984) *Oljen og norsk Økonomi*. Oslo: NKS forlaget.

Allison, Graham T. (1971) *Essence of Decision*. Boston: Little, Brown.

Andersen, Svein (1988) *Industrial Relations in British and Norwegian Offshore Industrial Relations*. London: Gower.

Arblaster, Anthony (1987) *Democracy*. Milton Keynes: Open University Press.

Blichner, Lars Chr. and Johan P. Olsen (1986) *Spørsmål i Stortinget. Sikkerhetsventil i petroleumspolitikken*. Bergen: Universitetsforlaget.

Bozeman, Barry (1987) *All Organizations are Public*. San Francisco: Jossey-Bass.

Bratbak, Berit (1980) *Regjeringens langtidsprogrammer 1953-1976*. Bergen: Manuscript.

Cohen, Michael D., James G. March and Johan P. Olsen (1972) 'A Garbage Can Model of Organizational Choice', *Administrative Science Quarterly*, 17:1-25.

Coronel, Gustavo (1983) *The Nationalization of the Venezuelan Oil Industry*. Lexington: Lexington Books.

Cyert, Richard M. and James G. March (1963) *A Behavioral Theory of the Firm*. Englewood Cliffs, NJ: Prentice-Hall.

Dahl, Robert A. (1987) 'Sketches for a Democratic Utopia', *Scandinavian Political Studies* 10(3): 195-206.

Dæhlin, Knut (1986) 'Myndighetenes ambisjoner og styring av norsk oljevirksomhet'. Oslo: *Marius*, no. 128.

Donaldson, Lex (1985) *In Defence of Organization Theory*. Cambridge: Cambridge University Press.

Downs, George W. and Patric D. Larkey (1986) *The Search for Government Efficiency. From Hubris to Helplessness*. Philadelphia: Temple University Press.

Egeberg, Morten and Inger Stigen (1985) 'The Management of Competing Norms and Decision Principles: The Organizational Context of Norwegian Directorates'. Oslo: Paper to the IPSA XIIIth World Congress, Paris.

Feldman, Martha S. (1983) 'Policy Expertise in a Public Bureaucracy'. Stanford, Ca.: Ph.D. Dissertation.

Grønlie, Tore (1977) 'Norsk Industripolitikk', pp. 99-166 in T. Bergh and H. Ø. Pharo (eds.) *Vekst og velstand*. Oslo: Universitetsforlaget.

Grønlie, Tore (1988) *Statsdrift*. Oslo: Tano.

Hall, Richard H. and R.E. Quinn (eds.) (1983) *Organizational Theory and Public Policy*. Beverly Hills: Sage.

Held, David (1987) *Models of Democracy*. Cambridge: Polity Press.

Hood, Christopher and Gunnar Folke Schuppert (eds.) (1988) *Delivering public services in Western Europe*. London: Sage.

Jenkins, Barbara (1986) 'Reexamining the 'Obsolescing Bargain': A Study of Canada's Decision-Making', *International Organization*, 40(1): 139-65.

Jepperson, Ronald L. (1987) 'Conceptualizing Institutions, Institutionalization, and Institutional Effects'. Stanford, CA.: manuscript.

Karl, Terry (1986) 'Oil Booms and Petro States'. Stanford, Ca.: manuscript.

Katzenstein, Peter J. (1984) *Corporatism and Change*. Ithaca: Cornell University Press.

Katzenstein, Peter J. (1985) *Small States in World Markets*. Ithaca: Cornell University Press.

Kaufman, Herbert (1964) 'Organization Theory and Political Theory', *American Political Science Review*, 58: 5-14.

Kingdon, John W. (1984) *Agendas, Alternatives, and Public Policies.* Boston: Little, Brown.

Klapp, Merrie G. (1987) *The Sovereign Entrepreneur. Oil Policies in Advanced and Less Developed Countries.* Ithaca: Cornell University Press.

Krasner, Stephen D. (1988) Sovereignty: An Institutional Perspective, *Comparative Politics*, 21: 66-94.

Krogh, Finn E. (1987) 'Reorganiseringen av Statoil'. Bergen: Dissertation.

Lægreid, Per (1988) *Oljebyråkratiet.* Oslo: Tano.

Lehmbruch, Gerhard (1984) 'Concertation and the Structure of Corporatist Networks', pp. 60-80 in John H. Goldthorpe (ed.) *Order and Conflict in Contemporary Capitalism.* Oxford: Claredon Press.

Lehmbruch, Gerhard (1987) 'Administrative Interessenvermittlung', pp. 11-43 in Adrienne Windhoff-Héritier (ed.) *'Verwaltung und ihre Umwelt'. Festschrift für Thomas Ellwein.* Opladen: Westdeutscher Verlag.

Leivestad, Roald (1986) 'Oljesektorens møte med den korporative kanal'. Bergen: Dissertation.

Lindblom, Charles E. (1977) *Politics and Markets.* New York: Basic Books.

March, James G. (1965) *Handbook of Organizations.* Chicago: Rand McNally.

March, James G. (1981a) 'Decision-Making Perspective. Decisions in Organizations and Theories of Choice', pp. 205-248 in Andrew H. Van de Ven and William F. Joyce (eds.) *Perspectives on Organization Design and Behavior.* John Wiley.

March, James G. (1981b) 'Footnotes to Organizational Change', *Administrative Science Quarterly*, 17: 563-577.

March, James G. (1988) *Decisions and Organizations.* London: Basil Blackwell.

March, James G. and Herbert A. Simon (1958) *Organizations*. New York: Wiley.

March, James G. and Johan P. Olsen (1975) 'The Uncertainty of the past: Organizational Learning under Ambiguity', *European Journal of Political Research*, 3: 147-171.

March, James G. and Johan P. Olsen (1976) *Ambiguity and Choice in Organizations*. Bergen: Universitetsforlaget.

March, James G. and Johan P. Olsen (1983) 'Organizing Political Life: What Administrative Reorganization Tells us about Government', *American Political Science Review*, 77: 281-96.

March, James G. and Johan P. Olsen (1984) 'The New Institutionalism: Organizational Factors in Political Life', *American Political Science Review*, 78: 734-749.

March, James G. and Johan P. Olsen (1986a) 'Garbage Can Models of Decision-Making in Organizations', pp. 11-32 in J.G. March and R. Weissinger-Baylon (eds.) *Ambiguity and command*. Marshfield, Mass.: Pitman.

March, James G. and Johan P. Olsen (1986b) 'Popular Sovereignty and the Search for Appropriate Institutions', *Journal of Public Policy*, 6(4): 341-370.

March, James G. and Johan P. Olsen (1989) *Rediscovering Institutions*. New York, London: Free Press

Marx, Karl (1963) *The Eighteenth Brumaire of Louis Bonaparte*. New York: International Publishers.

Merton, Robert (1957) *Social Theory and Social Structure*. Glencoe, Ill.: Free Press.

Milner, Henry (1987) 'Corporatism and the Microeconomic Foundation of Swedish Social Democracy: The Swedish Model Revisited', *Scandinavian Political Studies*, 10(3): 239-54.

Nardy, Cyntia (1987) 'The Contribution of Political Science to Organizational Behavior', in Jay W. Lorsch (ed.) *Handbook of Organizational Behavior*. Englewood Cliffs: Prentice Hall.

North, Douglas C. (1981) *Structure and Change in Economic History*. New York: Norton.

Nystrom, Paul C. and William H. Starbuck (eds.) (1981) *Handbook of Organizational Design, vol 2*. Oxford: Oxford University Press.

OECD (1987) *Administration as Service. The Public as Client*. Paris: OECD.

Offe, Claus (1984) *Contradictions of the Welfare State*. London: Hutchinson.

Offerdal, Audun (1988) 'Politisk ekspertise - finst den. Om politikarens plass i styringssystemet'. Bergen: manuscript.

Olsen, Johan P. (1981) 'Integrated Organizational Participation in Government', pp. 492-516 in P.C. Nystrom and W. H. Starbuck (eds.) *Handbook of Organizational Design, vol. 2*. Oxford: Oxford University Press.

Olsen, Johan P. (1983) *Organized Democracy*. Bergen: Universitetsforlaget.

Olsen, Johan P. (1985) 'Nyinstitusjonalismen og statsvitenskapen', *Statsvetenskaplig Tidsskrift* (Sweden), 88(1): 1-14.

Olsen, Johan P. (1988a) 'The Modernization of Public Administration in the Nordic Countries', *Hallinnon Tutkimus* (Administrative Studies, Finland), (Forthcoming).

Olsen, Johan P. (1988b) *Petroleum og politikk*. Oslo: Tano

Olsen, Johan P. and Harald Sætren (1980) *Aksjoner og demokrati*. Bergen: Universitetsforlaget.

Otterå, Magne (1985) *'Petroleumsvirksomhet og konfliktlinjer: En analyse av stortingskomiteenes behandling av petroleumsspørsmål'*. Bergen: Dissertation.

Palumbo, Dennis J. (1975) 'Organization Theory and Political Science', pp. 319-369 in Fred I. Greenstein and Nelson W. Polsby *Handbook of Political Science, Vol.2*. Mass.: Addison-Wesley.

118 *Johan P. Olsen*

Rainey, Hal G. (1983) 'Public Organization Theory: The Rising Challenge', *Public Administration Review*, 43: 176-182.

Rees, Judith (1985) *Natural resources*. London: Methuen.

Rokkan, Stein (1966) 'Norway: Numerical Democracy and Corporate Pluralism', pp. 70-115 in R.A. Dahl (ed.) *Political Oppositions in Western Democracies*. New Haven: Yale University Press.

Sait, E. M. 1938) *Political Institutions - a Preface*. New York: Appelton-Century-Crofts.

Sangolt, Linda (1984) *'Institusjonell endring - Sjøfartsdirektoratets tilpasning til petroleumsvirksomheten 1966-1984'*. Bergen: Dissertation.

Schattschneider, E.E. (1960) *The Semi-Sovereign People*. New York: Holt, Rinehart and Winston.

Selznick, Philip (1957) *Leadership in Administration*. New York: Harper & Row.

Simon, Herbert A. (1985) 'Human Nature in Politics: The Dialogue of Psychology with Political Science', *American Political Science Review*, 79(1): 293-320.

Simon, Herbert A. (1987) 'Politics as Information Processing', *L.S.E. Quarterly*, Winter 1987: 345-370.

Streeck, Wolfgang and Philippe Schmitter (1985) *Private Interest Government*. London: Sage.

Suleiman, Ezra N. (1987) 'State Structures and Clientelism: The French State versus the 'Notaires', *British Journal of Political Science*, 17: 257-79.

Tugwell, Franklin (1975) *The Politics of Oil in Venezuela*. Stanford, Ca.: Stanford University Press.

Waldo, D. (1961) 'Organization Theory: An Elephantine Problem', *Public Administration Review*, 21: 210-245.

Waldo, D. (1978) 'Organization Theory: Revisiting the Elephant', *Public Administration Review*, 38: 589-597.

Wheeler, Harvey (1968) *Democracy in a Revolutionary Era. The Political Order Today.* Middlesex, England: Penguin.

Wildavsky, Aaron (1987) 'Choosing Preferences by Constructing Institutions: A Cultural Theory of Preference Formation', *American Political Science Review* 81(1): 3-21.

Wolin, Sheldon S. (1960) *Politics and Vision.* Boston: Little, Brown.

V

The Organization of Society, Administrative Strategies, and Policy Networks

Elements of a Developmental Theory of Interest Systems[*]

Gerhard Lehmbruch

The contribution of *corporatist* theory to the study of modern political systems is disputed. Among the critical objections, two different lines of reasoning seem particularly pertinent. Some authors acknowledge the basic empirical validity of the theory, but question its theoretical relevance for the analysis of contemporary industrial democracies: In their view, *concertation* between government and the peak associations of business and labor (also called "macro-corporatism") may have played a certain role during the later stage of Keynesian economic policy. As for the rest, it remained confined to some relatively small countries and, moreover, appears now to be on the decline even here. However, as defenders of the theory point out, even if these observations were correct, corporatism continues to survive on other analytical levels, in particular as sectoral or *meso-corporatism*

[*] The following reflections originated in an earlier exchange of ideas with Philippe Schmitter and were further developed in the context of a research project on "administrative interest intermediation". I am particularly indebted to the contributions of Frans van Waarden and to critical suggestions of Erich Gruner.

(e.g., Schmitter 1989). But this defense does not invalidate a more fundamental objection: The recent versions of neo-corporatist theory continue to emphasize associational interest intermediation. And to the degree that associations apparently lose their central role in policy formation on the level of the national political system, the focus of research is then simply moved to the "meso" level where an analytical emphasis on associations may yet hold some explanatory power. Implicitly, however, this shift in research focus reveals inherent limits of corporatist theory in the analysis of interest intermediation on the (national) system level.[2]

This explains that more complex conceptualizations of the structure and process of interest intermediation *beyond corporatism* are attracting increasing attention. Among these are, for example, the metaphor of *policy networks* and typologies of *economic governance*. Such approaches go beyond corporatist theory without questioning its contribution to the study of industrial democracies. In particular, they may contribute to a better understanding of the role of the state or, to put it differently, of administrative strategies, in the emergence and in the dynamics of national and sectoral configurations in interest intermediation. This is the object of the following inquiry.

Interest Intermediation and the Notion of "Administrative Culture"

In cross-national public policy research, attention has repeatedly been drawn to empirical regularities in the interactions of public bureaucracies and organized interests. The frequency and the degree of legitimacy of such interactions are not uniformly developed in the highly industrialized liberal democracies. From an overview of the literature on "integrated participation" of organizations in government, J.P.Olsen (1983:166) has concluded that it "occurs more frequently in the Scandinavian countries than in Great Britain, and

---

2   The central importance of associations in the representation and intermediation of interests is, after all, not a discovery of neo-corporatist theory. It was one of the central tenets of later versions of the pluralist "group approach"; see, in particular, Truman (1951: 56 pp).

much more frequently than in the United States". But the difference is not only one of frequency. Public bureaucracies in different countries often apply quite different "standard operating procedures" (cf. Olsen, this volume) and strategies in their interactions with interest groups. Case studies on policy formation in Sweden and other Scandinavian countries, for example, point to the existence of particular strategies of interest intermediation on the part of the administration that are distinguished by a strong involvement of organized interests (and, in particular, peak associations) in policy formation and implementation and, at the same time, a relative strong attention to "integrative", trans-sectoral and "concerted" forms of handling complex social problems. In other political systems, more disaggregated, sectorally segmented approaches seem to be preferred. Moreover, the degree to which the participation of organized interests in government is considered legitimate varies considerably. Role orientations of the French bureaucratic elite, as Ezra Suleiman (1974:316-351) has shown, are characterized by a pronounced claim to autonomy from "lobbies": The administration is supposed to resist their "pressure", and the importance of consultation with "interest groups" is minimized. And whether an industrial association is considered as "representative" or "serious" appears to be at the administrators' discretion.

To be sure, institutional arrangements for the consultation of government with interest groups are found in practically all advanced industrial liberal democracies. It is apparently fairly common that in the earlier stages of the legislative process bureaucrats discuss bills and regulations with group representatives. Everywhere we encounter a multitude of advisory committees with the participation of group representatives, and it is not uncommon that similar bodies participate in policy implementation. But there is some evidence that these formal similarities may be quite superficial. Already the availability of information about the number and composition of advisory committees and the like varies considerably. In some cases this may be due to rules of administrative secrecy. But in others, the lack of information seems rather to indicate that consultative bodies play a symbolic rather than effective role. The Scandinavian countries, where according to most accounts their role in the policy process seems to be considerable, also furnish by far the most detailed and precise information about advisory committees and administrative commissions. Also, important characteristics such as the powers of committees and the frequency with which they meet are obviously far from uniform.

One important dimension on which industrial democracies differ seems to be the *degree of discretion which the bureaucracy has in determining whether and whom to consult.* Broad discretion does not necessarily indicate that the bureaucracy is more autonomous from interest groups than where it is constitutionally or legally bound to involve the organizations. It has more to do with the degree of legitimacy of such a relationship.

Another significant dimension in such patterns of consultation is the *degree of sectoral segmentation.* In some countries, administrative agencies will only consult the specialized organizations representing interests within the sector concerned. Elsewhere, the central peak organizations of the large producer groups are quite regularly involved in the preparatory stage of the legislative process in a broad ("transsectoral") spectrum of policy topics (Lehmbruch 1985).

It follows from these observations that cross-national variations in interest intermediation are not limited to *(intra)organizational properties* that played such an important role in much of the literature on *neo-corporatism.* One would also have to pay attention to patterns of inter-organizational relationships, or regularities in the interactions of organizations and public bureaucracies.

Sometimes empirical regularities of this sort are discussed as contributing to a specific *"administrative culture"* (Jann 1983) or *"policy style"* (Richardson 1982). That literature has certainly yielded some valuable descriptive information. But how these phenomena are related to the intermediation of interests in the policy process has not been systematically explored. All too often, "administrative culture" or "policy style" look like residual categories the theoretical relevance of which for the comparative analysis of political structures and processes is not quite clear.

Nevertheless, such attempts seem to indicate an awareness of what one might call the *"configurative"* aspect of interest intermediation: It is a structure made up of complex linkages between organizations, agencies, and other institutions the dynamic of which is not always sufficiently understood by isolating specific elements or relationships. If - in a first approximation - we see them as hanging together in complex "configurations", cross-national variations on this analytical level may become a research focus on its own right. To delineate a "policy network" approach in combination with an emphasis on institutionalization might then be a further step in trying to understand these configurative dynamics.

Understanding the variability of policy networks is particularly important for the analysis of attempts, repeatedly made in the last decades to remodel patterns of state intervention. Sometimes this happened in waves of transnational diffusion as, for example, with the adoption of planning techniques guided by "systems" approaches in the 1960s. Another case was the wave of "neo-conservative" market-oriented reforms aimed at reducing state intervention in the late 1970s and early 1980s. Outcomes of such attempts sometimes differed considerably from one political system to another. And cross-national research on the reforms undertaken in, e.g., telecommunications and health policy has shown that the specific configurations of policy networks have either supported or constrained such attempts at reform. These comparisons suggest at least partial explanations of the difference in outcomes between the countries under study (Lehmbruch et al. 1988; Lehmbruch 1989 a, b; Grande 1989; Döhler 1990).[3]

The problem of national configurations in interest intermediation and the concept of "networks"

In the literature on interest groups, "configurative" cross-national regularities were first discussed when the ethnocentric parochialism of the early *"group approach"* in American political science was over-

---

3 This project, with financial support from the Volkswagen Foundation, focussed on the United Kingdom, West Germany, and the United States.

come with the emergence of a systematic, and theory-conscious *comparative politics*. But works like Eckstein (1960) and LaPalombara (1964) were still very much indebted to the "pluralist" paradigm with its emphasis on "access" and on vectors of "influence", and when that paradigm was increasingly challenged, this line of inquiry somehow faded. Its successor, *neo-corporatist theory*, had from the beginning a much stronger comparativist orientation, in particular because of its early focus on "macro-corporatism" in economic policy. However, there was less interest in the cross-national variability of complex *systemic* configurations of interest intermediation than in singling out some key variables (such as organizational properties), and therefore much research effort went toward substituting them- in accordance with a methodological postulate of Przeworski/Teune (1970) - for the "proper names of systems".

Later, interest shifted toward sectoral *meso-corporatism*, an interesting parallel to *structural contingency* approaches in organization theory. As organization theorists explained variations in organizational structure from environmental *task contingencies* so did the students of corporatist inter-organizational relationships on the level of industrial sectors. But with this new research emphasis, attention was displaced away from the cross-national variability of "macro" phenomena such as complex systemic configurations.

There is, however, a different line of development in the theory of interest intermediation with a much stronger *configurative* orientation. Some of the advances made in the last decades in the analysis of the organization and intermediation of economic interests were accompanied by a significant shift in the metaphors used to describe these socio-political phenomena. Concepts taken from classical mechanics, such as the *vector sum* of influences, gave way to notions that emphasize interdependence, recursive relationships, and feedback. Particularly suggestive, the *"network"* metaphor conveys the idea of a *systemic* pattern of interorganizational linkages owing its cohesion, and its demarcation against the environment, to the sharing of meaning attached to interactions within the network.

Linked to this metaphor is the notion of variability in network patterns. It may to some degree be captured with such abstract conceptualizations as offered by (for example) graph theory. However, the political scientist interested in the comparative study of interest intermediation and its impact on policies will more often prefer verbal descriptions presumably more appropriate to preserve the multi-dimensionality and internal complexity that distinguishes *"policy networks"* (Katzenstein 1978) on the analytical level of national political systems. The degree of abstraction is then much lower than in the models of sociometric provenance. Rather, we encounter typological constructs highly "idiographic" in nature.

Moreover, differing from the sociometric research tradition, this variety of the *"network" concept* opens an *institutionalist* perspective. Not only are networks seen as emerging out of processes of collective social learning in institutional contexts.[4] Rather they become *institutionalized* themselves. And, as institutions tend to do, they then either constrain or facilitate political action. Thus, the collective bargaining network in the West German health system took shape in a long struggle over control of medical practice within the institutional framework of public health insurance created by Bismarck. And now its *institutional inertia* has become so strong that even under strong fiscal strain, as in the crisis of financing health costs in the 1980s, market-like mechanisms which had become important in other countries (as, for example, the "Health Maintenance Organizations" in the United States) stood no chance of being even taken into consideration (Döhler 1990). This is all the more remarkable since rehabilitation of the market had been a dominant theme in the political discourse of that time.

This interest in a *network approach* has of course also been inspired by neo-corporatist theory. But it is well known that in influential early versions of this theory the focus was much more on intra-organizational structures than on inter-organizational relationships. Schmitter's (1974) now familiar typology linked organizational properties with the relationship of interest associations and the state. But the latter was then still very much a black box. And how precisely organized interests are "specifically licensed, recognized, subsidized,

---

4   The importance of such learning processes in institutional contexts, in particular in public bureaucracies, was underlined by Heclo (1974).

created, or otherwise controlled in leadership election or interest articulation by the state", and eventually granted "a monopoly of representational activity within their respective categories" (Schmitter 1974), is a multidimensional phenomenon manifesting itself in extremely variable empirical configurations. How, in particular, are binary relationships between individual associations and government (or, eventually, individual agencies) aggregated into the network-like configurations mentioned above? How do we explain the regularities observed on the "network" or "system" level?

Still more, as methodological controversies about the operational description and measurement of *corporatism* have shown, the typology, when employed in cross-national comparison on the level of national political systems, did not lend itself easily to an easy agreement about indicators and the construction of indices. This was not so much the fault of the operability of the constructs. After all, the definitions emphasized organizational properties that could easily be translated in measurement concepts (degree of centralization, organizational density etc.) and, where employed in empirical research, proved to be reasonably robust (see, e.g., Schmitter 1981, Cameron 1984). But they represent only some dimensions of the more complex *configurations of "interest systems"* on the level of (national) political systems (Schmitter 1977). Although of central importance for the description and theoretical understanding of the intermediation of interests, organizational properties would have to be combined with additional analytical dimensions if one wanted to describe patterns of interest intermediation at the political system level.

To be sure, comparing *systems of interest intermediation* presents considerable analytical difficulties because of their "structural heterogeneity" (Schmitter 1977). Unlike political parties in a given political system, interest associations usually do not focus mainly on one set of - often tightly coupled - institutions, namely, parliament and cabinet. And already for the study of party systems it is obvious that their *structural heterogeneity* increases with looser coupling of the "focal" institutions, e.g. in federal states with strongly institutionalized "checks and balances". The resulting multidimensionality not only makes description and measurement much more complex but also complicates cross-national comparison and the building and testing of comparative hypotheses.

The "exchange" paradigm and "state interests" in "meso-corporatism"

But if progress in the cross-national comparative study of interest intermediation has slowed down in recent years, this seems not so much due to the methodological problems just mentioned. It has probably more to do with the shifting emphasis of much recent research in the neo-corporatist school from the "macro"- to the "meso"-level of interest intermediation.[5] Among the motives for this shift in research interests was a widespread belief that macro-corporatism had been linked to a specific agenda in economic policy that was now losing its immediate political relevance. Particularly with the decline of Keynesian macro-economic demand management, macro-corporatism on the level of the national (macro-)economy apparently tended to be superseded by (micro-)economic management on the "meso-level", as in industrial policy). Whether this view overemphasized the relationship of ("macro") corporatism and Keynesianism need not concern us here.[6] The new emphasis, while diverting research interests away from national configurations of interest intermediation, stimulated a growing body of empirical studies on the organization and representation of interests on the level of particular industries. Here it was clearly demonstrated that "sector" is an important dimension of variability. In highlighting sectoral regularities and *cross-sectoral variations*, it has made a significant contribution to the understanding of (national) *policy networks*, or *interest systems*, as pluridimensional configurations.

---

5   See, in particular, Cawson (1986). The distinction of different (namely, "macro", "meso", and "micro") "levels" of interest intermediation was originally introduced by Wassenberg (1982).

6   The discussion has not always avoided an overly narrow notion of "Keynesianism" as economic policy. The case for sectoral industrial policy was more often made within a general "Keynesian" framework to supplement rather than to supersede macro-economic policy.

The literature on meso-corporatism has brought important progress in understanding the emergence of stable linkages between the state and organized interests. It appeared that they might best be explained in the framework of an exchange paradigm. Something similar had originally been suggested as an alternative to attempts to explain the cooperation of labor unions in *tri-partite* wage policy in terms of a class-theoretical approach (as in Panitch 1977): Rather, unions should be regarded as rational (collective) actors guided by a self-interested "exchange calculus" (Lehmbruch 1979: 304). But such a calculus may of course be made by government agencies as well as by interest organizations as partners in a cooperative relationship (Olsen 1983:170 pp.). "The interest organizations may have the aggregated information and, most of all, the capacity to deliver the compliance of their members with respect to specific aspects of public policy". On the other hand, governmental agencies have "the capacity to provide attractive and selective rewards, and to accord public status to consenting organizations" (Schmitter 1986:44 pp.).

So the calculus refers to "specific aspects of public policy". And generalizations about such aspects suggest themselves most plausibly on the sectoral level: Meso-corporatism would be likely to emerge in sectors where "potential members are so large in number and dispersed in location that voluntary associability is severely impaired", or find themselves in a "particularly competitive and potentially ruinous" relationship, or where "categoric goods" (such as restrictions on entry) can only be produced reliably when backed by coercive authority (Schmitter 1986:45). And "state interests" suggest the recourse to corporatist relationships where the authorities "cannot obtain the necessary information on their own" or need "the active consent for the targeted groups" for implementing policies that intervene in matters related to production, investment, or employment" (op.cit. 46). Keeler (1987:255 pp.) has made this case for agricultural policy: The adoption of state interventionism in this sector resulted in a "corporatist imperative", since the large number of small producers would otherwise make interventionist schemes extremely difficult to administer.

As I indicated above, this line of reasoning thus leads to hypotheses that have a quite striking affinity to theories of "structural contingency" in research on industrial organizations, although their point of departure was different: Unlike earlier organization theories (in particular "scientific management") which regarded bureaucratic hierarchies and division of tasks in vertical authority structures as the most effective and efficient type of organization, contingency theorists expected organizations to adopt those structures that were most likely to guarantee their survival in an organizational environment defined by factors such as their specific tasks. The theory of meso-corporatism and the more recent organization theories thus converge in seeing structures related to environmental "task contingencies".

The organizational darwinism postulating the survival of the fittest has not remained the last word in contingency theory. In an influential version, organizational structure is mediated with the task environment in a process where the *dominant coalitions* within the organization have some latitude for *strategic choice* of alternatives. Among these alternatives is not only organizational design but also modifying the environment (e.g. switching to a different market) or manipulating the criteria of performance. And strategic choice can be determined by ideology (Child 1972). In a perspective of strategic choice the historical development of industrial organization can consequently be analyzed as a history of strategic adaptation to the environment (Chandler 1962, 1977; Lawrence/Dyer 1983).

A similar reasoning suggests itself in the context of a theory of meso-corporatism when structural variations are ascribed to the impact of sectoral *task contingencies* on an *exchange calculus* regarding associational and state interests. In an exchange framework, specific *state interests* may certainly be singled out as an explanatory variable for some cross-sectoral variations. They may also account for the impact which factors such as the size of countries and their degree of openness to international markets may have on some cross-national variations. But they do not easily explain cross-national variations in *standard operating procedures* or in the *strategies* of government bureaucracies dealing with organized interests. Therefore the predictive power of an *exchange calculus* hypothesis appears limited. We have to assume that the collective actors involved have some latitude for *strategic choice*, in the design of inter-organizational relations.

Sectoral contingencies and macro-level regularities in the structure of policy networks

In the literature on meso-corporatism, *sector* is sometimes employed as if it were synonymous with *industry*. But in the present theoretical context it has the more general meaning of *policy domain*, that is, "a set of actors with major concerns about a substantive area whose preferences and actions on policy events must be taken into account by the other domain participants" (Laumann/Knoke 1987:10).[7] So, when promotion of a particular industry becomes a "policy topic" (Olsen 1983:79), more durable, specific relationships of this industry with specific governmental agencies may be established, and a policy-related organization-set will thus emerge. In these circumstances, environmental *structural* or *task contingencies* may be responsible for the sometimes strikingly similar patterns observed across nations.

But *industries*, in our theoretical perspective, are only a special case of *sectors*. In other instances, an organization-set related to a *policy-topic*, or a *policy network*, may emerge around a governmental agency as its focal organization. Here, however, we sometimes encounter considerable cross-national variations. And this is apparently due to the fact that the range of strategic choice for governments is apparently much less constrained by environmental task contingencies than in the case of many industries.

A striking example are the different national health systems mentioned earlier: Different political strategies of health policy "network design" have obviously been much less constrained by environmental task contingencies. In the United States, where state

---

7   Related concepts are "issue area", or "arena", or J.P.Olsen's (1983:179) "policy topic's organization-set", that is, "a cluster of interdependent organizations which take interest in that topic". Within such an inter-organizational approach the introduction of the concept of "network" is a quite obvious next step..For a discussion of the concept of "sector" in inter-organizational terms, see also Scott/Meyer (1983).

regulation originally was either non-existent or incoherent, some medical schools and large foundations took the original leadership in an effort of professionalization that finally resulted in a system of "self-regulation" through an all-powerful "American Medical Association" (Starr 1982). Only more recent developments - first, the establishment of a public segment of health insurance, then the emergence of new corporate actors in a *medical-industrial complex* - have led to a diversification of that traditional pattern. A very dissimilar network structure developed in Britain with the creation of the state-controlled *"National Health Service"*. Both, in turn, differ strongly from the "corporatist" West German health system. Here, we have a pattern that is clearly not due to environmental "task contingencies" of health care, but rather to strategic decisions of different corporate actors at earlier historical junctures that then led to an institutional consolidation of the newly established linkage structures. In particular, protracted and often intense conflicts over professional control between the emerging medical associations and the decentralized public health insurance funds (where labor representatives has considerable influence) led the imperial government to intervene on behalf of the medical profession. The outcome was a sort of social peace agreement establishing a system of inter-organizational collective bargaining supervised by the government (Döhler 1990).

However, even where the cumulated findings of industrial sector studies in different (national) political systems indicate similar "task contingencies", some "meso level" variations can be observed that, on closer scrutiny, appear to be due to ("macro") systemic properties. As already indicated,in the agricultural "sector" we observe a distinctive "sectoral" pattern in quite different advanced industrial countries: Levels of organizational density of farmers associations are much higher than in the sector of industrial relations and thus seem to indicate the existence of an environmental "task contingency" (or "corporatist imperative") in agriculture (Keeler 1987:255 pp.). But closer inspection of the data (op.cit. 265) seems also to reveal quite significant differences in the organization of agriculture across nations, and these appear in turn related to variations found in industrial relations: The "corporatist" organizational pattern in agriculture seems to be more pronounced in countries with "corporatist" industrial relations, and less so in those where industrial relations correspond more to a "pluralist" pattern. And since the organizations of this sector in general do not in any decisive manner interact with those of agriculture, such correlations must be ascribed to some distinctive national patterns cutting across sectors.

As mentioned above, earlier research has tended to measure cross-national variations with the quite robust indicator of *organizational properties* - more precisely, with the organizational properties of labor unions for which comparable data were most readily available (e.g., Schmitter 1981). The underlying assumption was that these were correlated with the organizational properties of other important producer groups and, apparently, with important inter-organizational linkage patterns. Now, this may be a plausible explanation in a tightly coupled system of industrial relations where, moreover, government may be involved through some sort of bargained incomes policy. But to account for the apparent correlations between the organizational properties of labor unions and agricultural interest associations we would have to refer to some inter-organizational linkage patterns overarching the different sectors. This directs the analytical focus back from the "meso" level of sectoral interest intermediation to the "macro" level.

Thus it appears that the distinction between the "macro" and "meso" levels of interest intermediation may fruitfully be employed for analytical purposes that go beyond the more narrow difference found between "macro-" and "meso-"corporatism.[8] The latter distinction focuses, of course, on the specific pattern of interest intermediation through associations, and has more recently served as the point of departure for theories of "private interest government (Streeck/Schmitter 1985). Research about "networks" of interest intermediation, or "policy networks", represents a different line of inquiry where associations constitute only one type of corporate actors that eventually make up a network. Also the typological

---

8   Nor should it be narrowed down to the distinction of two specific policy patterns, namely, a "macro-corporatist" variant of keynesian demand management, and a "meso-corporatist" variant of sectoral industrial policy.

distinction between *"pluralism"* and *"corporatism"* would eventually have to be refined or replaced by more complex, pluridimensional typologies.[9] In such a pluridimensional framework, the distinction of "macro" and "meso" (sectoral) levels would constitute an important analytical dimension. In particular, it suggests that isomorphous patterns of interest organization and intermediation observed on the meso-level of economic sectors could eventually be attributed to systemic factors operating on the macro-level.

State Structures and Network Configurations: The Case of Switzerland

It follows that complex *"rule systems"* (in the sense of Burns/Flam 1987) and inter-organizational and institutional configurations, cannot fully be understood within an exchange paradigm. They come into being in processes of organizational and institutional learning during formative phases of historical development, and (to a larger or lesser degree) they may then become dissociated from the strategic choices of that formative phase and survive as institutional residues of past organizational options. Such historical dissociations between strategy and structure suggest a genetic approach that focuses on the role of public bureaucracies and governments in the emergence and further evolution of systems, or "networks" of inter-est intermediation. "Interest systems" or macro-level "policy net-works", I submit, are complex configurations that can be analyzed in an evolutionary perspective not unlike "party systems" (Lipset/Rokkan 1967). They have grown and been transformed through interrelated - but not necessarily synchronized - develop-mental sequences of different subsystems, and in critical junctures state bureaucracies have often played an important formative part of their own. Some examples will follow below.

As indicated earlier, interactions of government bureaucracies with associations or other corporate economic actors seem to be of

9   An interesting attempt has been made in this direction that combines concepts of "governance" taken from transaction cost economics (Williamson 1975; Ouchi 1980) with a "neo-corporatist" approach (Hollingsworth/Lindberg 1985).

crucial importance in linking the macro- and meso-levels and result in the emergence of network configurations which eventually become institutionalized. This hypothesis should not be confounded with the proposition that organized interests tend to adapt their strategies and structures to the institutional framework of the particular system of government. In an important early study, Eckstein (1960) extrapolated from the case of the United Kingdom, as compared to the United States, that in a parliamentary system with a strong leadership position of the executive, organized interests will seek access to the latter instead of parliament. And one might then add that their organizational structure will be adapted to addressing this "target structure". From such a hypothesis one would also predict that interest associations operating in a decentralized political system will tend to develop a decentralized structure themselves so that, among others, peak organizations would be rather weak. The case of the United States seems to confirm such a prediction.

However, if we look at the experience of Switzerland a similar expectation is not borne out: As many students of Swiss politics have emphasized this country has a decentralized form of government and a very decentralized party system, but the large economic interest groups are organized in quite influential peak associations. This does not necessarily imply that Eckstein was outrightly wrong: Until the 1870s the fragmentation of Swiss interest groups mirrored the decentralization of the political system as predicted by the hypothesis.[10] But with its focus on "access", this central theoretical category of pluralist interest group theory, the hypothesis falls short in explaining the evolutionary complexity of policy networks. The contemporary Swiss system rather has to be understood as the out-

---

10 The popular term to designate the peak association of business, "Vorort", continues to serve as a reminiscence of this decentralized past: Like in the old Swiss Confederation (before 1798), where different cantons alternately served as "Vorort", that is to say, they were charged with the presidency of the diet, so in the 19th century there was a loose coalition of regional business associations in which the conduct of administrative matters rotated. Later on, the seat of the Union of Commerce and Industry remained with the association of Zürich, as a permanent "Vorort", and the name was subsequently transferred to the headquarters of the "Union" as a (now bureaucratized and more centralized) business peak association.

come of a *"strategic choice" on the part of political elites* in a critical juncture to restructure a trade policy network adapted to new international contingencies with which the traditional state structures were not fit to cope.

This critical juncture for development away from the decentralized notables' associations arrived in the last quarter of the 19th century when, with the onset of what has sometimes been called the *"great depression"*, the European free trade system disintegrated. This led to a process of bureaucratization and centralization of organized interests that finally gave the peak associations a clear organizational lead over other collective political actors, in particular political parties. This development, however, cannot be seen simply as the outcome of an endogenous transformation of the system of interest groups. The antagonism between free-traders and protectionists in the Swiss industry led to *demands for an encompassing system of interest intermediation*, eventually some sort of compulsory corporatist organization (Gruner 1954). The strength of the liberal tradition prevented the realization of such a design. Under these circumstances, the "natural", i.e. endogenous reaction to the breakdown of the European free trade system might rather have been the formation of two rival associations as it happened, for example, in neighbouring Germany.[11] In Switzerland this was avoided because the federal government intervened in favor of the formation of *representational monopolies of peak associations* (Bücher 1888, Gruner 1954). This intervention was motivated by the peculiar structure of the Swiss state. Because of its institutional decentralization and, at that time, its extremely weak administrative capacities, the government of the federation found itself not well equipped to reconcile the conflicting interests in foreign trade and conduct successful international negotiations on tariffs. Therefore it proposed to the "Vorort" (hitherto an association run by leading businessmen in a honorary capacity) and to the Swiss Union of Articrafts and Trades (small business) financial

---

11 Here, the protectionist "Centralverband Deutscher Industrieller" was opposed by the peak association of some export-oriented industries, the "Bund der Industriellen". Both merged after the First World War, as a result of developments to which I will come back.

grants to employ full-time secretaries for the establishment of trade statistics and other documentation needed by the government. After this precedent, full-time secretaries paid from public funds were later also appointed for organized agriculture and for labor. As a condition for these subsidies, the government demanded the establishment of unified peak associations, even for the trade unions divided into separate and competing socialist and denominational associations.[12]

The emergence of strong economic peak associations in Switzerland thus looks like a case of "political design" where "the intervention of organized interests ... is to some extent intentionally created, structured and institutionalized through state action" (Anderson 1977:129). However, the solution originally chosen under particular historical circumstances has then become dissociated from its historical origins and became self-sustaining through its acquired institutional momentum.

On the face of it, the Swiss case fits a corporatist "exchange paradigm" where the government grants a representational monopoly and organizational resources to centralized associations in order to discharge on these the tasks that they are better qualified to assume than a government bureaucracy. But why did that happen just in Switzerland? Here we encounter a *strategic choice* that appears to have been motivated by the peculiar structure of the Swiss state: Owing to complex historical reasons, Swiss political elites have been extremely reluctant to provide their government with administrative resources such as a strong permanent professional bureaucracy. The preferred alternative was, as Swiss commentators like to say, *"militia administration"*. This term of course refers to the militia type organization of the Swiss army, but that favourite reference in turn implies that this is part of a specific Swiss *"rule system"* for organizing the polity. Put otherwise, it implies an elite consensus about the social

---

12 The inclusionary logic of the Swiss pattern is strikingly illustrated by this co-option of organized labor: Originally a purpose of the establishment of this peak association "Worker's League" was to neutralize the influence of the Social Democrats. However, when a leading Social Democrat Hermann Greulich served as "labor secretary", he succeeded to transform it into a pressure group for reforms in labor and social policy.

meaning of institutions that evolved from historical experience. Swiss elites often continue to uphold a "militia" interpretation of their administrative system although in the meantime a competent and professionalized - though relatively small - federal bureaucracy has developed. This then serves to justify the privileged position of interest associations in the policy networks although these are today better understood as the product of a process of institutionalization in which the structures have since long become dissociated from their strategic origins.

National Paths in the Growth of Policy Networks as Sequential Interaction of the Organization of State and Society

The breakdown of the European free trade regime, which led to the Swiss developments just described, was a critical juncture in the development of organized interests in other countries as well. It is well known that this development took often place in waves linked to major political-economic crises. In the language of pluralist interest group theory, such crises disrupted the "established patterns of behavior". New patterns of association would therefore develop, and because in modern complex societies "the means of adjustment are beyond the resources of direct action by the groups involved", these associations would then inevitably "gravitate toward government" (Truman 1951:104). The theoretical weakness of this interpretation in terms of an endogenous logic of organizational growth is generally recognized today. And the emergence of inter-organizational linkages between associations and the government would rather be seen as an exchange between organized interests and government in which both sides are guided by strategic considerations than as the restoration of an "equilibrium" of interest groups presumably gotten "disturbed". This strategic interaction, however, leads to highly variable national configurations. Although the breakdown of the free trade regime and the "great depression" confronted the European countries, their governments, and the large producer groups with some largely similar new "task contingencies", their strategic responses show significant variations: Whereas in Switzerland the government obtained the formation of encompassing peak associations, in neighbouring countries such as Germany and Austria free-traders and protectionist established rival pressure groups.

In these countries, the organizational concentration of business peak associations resulted from the next trans-national "wave" in the development of state-interest networks, the first world war. It is well known that in the major belligerent countries the organizations of business were co-opted into the administration of the war economy. This organizational mobilization of business by the state was often extended to labor unions, in particular with the "institutionalization of class conflict" through regular procedures of collective bargaining. The Second World War had similar consequences, and again we encounter some remarkably parallel developments in different countries (Grant , Nekkers, and van Waarden 1991).

Corporatist theory has been attentive to these "waves" and has linked them quite plausibly to environmental contingencies emerging in most of the advanced industrial countries. Yet, on the other hand, we observe also characteristic differences in the responses of individual countries to (more or less) similar external challenges.[13] Not all of them chose the "corporatist" solution of co-opting the peak and trade associations of business for the administration of the war (and post-war) economy. Already in the First World War, business trade and peak associations played a central role in Germany, while in the United States' "War Industries Board", industries not organized in associations were mobilized "through their established leaders to the extent that such were quickly discoverable" (McConnell 1966:61). For the Second World War, van Waarden (1991) distinguishes four types of state-business relations, namely "captured etatism" (the state "captured" by businessmen who are in charge of running the war economy, as in the United States and Canada), "state

---

13 The first major study of these variations, a comparative analysis of the war economy during the Second World War, will be published shortly (Grant, Nekkers and van Waarden 1991)

corporatism" (Germany and the occupied countries),[14] "societal meso-corporatism" (Britain), and "societal macrocorporatism" (Sweden and Denmark). Moreover, the government may directly intervene into industry structures.[15]

To these differences in network configurations correspond differences in *institutional stability*. In some countries the war-time networks disintegrated soon after the end of the crisis. In others, on the contrary, they became so firmly institutionalized that they survived under changing circumstances. In particular, the cooptation of organized labor into national bargaining mechanisms proved durable in some countries while others reverted to older, more conflictual structures. The United States may serve as an illustration for the latter path. On the other hand, in several smaller European nations the "tripartist" patterns displayed a remarkable continuity. Austria, with its historical burden of violent internal conflict in the twenties and thirties, is a particularly salient case: Although here, as elsewhere, the tripartist patterns of the late forties declined in importance in the first half of the following decade, their institutional continuity remained strong enough to serve as the nucleus for the more complex bargaining system of Keynesian economic "concertation" in the sixties and seventies.[16]

Are these variations simply to be understood as "oscillations" around a trans-national path of development, amenable only to

---

14 For the case of Germany, however, this interpretation - based on Hajo Weber, chapter 5 in Grant et al. (1991) - is contestable. To be sure, specific sectors of the economy were governed by hierarchically structured compulsory associations. But Weber ignores that the design of a "corporatist order" was abandoned soon after the nazi-seizure of power in 1933: Such an overarching hierarchical organizational macro-structure would have been incompatible with the highly personalist style of Hitler's rule. In the "polycratic" power structure of the regime, the German equivalent of the "One-dollar-a-year man" had a prominent place: From 1938 to 1945 Carl Krauch, chairman of the supervisory board of the IG Farben corporation, served as "general commissioner" for the chemical industry, a top position of the economic planning bureaucracy, without ever being on the public payroll (Broszat 1969, 372 pp.).

15 Examples are the reorganization of the Japanese electric power industry by the Electric Power Control Law of 1938 (Johnson 1982: 126) or the establishment of the Hermann-Göring-Werke in Nazi Germany

16 See the longitudinal analysis in Halle (1987:117 pp.)

"idiographic" (or ad hoc) explanation from peculiar country-specific circumstances? Or do they represent country specific empirical regularities that cut across the "task contingencies" discussed before? I submit that such regularities are indeed present, and that they can be integrated into a *developmental model of national, or macro-level, policy networks*. The constitutive elements of such a model are, on the one hand, "state structures" (to use a rather summary term), corresponding administrative strategies, and interpretations of social reality guiding "strategic choices" of state elites. These elites interact, in situations of strategic choice, with specific patterns of social organization, in particular with the organization of interests in the national economy.

Such situations of choice are, in particular, crises in which the *institutional capacities of the state* are challenged by fundamental changes or disruptions of its economic environment. A first important institutional switching point that in some of the Western countries shaped the future configuration of their policy networks was the period when the nation-state organized a nation-wide capitalist market and had to cope with the economic and social changes brought about by the industrial revolution. Hence, by and large, some fundamental patterns of the national policy networks of the more advanced European countries took their shape in (or around) the 19th century. As they entered this watershed, however, their political-administrative institutions on the one hand and their societal differentiation and organization on the other, had moved through varying sequences of development. And the "sequential interaction"[17] of state structures and the organization of society then had a crucial impact on the future configuration of their policy networks. In particular, it made an important difference whether a centralized bureaucracy was inherited from the pre-industrial age (as in France, Germany, Austria, or Sweden) or was grafted on an already highly differentiated entrepreneurial industrial economy (as in Great

---

17 The term is taken from Lipset/Rokkan (1967: 34). As indicated above, the construction of a developmental model of "interest systems" can fruitfully employ some central elements of the logic of their model of party systems.

Britain or, at a more advanced stage of economic development, in the United States).

In later periods, in particular with the internationalization of markets and increasing international interdependence of the economy, some major crises too had an international impact. Of particular importance, as already mentioned, were the breakdown of the free-trade system or the two world wars. This led to the new phenomenon, already discussed, of a restructuration of national policy networks being subject to similar environmental "task contingencies" and taking place in *waves across nations*. But to the degree that the national networks have already developed highly differentiated configurations, in a longitudinal perspective we continue to observe different national paths of development, where the strategic interaction of state and administrative elites, on the one hand, and the elites of the organized society, on the other, responds to the new environmental challenges within a range of available strategic options determined by the institutional sedimentations inherited from the earlier developmental sequences. And, not dissimilar to the "freezing" of party systems (Lipset/Rokkan 1967), these network patterns may then form new sediments, that is, acquire institutional momentum and become self-sustaining.

Detailed elaboration of this model is beyond the scope of the present article. But some cases may be discussed to illustrate the guiding hypotheses. Let us first return to Switzerland, as a somewhat deviant case in the development of policy networks in Western Europe. Here, the weakness of administrative resources of the Swiss state, and traditional Swiss distrust of a strong central power, interacted with a powerful tradition of *corporate social organization* (albeit on a local and regional level). When the challenge of the free-trade crisis necessitated the establishment of new administrative capacities, "militia administration" through corporate groups on the national level was a strategic choice appropriate to those structural preconditions, and this led - through a process of "freezing" - to the strategic centrality of interest associations characteristic of contemporary Switzerland.

Since this was the outcome of the "sequential interaction" of state structures and the organization of society, the deviant Swiss case does not warrant the simple inference that, conversely, other European "strong states" with a powerful bureaucratic tradition, would in general tend to keep "interest groups" at arms length. We rather have again to ask how state structures interacted with the organization of society. A significant comparison here are two European countries with an old and important bureaucratic heritage, France and Sweden. Their paths of institutional development parted in the period of late absolutism: Sweden retained the collegial form of administration which at that time served as an institutional linkage to powerful societal interests. France, on the other hand, began to supersede the traditional collegial administration with the *monocratic* type of bureaucratic organization[18] that finally triumphed in the hierarchical structure of the Napoleonic state. If we accept Tocqueville's famous hypothesis about the impact of this administrative tradition on the state-society relationship in France,[19] it follows that a state structure characterized by centralized government and a strong bureaucracy interacted with a weak corporate organization of society. Suleiman's observations about the perception of "pressure groups" by the French bureaucracy indicate that this pattern has been remarkably persistent, at least in the interpretation of social reality by the bureaucrats themselves.

In Sweden, on the other hand, a centralized state and strong bureaucracy were linked, through the maintenance of *collegial administration*, to a strong corporate organization of society. This collegial structure of the Swedish administration seems to have served as an important institutional nucleus for the development of "corporatist" linkage structures: When Sweden entered the period of rapid industrialization, its institutional patterns adapted to the new

18 About the importance of the *commissaire*, see Hintze (1970) and, already, Tocqueville (t.II * , 1952 {L'Ancien Régime et la Révolution, first published in 1859}, 109)

19 "Le pouvoir central en France n'a pas encore acquis au dix-huitième siècle cette constitution saine et vigoureuse que nous lui avons vue depuis; néanmoins, comme il est déjà parvenu à détruire tous les pouvoirs intermédiaires, et qu'entre lui et les particuliers il n'existe plus rien qu'un espace immense et vide, il apparaît déjà de loin à chacun d'eux comme le seul ressort de la machine sociale, l'agent unique et nécessaire de la vie publique" (Tocqueville, op.cit. 135). This interpretation was taken up by Crozier (1963:275 pp.)

environmental challenges by co-opting the emerging modern interest associations into the collegial structures.[20] Therefore, different from France, "corporatist" linkages acquired a high degree of legitimacy.

Other countries recently classified as "corporatist", Austria and the Netherlands, have an administrative tradition more germane to the French model: The monocratic type of bureaucratic organization became dominant in the 18th or 19th century. However, if we look into the sequential interactions of state structures and the organization of society we find a pattern roughly equivalent to the Swedish path of development. The Dutch Republic had an extremely weak central government, but a strong corporate organization of society. Although the occupation by the armies of revolutionary France destroyed much of these structures (notably the guilds) the transformation of society never went so far as to eradicate the corporate traditions. It was upon this institutional heritage that the era of Napolenonic rule grafted the French model of bureaucratic administration (Daalder 1966). Thus, through a different historical path, the Netherlands , too, combine a tradition of strong centralized administration with a strong corporate organization of society (van Waarden 1990).

In Austria, finally, the interaction of developmental sequences was again somewhat different but the outcome similar. Here the 18th century was characterized by the triumph of centralizing government and monocratic administration. In the 19th century, to shield this regime against demands for popular representation, a system of political consultation through *chambers* (in particular, the regional chambers of commerce) developed as a surrogate for parliamentarism. When finally parliamentary government was introduced, this did not mean the final victory of liberal individualism since the symbiosis of bureaucratic rule and corporate representation was already firmly established. After the highly conflictual interlude between the

---

20 This has been well illustrated by Hans Meijers studies of the development of the Swedish committee system (Meijer 1956, 1969). Today, the Labor Market Board is the best-known example of associational representation in collegial administrative authorities.

two world wars, party government finally became the overarching linkage structure of this corporatist network (Lehmbruch 1976, 1984).

What Sweden, Austria, and the Netherlands have in common is thus the conjunction of centralized government,[21] strong professional administration, and a strong corporate organization of society. This conjunction, I submit, was the historical precondition that permitted these countries after the Second World War to develop systems of strong "corporatist" concertation of policies between government and the peak interest associations - systems, moreover, that enjoyed widespread legitimacy.[22] I do not pretend that it was the necessary condition for the emergence of strong corporatism: Spatial diffusion (e.g. between Scandinavian countries) may also lead to this outcome. However, the combination of a strong central professional administration and a strong associational system seems to be required for the continued functioning of a corporatist system in that sense. In Germany these conditions were not fulfilled insofar as it never (except during the Hitler regime) experienced centralized government. Although a strong associational system developed since the late 19th century the decentralized patterns of policy formation in the "semi-sovereign state" (Katzenstein 1987) hampered the successful introduction of corporatist concertation. Instead, Germany developed a hybrid and rather unwieldy network configuration that was characterized (Scharpf et al. 1976) as *Politikverflechtung* (interlocking politics).

Our central contrast was between countries that entered the age of emerging industrial capitalism with a strong and centralized bureaucratic state apparatus, and those that did not. For the latter class, our only example so far was Switzerland. Another case is, of course, the United States. As Skowronek (1982) has pointed out, it would be inexact to call the US a "stateless society". Rather, the

---

21 In this context, the federal structure of the Austrian Republic can be neglected, for decentralization is largely limited to policy implementation whereas policy-formation remains essentially centralized.

22 Van Waarden (1990) makes a similar point for the Dutch case. As argued here, however, Sweden and Austria arrived at equivalent network configurations through different "sequential interactions" of state structure and societal organization.

"expansion of national administrative capacities" in the United States was a late developmental sequence, and one that only incoherently superseded an earlier state structure, very dissimilar to the experience of the European bureaucratic states, namely a "state of courts and parties". Moreover, the timing of the respective sequences in the development and state structure and the organization of society was distinctly different. In the above mentioned European states bureaucratic administration was firmly established before the emergence of the bureaucratized private business corporation. In America the relationship was rather inverse. And this different timing was not only a matter of coincidence. Rather, the growth of administrative capacities - in particular the regulatory agencies - was a response to the *challenge of "private government"* (McConnell 1966) constituted by the big corporation. Confronted with an older and different state tradition and, at the same time, with a highly developed bureaucratic organization of society, the "administrative state" never achieved that relative unity and organizational coherence and the corresponding perception of administrative roles developed in the continental European model.[23] Attempts of government officials to further the establishment of business associations (as undertaken by Herbert Hoover when he was secretary of commerce), never led to an overarching organization of the economy as obtained in Sweden, Austria or Germany. The major attempt of this order, the establishment of the *National Recovery Administration* in the early *New Deal*, ended in failure. This setback clearly demonstrated the resilience of a pattern of state-society interaction characterized by the relative encapsulation of small constituencies (McConnell 1966:336 pp.), the prominence of the business corporation (rather than the association), and of collective interpretations of the state-economy relationship developed before the growth of (presumably) "big government". Thus it appears that "American exceptionalism" in the configuration of policy networks (Salisbury 1979, Wilson 1982) may also be explained in a

---

23 Moreover, while European civil servants inherited a high social status from the Old Regime, the emerging American bureaucrats never came to enjoy a similar respect on the part of business elites (Vogel 1986).

framework of sequential interactions of state structure and the organization of society.

Collective Interpretations of Social Reality in the Development of Policy Networks

Strategic orientations of the actors in policy networks are guided by
collective interpretations of social reality, developed by the political,
administrative, and economic elites. To understand a national "policy
network" is not simply to describe inter-organizational linkages, but
includes the reconstruction of meanings or interpretations that
support their institutionalization. In this very large sense, policy
networks have to be understood as products of collective historical
experience.

To the degree that public bureaucracies occupy a central position
in the strategic interaction of the elites, their world-view and its
feedback on strategic codes is an important element in the analysis of
network configurations. Within the developmental analytic framework suggested here, one might conclude that interpretations developed by the bureaucracy in the formative phase of the emerging
policy networks tend over time to petrify into ideological sediments
that guide much of the interpretation of later crises and structural
adaptations.

John Armstrong (1973), in his comparative study of European
bureaucracies, stressed the importance of dominant *"development
doctrines"* in the organizational socialization process of national
administrative leadership groups. However, if this hypothesis is
plausible, an obvious conclusion would be to enlarge this perspective
and to focus on the incipient codes of the administration for strategic
interaction in the emergent state-society policy networks, in particular for its relationship with economic interests. Fundamental beliefs
about the legitimacy of specific patterns of strategic interaction have
probably been formed in that watershed period. Suleiman's observations about the role perceptions of French top bureaucrats are probably best understood in this perspective.

To illustrate this hypothesis, the notion of bureaucratic autonomy as developed in the Prussian administrative tradition is particularly appropriate. For it became exposed in the framework of an elaborate doctrine that continued to exert its influence beyond the formative phase of the German type of policy network. Its main exponent was the political philosopher of the Prussian reform, Hegel, and the contemporary social background of this strategic code is apparent from Hegel's own text.

Hegel's theory of administrative interest intermediation was fully developed in his "Philosophy of Right" (1821). It has its intellectual roots in Hegel's lecture of classical economics. The economy, or "system of wants" (System der Bedürfnisse) is the "mediation and satisfaction of wants" of the individual by his labor, and by the labor and the satisfaction of the wants of all other individuals (§ 188). The division of labor results in mutual dependence in production and exchange, but these interrelations are differentiated into "particular (besondere) systems of wants", of their means and efficacy, the ways of satisfying them as well as the issue of theoretical conceptualization and practical relevance. To these Hegel gives (perhaps somewhat surprising after his implicit reference to the economics of Adam Smith) the traditional name of "estates" (§ 201).

The particular ends and interests of the individual living in civil society are thus aggregated into "common particular interests", and these are taken care of by the institution of the "corporation". This is a modernized, more open version of the pre-revolutionary guild, under state tutelage. The corporation bestows on its member social "recognition" and thus the "honor" that goes with belonging to the estate.

Distinguished from the "common particular interests" in civil society is the "general interest of the state". To attend to this general interest of the state and to the principle of legality in the pursuit of individual rights is the task of the executive, represented by the civil service and government agencies. "Whereas bourgeois society is the battleground of the individual private interest of all against all, this is the place of the conflict of the private interest against the common particular concerns, and of both together against the higher viewpoints and regulations of the state". But insofar as the state preserves "the particular spheres, their justification and authority as well as their welfare", he is assured of the loyalty of the citizens (§289).

The corporation at the same time is important with regard to the division of labor within government itself. Because of the necessity of specialization the problem is how to integrate the differentiated business of government both at the top and at the bottom. Integration at the top has been achieved by the modern ministerial organization as introduced by Napoleon. But in order to prevent atomization at the bottom, an "organic state" of the "particular spheres" (of society) is needed (§ 290).

The civil service itself is an "estate" insofar as its members constitute a "particular system" in an economy characterized by the division of labor. But they are distinguished from the other estates insofar as their business are the "general interests of the social order (gesellschaftlicher Zustand)".Therefore they have to be relieved from the direct labor intended to satisfy their individual wants - either by private wealth, or by remuneration from the state making use of their labor. Thus their private interest is satisfied in its work for the general interest (§ 205). The members of government and the civil service form the main part of the "middle estate" (Mittelstand), comprising mainly the educated intelligentsia, who have the sense of the state and of legality. The existence of such a "Mittelstand" is the mark of a highly developed state (§ 290 supplement).

Hegel's theory thus emphasized two important interpretational concepts that were to serve as a normative reference point for future bureaucratic generations. But at this point it also becomes clear that this theory is strongly anchored in a distinct period of the social history of Prussian administration. This was clearly perceived, two decades later, by the young democratic journalist Karl Marx who, in his "Critique of the Hegelian Law of the State" (1843), stressed the "empirical" character of Hegel's description of the bureaucracy as the main part of the educated middle classes in contemporary Prussia. In his history of the Prussian reform, Reinhard Koselleck (1967) has shown how this emphatic conviction with which the reform bureaucracy perceived its own mission as the autonomous guardian of the general interest (Hegel's *allgemeiner Stand*) was the product of a situation when the Prussian society lacked any strong autonomous organization. In a state lacking religious, ethnic, legal, and geographic unity, the civil service was the only integrating element and, at the same time, driving force of social transformation.

One generation later new patterns of social organization emerged with the growth of a commercial and industrial economy. Now, of the prescriptive elements contained in Hegel's analysis, the one that had the strongest impact was certainly the notion of *autonomy of the administration* which, as representative of the general interest, was now supposed to *integrate a conflictual society into the state*. This adaptation of the world-view of the civil service to the emergence of a (proletarian) "social movement" was due, in particular, to the influential Hegelian Lorenz von Stein (1850). His vision of an "administration of social reform" was transmitted, in particular, to the bureaucratic social reformers at the time of Bismarck, and found an echo in the idea which these administrative elites had of their mission. Max Weber's notion of an instrumental civil service still presupposes this disinterested character of the bureaucratic ethos which we found in Hegel's vision.

However, Weber's ideal type civil servants are no longer (as Marx put it in his critique of Hegel) "supraordained, as the knowing spirit, to the materialism of bourgeois society". Already in Lorenz von Stein's conservative-reformist theory the state and its administration was in danger of falling under the control of a dominant non-laboring class of proprietors. Weber, writing in an environment of a developed capitalist economy, became aware that bureaucratic organizations may place themselves at the disposal of exclusively economic interests, thus contributing to a "crypto-plutocratic distribution of power" (Weber 1976, 571). Thus, within this interpretation of social reality which originated with the Prussian reform bureaucracy, the vision of an "autonomous" civil service now finds its counterpart in the negative vision of *bureaucratic "capture"*. Whether such a world-view is still an adequate representation of reality may be open to question. But it remains a powerful legitimizing collective image for strategic interaction and in this sense it constitutes an important aspect of the configuration of policy networks.

References

Anderson, Charles W. (1977) 'Political Design and the Representation of Interests' *Comparative Political Studies* 10:127-152.

Armstrong, John (1973) *The European Administrative Elite.* Princeton: Princeton University Press.

Broszat, Martin (1969) *Der Staat Hitlers.* München: Deutscher Taschenbuch Verlag.

Bücher, Karl (1888) 'Die wirtschaftliche Interessenvertretung in der Schweiz' *Zeitschrift für die gesamte Staatswissenschaft* 44:346-382.

Burns, Tom R. and Helena Flam (1987) *The Shaping of Social Organizations.* London: Sage.

Cameron, David (1984) 'Social Democracy, Corporatism, Labour Quiescence, and the Representation of Economic Interest in Advanced Capitalist Society', pp. 143-178 in John Goldthorpe, (ed.) *Order and Conflict in Contemporary Capitalism.* Oxford: Clarendon Press.

Cawson, Alan (1986) *Corporatism and Political Theory.* Oxford: Basil Blackwell.

Child, John (1972) 'Organizational Structure, Environment and Performance: The Role of Strategic Choice' *Sociology* 6:1-22.

Chandler, Alfred (1962) *Strategy and Structure: Chapters in the History of the American Industrial Enterprise.* Cambridge, Mass.: MIT Press.

Chandler, Alfred (1977) *The Visible Hand: The Managerial Revolution in American Business.* Cambridge, Mass.: Harvard University Press.

Crozier, Michel (1963) *Le Phénomène Bureaucratique.* Paris: Éditions du Seuil.

Daalder, Hans (1966) 'The Netherlands: Opposition in a Segmented Society', pp. 188-236 in Robert Dahl (ed.) *Political Oppositions in Western Democracies.* New Haven: Yale University Press.

Döhler, Marian (1990) *Gesundheitspolitik nach der "Wende". Policy-Netzwerke und ordnungspolitischer Strategiewechsel in der Bundesrepublik, Großbritannien und den USA.* Berlin: edition sigma.

Eckstein, Harry (1960) *Pressure Group Politics: The Case of the British Medical Association.* London: Allen and Unwin.

Grande, Edgar (1989) *Vom Monopol zum Wettbewerb? Die neokonservative Reform der Telekommunikation in Großbritannien und der Bundesrepublik Deutschland.* Wiesbaden: Deutscher Universitätsverlag.

Grant, Wyn, Jan Nekkers, and Frans van Waarden (eds.) (1991) *Organizing Business for War. Corporatist Economic Organization during the Second World War: a Comparison of Nine Countries.* Oxford, Prov.: Berg-Publishers.

Gruner, Erich (1954) 'Wirtschaftsverbände und Staat. Das Problem der wirtschaftlichen Interessenvertretung in historischer Sicht' *Schweizerische Zeitschrift für Volkswirtschaft und Statistik* 90:1-27.

Halle, Axel (1987) *Politik im Netzwerk: Parteien, Parlament und Verbände in Österreich.* Konstanz: Wisslit Verlag.

Heclo, Hugh (1974) *Modern Social Politics in Britain and Sweden: From Relief to Income Maintenance.* New Haven: Yale University Press.

Hegel, Georg Wilhelm Friedrich (1821) *Grundlinien der Philosophie des Rechts, oder Naturrecht und Staatswissenschaften im Grundrisse.* Werke Band 8, edited by Eduard Gans. Berlin 1833: Duncker und Humblot.

Hintze, Otto (1970) 'Der Commissarius und seine Bedeutung in der allgemeinen Verwaltungsgeschichte', pp. 242-274 in Otto Hintze *Staat und Verwaltung.* Göttingen: Vandenhoeck & Ruprecht.

Hollingsworth, Rogers C. and Leon Lindberg (1985) 'The Governance of the American Economy: The Role of Markets, Clans Hierarchies, and Associative Behavior', pp. 221 - 252, in Wolfgang Streeck and Philippe C. Schmitter (eds.) *Private Interest Government*. London, Beverly Hills: Sage .

Jann, Werner (1983) *Staatliche Programme und Verwaltungskultur. Bekämpfung des Drogenmißbrauchs und der Jugendarbeitslosigkeit in Schweden, Großbritannien und der Bundesrepublik Deutschland im Vergleich*. Opladen: Westdeutscher Verlag.

Johnson, Chalmers (1982) *MITI and the Japanese Miracle: The Growth of Industrial Policy, 1925-1975*. Stanford, CA.:Stanford University Press.

Katzenstein, Peter (1978) 'Conclusion: Domestic Structures and Strategies of Foreign Economic Policy', pp. 295-336 in Peter Katzenstein (ed.) *Between Power and Plenty: Foreign Economic Policies of Advanced Industrial States*. Madison. Wisc.: University of Wisconsin Press.

Katzenstein, Peter (1987) *Politics and Policy in West Germany: The Growth of a Semi-Sovereign State*. Philadelphia: Temple University Press.

Keeler, John (1987) *The Politics of Neocorporatism in France: Farmers, the State, and Agricultural Policy-Making in the Fifth Republic*. New York: Oxford University Press.

Koselleck, Reinhard (1967) *Preußen zwischen Reform und Revolution. Allgemeines Landrecht, Verwaltung und soziale Bewegung von 1791 bis 1848*. Stuttgart: Klett-Cotta.

LaPalombara, Joseph (1964) *Interest Groups in Italian Politics*. Princeton, N.J.: Princeton University Press.

Laumann, Edward and David Knoke (1987) *The Organizational State: Social Choice in National Policy Domains*. Madison, Wisc.: University of Wisconsin Press.

Lawrence, Paul and Davis Dyer (1983) *Renewing American Industry: Organizing for Efficiency and Innovation*. New York: Free Press.

Lehmbruch, Gerhard (1976) 'Liberal Corporatism and Party Government' *Comparative Political Studies* 10:91-126.

Lehmbruch, Gerhard (1979) 'Concluding Remarks: Problems for Future Research on Corporatist Intermediation and Policy-Making', pp. 299-310 in Philippe Schmitter and Gerhard Lehmbruch (eds.) *Trends Toward Corporatist Intermediation.* London: Sage.

Lehmbruch, Gerhard (1984) 'Concertation and the Structure of Corporatist Networks', pp. 60-80 in John Goldthorpe (ed.) *Conflict and Cooperation in Contemporary Capitalism.* Oxford: Clarendon Press.

Lehmbruch, Gerhard (1985) 'Österreichs sozialpartnerschaftliches System im internationalen Vergleich', pp. 85-107 in Peter Gerlich , Edgar Grande , and Wolfgang C. Müller (eds.) *Sozialpartnerschaft in der Krise.* Wien: Böhlau.

Lehmbruch, Gerhard, Marian Döhler, Edgar Grande, and Otto Singer (1988) 'Institutionelle Bedingungen ordnungspolitischen Strategiewechsels im internationalen Vergleich', pp. 251-283 in Manfred G. Schmidt (ed.) *Staatstätigkeit.* Opladen: Westdeutscher Verlag.

Lehmbruch, Gerhard (1989a) 'Marktreformstrategien bei alternierender Parteiregierung: Eine vergleichende institutionelle Analyse', pp.15-45 in *Jahrbuch zur Staats- und Verwaltungswissenschaft 3.* Baden-Baden:Nomos Verlag.

Lehmbruch, Gerhard (1989b) 'Wirtschaftspolitischer Strategiewechsel und die institutionelle Verknüpfung von Staat und Gesellschaft', pp. 222-235 in Hans-Hermann Hartwich (ed.) *Macht und Ohnmacht politischer Institutionen.* Opladen: Westdeutscher Verlag.

Lipset, Seymour Martin and Stein Rokkan (1967) 'Cleavage Structures, Party Systems, and Voter Alignments: An Introduction', pp. 1-64 in Seymour Martin Lipset and Stein Rokkan (eds.) *Party Systems and Voter Alignments: Cross-National Perspectives.* New York: Free Press.

Marx, Karl (1843) 'Kritik des Hegelschen Staatsrechts', pp. 401-553 in *Marx/Engels Gesamtausgabe, 1. Abteilung, 1/1.* Frankfurt a.M.: Marx-Engels-Archiv Verlagsgesellschaft.

McConnell, Grant (1966) *Private Power and American Democracy.* New York: Knopf.

Meijer, Hans (1956) *Komittépolitik och komittéarbete.* Lund:Gleerup.

Meijer, Hans (1969) 'Bureaucracy and Policy Formulation in Sweden' *Scandinavian Political Studies* 4:103-116.

Olsen, Johan P. (1983) *Organized Democracy: Political Institutions in a Welfare State - the Case of Norway.* Bergen: Universitätsvorlage Bergen.

Olsen, Johan (1983) ' Integrated Participation in Government', pp. 492-516 in Nystrom Paul C. and William H. Starbuck (eds.) *Handbook of Organizational Design, vol. 2.* Oxford 1981: Oxford University Press.

Ouchi, William (1980) 'Markets, Bureaucracies, and Clans' *Administrative Science Quarterly* 25:129-141.

Panitch, Leo (1977) 'The Development of Corporatism in Liberal Democracies' *Comparative Political Studies* 10:61-90.

Przeworski, Adam and Henry Teune (1970), *The Logic of Comparative Social Inquiry.* New York: John Wiley & Sons.

Richardson, Jeremy (ed.) (1982) *Policy Styles in Western Europe.* London: Allen and Unwin.

Salisbury, Robert (1979) 'Why No Corporatism in America', pp. 213-230 in Philippe C. Schmitter and Gerhard Lehmbruch (eds.) *Trends Towards Corporatist Intermediation.* London, Berverly Hills: Sage.

Scott, Richard and John W. Meyer (1983) 'The Organization of Societal Sectors', pp. 129-153 in Scott, Richard and John. W. Mayer (eds.) *Organizational Environments: Ritual and Rationality*, Beverly Hills and London: Sage.

Scharpf, Fritz, Bernd Reissert, and Fritz Schnabel (1976) *Politikver-flechtung: Theorie und Empirie des kooperativen Föderalismus in der Bundesrepublik.* Kronberg/Ts.: Scriptor.

Schmitter, Philippe (1974) 'Still the Century of Corporatism?' *Review of Politics* 36:85-131.

Schmitter, Philippe (1977) 'Modes of Interest Intermediation and Models of Societal Change in Western Europe' *Comparative Political Studies* 10:7-38.

Schmitter, Philippe (1981) 'Interest Intermediation and Regime Governability in Western Europe and North America'. pp. 287-330 in Suzanne Berger, (ed.) *Organizing Interests in Western Europe.* Cambridge: Cambridge University Press.

Schmitter, Philippe (1986) 'Neo-corporatism and the State', pp. 32-62 in Wyn Grant, (ed.) *The Political Economy of Corporatism.* London: Macmillan.

Schmitter, Philippe C. (1989) 'Corporatism is Dead! Long Live Corporatism' *Government and Opposition* 24:54-74.

Skowronek, Stephen (1982) *Building a New American State: The Expansion of National Administrative Capacities, 1877-1920.* Cambridge: Cambridge University Press.

Starr, Paul (1982) *The Social Transformation of American Medecine.* New York: Basic Books Inc..

Stein, Lorenz von (1850) *Geschichte der sozialen Bewegung in Frankreich von 1789 bis auf unsere Tage.* 3 vols.. Re-edited by Gottfried Salomon. München 1921: Drei-Masken Verlag.

Streeck, Wolfgang and Philippe Schmitter, Philippe (1985) 'Community, Market, State - and Associations? The Prospective Contribution of Interest Government to Social Order', pp. 1-29 in Wolfgang Streeck and Philippe C. Schmitter (eds.) *Private Interest Government: Beyond Market and State.* London: Sage.

Suleiman, Ezra (1974) *Politics, Power and Bureaucracy in France.* Princeton, N.J.: Princeton University Press.

Tocqueville, Alexis de (1952) *Oeuvres complètes.* Edited by J.P. Mayer. Paris: Gallimard.

Truman, David (1951) *The Governmental Process: Political Interests and Public Opinion.* New York: Knopf.

Vogel, David (1986) *National Styles of Regulation: Entvironmental Policy in Great Britain and the United States.* Ithaca, N.Y. and London: Cornell University Press.

Waarden, Frans van (1991) 'Wartime Economic Mobilization and State Business Relations. A Comparison of Nine Countries', forthcoming in Wyn Grant, Jan Nekkers , and Frans van Waarden (eds.) *Organizing Business for War. Corporatist Economic Organization during the Second World War: a Comparison of Nine Countries.* Oxford, Prov.: Berg-Publishers.

Waarden, Frans van (1990) *'Genesis and Institutionalization of Nationally Specific Policy Networks between State and Societal Interests: A Model for Analysis and some Historical Comparisons between the USA and the Netherlands'* (ECPR, Joint Sessions of Workshops, Bochum; mimeographed).

Wassenberg, Arthur (1982) 'New Corporatism and the Quest for Control: The Cuckoo Game', pp. 83-108 in Gerhard Lehmbruch und Philippe C. Schmitter (eds.) *Patterns of Corporatist Policy-Making.* London, Berverly Hills: Sage.

Weber, Max (1976) *Wirtschaft und Gesellschaft*, 5. Aufl. Tübingen: Mohr-Siebeck.

Williamson, Oliver E. (1975) *Markets and Hierarchies. Analysis and Antitrust Implications. A Study in the Economics of Internal Organisation.* New York: Free Press.

Wilson, Graham (1982) 'Why is There No Corporatism in the United States?', pp. 219-236 in Gerhard Lehmbruch und Philippe C. Schmitter (eds.) *Patterns of Corporatist Policy-Making.* London, Berverly Hills: Sage.

Part two

The Politics of Collective Action

VI

Interest Heterogeneity and Organizing Capacity Two Class Logics of Collective Action?*

Wolfgang Streeck

Introduction

One of the problems that have from early on figured prominently among the concerns of the "corporatist community" is the question of *symmetry* between capital and labor. In Gerhard Lehmbruch's work, this theme is addressed primarily in terms of the *outcomes of political exchanges* at the national level, in particular in the context of incomes policies. Others have looked at the *organizing capacities* of the two classes in an attempt to determine whether there are differences in their ability to act as organized social categories: to formulate collective strategies, negotiate collective obligations, and implement collective policies by preventing free riding of individual class members

---

* This paper draws heavily on ideas developed and accumulated during years of close collaboration with Philippe Schmitter. Moreover, it uses material from a joint book that we have for long been trying to complete. I am therefore quite uncertain to what extent, if at all, I can claim any property right to the following arguments. Were it not for the logistical difficulties between Berlin, Florence, Madrid and San Francisco that have made our lives generally so difficult, the paper should properly have been co-authored. But the way things are, there is one author exclusively to be held responsible for whatever flaws and distortions the reader may find.

on the efforts and sacrifices of others in the pursuit of collective interests.

There always were suspicions that the two dimensions of symmetry, political and organizational, were in some way related, and that in both of them, capitalists were better placed than their opponents. From early on, students of incomes policy have pointed to the fact that it was usually only one kind of income, wages, that became subject to regulation, while prices, profits, and dividends remained free to rise either by design - where incomes policies were intended to reduce the real wage - or because of the lack of an adequate enforcement machinery. Perhaps for this reason, incomes policies often included deals between trade unions and the state - e.g., on taxation or social policy - that were to compensate labor for wage restraint in the absence of price or profit restraint, or of binding commitments on employment and investment (Lehmbruch 1979, 1984). But doubts remained as to the equity of such exchanges. More recently, the very necessity of political rewards for trade union conformity with restrictive policies has been questioned, most forcefully by the theoretical and practical proponents of monetarism but also, at least implicitly, by Fritz Scharpf (1987).

As indicated, economic asymmetry was thought by some to be related to the two classes' respective organizing capacities. Sometimes trade unions demanded that prices and profits, or employment and investment, be included on the agenda of national incomes policies and tripartite negotiations. But invariably they were told by their direct counterparts, the national peak associations of business, that these were not among the subjects for which business associations have a mandate from their members to negotiate. While firms were, more or less enthusiastically, willing to engage in collective regulation of the *labor market*, this in their view was and had to remain an exception. Under the rules of a market economy all other prices and incomes were to be determined by the individual decisions of competing firms, which were to judge their market environments independently.

This organizational delimitation of the scope and domain of incomes policies, modified only in such exceptional cases as the

Austrian *Paritätische Kommission*, always appeared as an important source of strength for capital and contributed to the impression of political and economic asymmetry. The remarkable thing was that, in this case, *political strength* seemed to be associated with and protected by *organizational weakness*. This was reflected in the strict limitation of the mandate under which business associations were permitted by their members to take part in tripartite negotiations. More precisely, the structural power of the capitalist class, expressed in its ability to pursue important objectives through *individual action* in the market, translated into *political power* through an absence of *organizational power* at the level of *collective action*. Being located in a privileged market position, capitalists could afford weak associations. They thus could escape the dialectical logic of interest intermediation that might turn against its original beneficiaries by subjecting them to negotiated discipline. *Organizational weakness*, in that it prevented a spill-over of collective-political intervention to subjects of "managerial" or, for that matter, "proprietorial privilege", thus served, paradoxically, as a *source of strength*.

If this was so, however, an intriguing question was bound to arise. If the equity problems of incomes policies - and generally of a negotiated trilateral management of democratic capitalism in the 1970s and 1980s - were related to limitations on the scope of corporatist political bargaining; and if such limitations derived at least in part from deficiencies of capitalist associations in intermediating the full range of interests of their members: should it not then in principle be possible to increase the *symmetry*, and thereby the *legitimacy*, and as a consequence the *efficiency*, of the "bargained economy" by strengthening the organization of capitalists? Was it not then, to add to the paradoxes, in the interest of trade unions and Social-Democratic governments to increase the organizational power of business associations as a way of controlling the market power of the individual capitalist? *To weaken* - or discipline - *capital by strengthening its associations*?[2] The answer depended on how one resolved a

---

2   "Perverse" projects of this kind came to be far more than just speculation. Well in advance of the 1987 general election in Britain, a group of economists and social scientists close to the leadership of the Labour Party were working on an

theoretical problem located at that crucial intersection between class theory, organization theory and political science that had been notoriously neglected by the mainstreams of the various disciplines bordering on it: the problem of whether the organization of capitalists is just *lagging behind* the organization of workers for some reason of historical sequence or due to lack of attention paid to it by governments and states as principal agents of political-organizational design - or, alternatively, whether there is a specific *class logic* behind capitalists' organizational weakness that makes for categorical differences in organizational forms and dynamics between capital and labor. While in the first case, the deficits of interest intermediation, incomes policy and, ultimately, neo-corporatism, might be rectifiable, in the second the prospects of doing much about both the organizational asymmetry of capital and labor and the resulting lopsidedness of the political management of capitalist economies would appear extremely inauspicious.

Astonishingly enough, the question of a class *logic of interest associability* has received little explicit and systematic attention, probably because the subject is so very difficult. One important exception is the much-quoted essay by Claus Offe and Helmut Wiesenthal entitled "Two Logics of Collective Action: Theoretical Notes on Social Class and Organizational Form" (Offe/Wiesenthal 1980) which comes down strongly in favor of inherent, class-specific differences in organizational capacity, precluding by implication an equitable corporatist management of advanced capitalism through tripartite bargaining. The present paper will relate some of Offe and

economic policy for the first year after a potential Labour victory. Central to their considerations was a return to the Keynesian full employment commitment of the time before the Conservative government - which, if successful, would certainly have curtailed the power of employers in the labor market. To prevent expansionary policy measures from resulting in another outburst of inflation, an incomes policy was seen as indispensable. Aware of the limited capacity of trade union leaders to keep their members from settling old bills with their employers to make up for their income losses since 1979, the group discussed methods of improving the organizational strength of the CBI, the British peak association of business, and in particular its control over the wage-setting behavior of the 100 or 200 largest British firms, as a way of precluding these making concessions to their workforces that would have preempted an increase in employment.

Wiesenthal's propositions to a body of empirical evidence. While it will arrive at conclusions quite different from the hypotheses put forward in the 1980 essay, this is not to detract from its importance or, indeed, its theoretical accomplishment. In fact, this paper deliberately abstains from offering a final judgement on the project of a class theory of organizational form as such; if at all, it argues that the substantive propositions of such a theory will be likely to differ from those suggested by Offe and Wiesenthal, but in the light of the pioneering status of their effort, this is far from surprising. (In any case, given the limited scope of the evidence available and the measurement difficulties involved, a claim to have empirically rejected a theory of this breadth and sophistication would be more than premature.)

Taking Offe and Wiesenthal (1980) as a point of departure, the present paper will, however, try to throw some light on the problem that dominated so much of the political and social science debate in the 1970s: the possibility of symmetrical corporatist management. In a nutshell, it will argue that at least under the historical circumstances of the 1980s and 1990s, there may well be a degree of convergence in organizational form between capital and labor, albeit *not* in the sense of a corporatist transformation of business associability but *vice versa*: with labor organizations undergoing transformation on the model of capitalist associations. While it is not at all clear what the possible implications of this may be for the distribution of political power, such a development would seem to reflect more general changes, which are likely to preclude a resurgence of the kind of economic policy that was at the center of the "corporatist debate" in the 1970s. As a consequence, the problem of symmetry in incomes policy in particular and in centrally bargained economies in general, rather than being resolved by organizational convergence, would fall by the wayside *due to convergence occurring in an unexpected direction*. This would not necessarily eliminate corporatism as a form of interest organization and policy coordination. But it certainly points to it assuming a more fragmented, decentralized and functionally specialized structure ("local", "sectoral", or "policy arena" corporatism).

A Class Theory of Organizational Form

The central message of Offe's and Wiesenthal's (1980) essay can be summarized as yet another paradox adding to that of organizational weakness and political strength: a supposed coincidence, in the case of business interests, of a *lower need for* with a *greater ease of* interest organization. For Offe and Wiesenthal's *class theory of organizational form*, the new paradox is what the old one was for the *class theory of political exchange*; in fact, both reflect the same underlying condition projected on different conceptual planes. Since capitalists can successfully pursue most of their interests individually through market relationships, they need collective action and organization only for a subset of their interests. In this sense, capitalist associations are organizationally *weaker* than trade unions. At the same time, the interests they have to represent are less complex and thus comparatively less demanding to treat inside collective organizations. Capitalist interest associations should therefore find it easier than trade unions to become *strong* organizations, as building and maintaining an organization of which little is expected, is likely to be less difficult than building and maintaining an organization that has to perform important functions. As a consequence, capitalists - also because they have superior material resources - tend to be *better organized* than workers given the *limited purposes their associations are to serve*, and this holds true despite the fact that they require collective interest representation much less urgently.

Why exactly is it that capitalists *need interest associations less* than workers? Rooting their analysis firmly in the Marxist theory of the capitalist class structure,[3] Offe and Wiesenthal (1980) start from the fundamental condition of inequality underlying the formally equal contract of employment: the fact that the commodity traded in labor markets, labor power, is not detachable from its seller. Wage labor therefore inevitably gives rise to a relationship of social control and domination between a small number of owners of "dead labor" who, in organizing the labor process, combine their physical capital with

---

3   In fact, as will become apparent, they use a rather more orthodox version thereof than is normally invoked in the writings at least of the senior author.

the "living labor" of a large number of workers - whereby the latter, to become party to an "equal" and "voluntary" commercial exchange, have to accept a subordinate position in a relationship of authority. Small group size and control over the labor process, Offe and Wiesenthal argue, each give capitalists access to a specific "form of collective action" that workers do not have at their disposal: "informal cooperation" on the one hand, and "the firm itself" on the other (Offe/Wiesenthal 1980:75). For capitalists, interest associations are therefore just one of three alternative instruments "to define and defend (their) interests" (*ibid.*), and compared to capitalists' everyday command over the organization of the enterprise, they are unlikely to be regarded by them as very important.

This is different for workers. Large group size, Offe and Wiesenthal imply, increases dependency upon formal arrangements for collective action. Moreover, as trade unions are organizations of those who have no power over the organization of work and the enterprise, they are the *only* organizational means available to their members to protect their interests - given that the labor "market" and the "free" employment contract are inevitably biased against the "seller". While business associations cover, process, and pursue only a limited segment of the total interest range of their members, "unions are confronted with the task of organizing the entire spectrum of needs that people have when they are employed as wage workers" (Offe/Wiesenthal 1980:75).

The narrow range of interests that need to be fed into and represented by capitalist associations provides, according to Offe and Wiesenthal, for a *comparatively homogeneous organizational* input that does not make difficult demands on the organizational *process* (see figure I). On the labor side, by comparison, organizational input is highly *heterogeneous*, and its processing requires *more complex arrangements* that are always in risk of failing or breaking down. In particular, Offe and Wiesenthal suggest three mechanisms that reduce input heterogeneity for capital associations and increase it for trade unions:

- the fact that "the powerful are fewer in number" and are therefore "less likely to be divided among themselves" (Offe/Wiesenthal 1980:78);

- the "multitude of needs of 'living' labor" - the complexity of life interests as opposed to capital interests, and of a life world entangled in a relationship of social control by the inseparability of labor as a commodity from the person of its seller - which, if only "for quantitative reasons", is "comparatively more difficult to organize" (Offe/Wiesenthal 1980:75);
- the asymmetrical dependency of workers' interests on capitalists' interests - being just another expression of the basic asymmetry of a class society - forces workers to consider and take into account the interests of capitalists much more than capitalists in turn have to consider the interests of workers. This "increases the lack of homogeneity of those interests that working class associations have to accommodate and the concomitant difficulties of the intra-organizational decision-making process..." (Offe/Wiesenthal 1980:76)

Differently heterogeneous *inputs*, then, result in differently demanding organizational *process* requirements. The small group size of the capitalist class entails low transaction costs and less divergent interests needing internal reconciliation; high functional specificity of interest associations and the absence of contamination by the opponent's interests further relieve the internal process. It is here that Offe and Wiesenthal ground their idea of two different *class logics of collective action*. To the extent that interests become the subject of organized representation, those in a dominant structural position are argued to have *far simpler interests* that can be handled in what Offe and Wiesenthal call a *"monological" mode of interest politics*. Domination generally implies "a clearer view of what (one wants) to defend" (Offe/Wiesenthal 1980:78) as interests can be largely *negatively defined* in terms of a preservation of the *status quo*. A dominant capitalist class, in particular, has an especially simple and easy-to-apply criterion by which to define its interests since "all the relevant questions can therefore be reduced to the unequivocal standards of expected costs and returns, i.e. to the measuring rod of money" (Offe/Wiesenthal 1980:75). Capitalist interest politics, strictly speak

Figure I:

The Class Theory of Interest Organizational Form: An Ideal Typology of Differences Between Capital and Labor *

Capital	Labor
### Class Structural Conditions	
Small Group Size	Large Group Size
More Important Alternative Modes of Collective Action: Firm, Collusion	No Alternatives Modes of Collective Action
### Organizational Input	
Narrow	Broad
Homogeneous	Heterogeneous
Specific	Diffuse
"Pure"	"Contaminated"
### Organizational Process ("Logic")	
Simple	Complex
Bureaucratized	Political
Empirical	Discursive
"Monological"	"Dialogical"
### Substantive Interest Definitions	
Given	Chosen
Negative	Positive
Quantitative	Qualitative
Additive	Non-Additive
Individualistic	Collectivistic
Utilitarian	Normative

* Abstracted from Offe and Wiesenthal (1980).

ing, can be conducted *without a preceding or accompanying political discourse*. In the limiting case, determining and aggregating the interests of capitalists can be delegated to a staff of experts, and indeed according to Offe and Wiesenthal, capitalist collective interests, narrow as they are, lend themselves particularly well to "rational" and "efficient" processing inside highly bureaucratized associations that are, and can be,

> confined to the function of aggregating and specifying (...) interests of members which, from the point of view of the organization, have to be defined as given and fixed, the formation of which lies beyond the legitimate range of functions of the organization (Offe/Wiesenthal 1980:79).

Offe and Wiesenthal admit that the capitalist class, "under the competitive pressure that its individual members put upon each other, has to seek constantly to find the *means*, or the most rational purposive behavior, by which its interest is to be met..." However,

> the interest itself (the end) can safely remain remote from any conscious reflection or effort to learn on the part of class members (since) in order for his interest to be his 'true' interest, the individual capitalist does not have to consult with other capitalists in order to reach a common understanding and agreement with them as to what their interests are. In this sense, the interest is "monological". (Offe/Wiesenthal 1980:91)

Non-political, bureaucratic, "individualistic and purely instrumental", or "utilitarian" associability (Offe/Wiesenthal 1980:78) is not a liability for capital but its natural and optimal form of collective action. Labor, on the other hand, is described as depending on a *"dialogical"* mode of interest politics as the only way of dealing to its political advantage with the wide and heterogeneous range of "life interests" arising from workers' disadvantaged position in the labor market and the class structure. Labor, therefore, is the truly *political* class in that the "real" interests of workers cannot be determined empirically but, unlike those of capital, *"can only be met to the extent they are partly redefined"* in a political discourse (Offe/Wiesenthal 1980:79; authors' italics). Not only do trade unions face a much greater heterogeneity of interest "inputs" than business associations; what is more, since the interests of workers are functionally diffuse and need to be positively clarified in terms of some normatively acceptable alternative to the status quo, there is no simple "common denominator to which all these heterogeneous and often conflicting needs can be reduced..." (Offe/Wiesenthal 1980:75). Moreover, because of their structural position of dependency, workers are much more likely to perceive their interests in a "distorted" way, and unless such distortions are "rationalized" in a political dialogue, collective action through trade unions is more likely to prolong than to overcome labor's disadvantaged position in the class structure.

Interest heterogeneity, then, makes "the problem of creating and maintaining unity among members and of mobilizing members' resources (...) considerably more serious" for labor than for capital associations (Offe/Wiesenthal 1980:83). In addition, the substantive content of working class interests and its normative contestability require a *dialogical internal process* which, especially if the number of participants is large, is intrinsically more difficult to operate and more likely to fail. Associative action of labor is thus handicapped not just by higher underlying *interest heterogeneity* but also and at the same time by lower *organizing capacity*. This interpretation is confirmed by Offe and Wiesenthal's use of the concept of "opportunism" (1980:103 pp.). Trade unions, the authors observe, tend to fall victim to a temptation to adopt the same "monological" and "bureaucratic" organizational process that serves capitalist interests so well, in an attempt to avoid the effort required by, and the crises inherent in, the dialogical mode. In this way they expand their *organizing capacity* in relation to their heterogeneous interest base. But this, Offe and Wiesenthal argue, comes at a high political price. While an "opportunistic" shift to a monological process may indeed enable labor to overcome some of its comparative *organizational* disadvantages, it inevitably eliminates the categoric difference between capital and labor interests, reducing the *political quality* of the latter to that of the former. The result is a *formal-organizational*, i.e., superficial symmetry between capital and labor which places the latter at a *political* disadvantage, thereby reproducing the underlying *structural* asymmetry. This is why "opportunistic" trade unionism is bound to be unstable: it is subject to cyclical crises and transformations as suppressed needs for normative interest definition revolt against the monological suspension of politics in a more than technocratic sense (Offe/Wiesenthal 1980:103 pp.)

Implications for Encompassing Organization: Mobilizing Empirical Evidence

There are a number of ways in which one could discuss a theory as wide-ranging and ambitious as that of the "two logics of collective action". One possible, and quite plausible, approach would be to scrutinize Offe and Wiesenthal's various assertions on the structure and internal life of trade unions. This is not what the present paper will do.[4] Having reconstructed in some detail the Offe and Wiesenthal theory, the argument will instead focus on one specific implication of that theory that appears to be empirically testable. This relates to differences in the capacities of capital and labor to set up what in Mancur Olson's widely used terminology are called "encompassing organizations" - organizations which both include a large proportion, and ideally all members, of their social category and are capable of developing and implementing a centrally determined, common policy for their entire constituency (Olson 1982).

While Offe and Wiesenthal (1980) do not explicitly address the subject of encompassing organization, it should be clear from our account that *on their premises, the capitalist class is likely to find it much easier than the working class to build and maintain encompassing organizations*. This follows directly from the theory's two main propositions, the lower *interest heterogeneity* among capitalists - at least insofar as interests enter the arena of collective action - and their higher *organizing capacity*, as expressed in the greater ease and confidence with which capital can allegedly make use of the "monological" social

---

4   Nor will it deal with the question whether economic "profit" objectives are in fact as clear cut and easy to define, at both the individual firm and the collective class level, as Offe and Wiesenthal believe - which would be another promising line of attack.

technology of functionally specific, bureaucratic organization. Centrifugal tendencies that give rise to pluralistic organizational fragmentation and internal decentralization should therefore be weaker among capitalists than among workers; internal conflict and dissensus resulting in secession and separate organization should occur comparatively rarely; there should in any population of capitalist interest organizations be fewer lines of inter-organizational differentiation reflecting structural interest cleavages; and thus *the number of capitalist associations in any given "interest space" should be clearly lower than the number of trade unions.*

Extracting empirically testable propositions from a complex theory is always hazardous. However, in the present case the authors themselves which, if only by implication, offer strong confirmation. This is where they attribute, by logical deduction rather than on empirical evidence, a different "optimal size" to trade unions and business associations. The latter, Offe and Wiesenthal argue, can grow almost indefinitely since, due to the high simplicity and commensurability of capitalist interests, increasing size does not add much to their internal heterogeneity. (Put in a more technical language, business associations have more favorable *economies of scale* than trade unions.) Another reason why business associations can grow without limits is that they do not depend on their members' *marginal propensity to act* - as opposed to *pay* - to mobilize sanctioning power against their opponents. "What there *is* in terms of sanctioning potential of the (business) organization," Offe and Wiesenthal (1980:80) maintain, "can be put into effect by the *leadership* of the organization alone..." By contrast, the sanctioning potential of trade unions "becomes effective only through the organized members and their explicitly coordinated action" (i.e., the strike; W.S.). From this results a curvilinear relationship between organizational size and organizational effectiveness:

> As union size increases, heterogeneity of members' positions, occupations, and immediate interests tends to increase, too, which makes it more difficult to formulate generally agreed upon demands and to mobilize a common willingness to act

that flows from a notion of shared, collective identities and mutual obligations of solidarity (Offe/Wiesenthal 1988:81).

The maximum size of a trade union is therefore not its optimal size. Limits exist for the growth of union organizations that do not exist for business associations. There is, according to Offe and Wiesenthal (1980:81), an "optimum size beyond which union power decreases", and there is a dilemma "between size and collective identity" (Offe/Wiesenthal 1980:82) that is quite unknown to business.[5] From this it follows, as Offe and Wiesenthal themselves indicate (1980:111), that membership density should generally be lower for trade unions than for business associations, as *organization size* can come much closer to *group size* among capitalists than among workers. But given the significant economies of scale that exist for bureaucratic formal organizations, the optimal size argument also implies that, *everything else being equal,* the higher aggregate organizational density among capitalists is likely to be achieved *by a smaller number of more encompassing organizations.* A trade union, by comparison, can achieve, and in fact afford, high density only if it defines its organizational domain narrowly and specifically, thereby excluding from it potentially large segments of the working class which then can, and have to, be organized by other, competing unions. For the working class as a whole, this means that it can reach a high level of aggregate density - which will be likely to remain lower than aggregate density among capitalists - only if it organizes itself in *a large number of small organizations* rather than, like capital, in *a small number of large organizations.* It also implies that however labor may at some point escape from its position of structural disadvantage, it will *not* be able to do so through the use of encompassing organization. It is at this point that Offe and Wiesenthal's theory deviates most strongly from the mainstream of the neo-corporatist debate.

---

5   And that, as we have seen, can at most be temporarily removed by "opportunistically" suspending the dialogical organizational process, at the price of assimilating the political quality of worker interests to that of capitalist interests, thereby eliminating the very specificity of the interests of a subordinate as opposed to a dominant class, with the result of submission to capitalist hegemony.

How can one mobilize empirical evidence, keeping "everything else equal", on the relative degree of organizational encompassingness of social groups as different as capital and labor? For example, it seems self-evident that capitalists are always "fewer" in number than workers, so even if their "logic of collective action" or the political quality of their interests were not different from labor, they should have both "fewer" interest organizations and, due to lower transaction costs, "higher" organizational density. (This point is, in fact, made by Offe and Wiesenthal themselves, although group size, as we have seen, is not their most important explanatory variable.) But to make sense for empirical analysis, comparative terms like "fewer" or "higher" must refer to some *common universe*. Which collectivity of capitalists is to be compared to which collectivity of workers? If the comparison is to be valid, the respective populations of capitalists and workers must be so defined that they in some way *correspond* to each other. For one thing, this raises the question *of what a capitalist is* - rather a tricky one indeed. Secondly, it requires identification of social spaces - defined as sets of economic processes and political activities - in *which coterminous sets of capital and worker interests* can be assumed to emerge that can meaningfully be compared in terms of their scope, complexity, heterogeneity etc.; these will in the following be referred to as *interest spaces*. And, thirdly, to count the number of interest associations on either side of the class divide, a common criterion is needed as to *what an association is* and, in particular, where it ends: at which point, in other words, a set of interrelated organizational units begins to constitute one encompassing organization, rather than a system of several independent organizations.

The empirical evidence introduced in this paper is based on the following operational decisions (Schmitter/Streeck 1981):

1. "Capitalists" are ideal-typically not individuals but *firms*. The paper will be looking exclusively at such capitalist associations under whose rules members are defined as, or stand for, independent production units competing in markets for goods and services. While this, as any, decision may appear debatable, it is clearly in line with Offe and Wiesenthal's description of capitalist interests as function-

ally specific, impersonal, and dissociated from the life-world of individuals. In any case, defining capitalists in this way places, as it should, the theory being tested at an advantage since it eliminates from the universe of capitalist associations those based on the *Weltanschauung*, religious beliefs, gender, leisure activities etc. of individual members of the capitalist class - inclusion of which would increase the observed degree of organizational fragmentation.

2. A possible "interest space" for comparing organizational patterns of capital and labor could be a country as demarcated by the boundaries of a nation state. However, given Offe and Wiesenthal's close recourse to Marxist class theory, what appears even more appropriate are *economic sectors*, defined as *any population of firms producing a similar range of products for the same product market using similar inputs of raw materials, technology and labor*. Assuming, as class theory undoubtedly does, that an actor's position in the division of labor and the system of economic exchange significantly affects his interests, the set of capitalist interests originating in a given sector can plausibly be regarded as "corresponding" to the set of workers' interests originating in the same sector.

3. Finally, in distinguishing between the borderline cases of a specialized associational subunit on the one hand, and an independent association affiliated to an association of associations (or "higher order" association) on the other, the criterion will be the presence or absence of a statutory or customary *right of the lower-level unit to secede from the higher-level unit*. A highly decentralized interest organization whose subunits do not have a right to secede is thereby counted as a unitary, and potentially encompassing, organization. A highly centralized "association of associations", on the other hand, whose affiliates can however decide to disaffiliate, is treated as a set of different, autonomous organizations. The assumption is that the reservation by organized subgroups of a right to secede is a meaningful tool to protect their interest-political autonomy, and that it therefore is likely to reflect a higher degree of interest heterogeneity than even the most advanced decentralization inside a unitary organization.

To test one aspect of the Offe and Wiesenthal theory, then, this paper will compare the number of trade unions and business associations representing the interests of capitalists and workers located and pro- ducing in identical economic sectors. To control for the impact of special market conditions and technologies, the paper will look at seven different sectors: chemicals, pharmaceuticals, construction, dairy, meat processing, fruit and vegetable packing, and machine tools. To control further for the influence of national specificities and peculiarities, the paper will use evidence from sectoral associational systems of nine countries, Austria, Canada, Italy, West Germany, the Netherlands, Spain, Sweden, Switzerland, and the United Kingdom.[6] Class theory of organizational form predicts that sectoral interest spaces will be populated by clearly more trade unions than business associations, with business associations being more encompassing with respect to their sectoral interest base than trade unions. It also predicts that the capitalist class will achieve a higher organizational density ratio. Since this prediction is derived from a general theory of the class structure under capitalism, by and large the same results should be expected in all countries and sectors.

Size, Fragmentation and Density: The Role of Domain Choice

At first glance at least, it is hard to see how empirical data could more forcefully contradict a theory than in the present case. In the 56 sectors on which data are available, *there are on average no fewer than 16.4 business associations to one trade union.* Even if the two extreme cases are deleted - two West German sectors with a high number of local artisanal associations - the relationship reduces only to 8.1 to 1. More unions than business associations can be found only in three cases: the machine tools industries of Austria, Canada and Switzerland. These, however, are clearly exceptional in that they are

---

6   Due to missing values, the number of cases available is not 9 x 7 = 63, but only 56. The data were collected in the course of the "Organization of Business Interests" research project directed by Philippe Schmitter and this author (Schmitter and Streeck 1981).

extremely small and narrowly defined subsectors of the metal-
working industry.[7] The basic numerical relationship between business associations and trade unions remains unchanged even if
"associations of associations" - or "higher-order associations" - are excluded. In this case, the ratio of business associations over trade
unions declines to 6.7 to 1.[8]

Assuming that sectoral interest spaces for business and labor are
comparable, the observation that on the labor side a given interest
space is populated by far fewer associations than on the business
side would seem to justify the conclusion *that trade unions are more,
rather than less, encompassing than business associations.* Taking into account that the number of firms in a given sector is always much
smaller than the corresponding number of workers, it appears that
either the range of interests represented by business associations is
much more *heterogeneous* in spite of it being associated with a smaller
number of individuals - so that a capitalist association that was of the
same size as a trade union would incorporate much greater interest
variety - or the *organizing capacity* of business associations is much
lower than that of trade unions, resulting in *disproportionately greater
aversion to heterogeneity,* or both. This follows if one assumes, as Offe
and Wiesenthal do, that organizational boundaries are determined
by limits to the internal heterogeneity that an organization can process. Put otherwise, *the addition of one more member to a capitalist association seems to increase its internal heterogeneity to a much greater extent
than the addition of one more member to a trade union.* In fact, since there
are many *more* business associations than trade unions for *fewer*
capitalists than workers, the extent to which *one marginal member* of a
business association detracts from its internal cohesion exceeds by a
factor of at least 7 the centripetal effect in a trade union caused by a
group of marginal members equal in size to the average number of
workers per firm.

7   In fact, the machine tools sector as defined for the purposes of data collection
     comprises only two types of machines, metal and wood working machinery
     (Schmitter/Streeck 1981).

8   Since associations of associations are more likely to exist where there are many
     independent associations, their inclusion increases the difference between large
     and small sectoral associational systems.

There are no good data available on the comparative organizational *density* of capitalists and workers by sector. However, assuming for the sake of argument that Offe and Wiesenthal are right and that capitalists are universally more densely organized than workers, the strongly different patterns of organization that we have found suggest quite a different explanation from the one offered by class theory. If capitalists do achieve higher density, this seems to be because their interest organizations are *much more fragmented than trade unions*, enabling them to make *disproportionate use of their general advantage of small numbers*. Rather than being due to "the dual advantage of greater commensurability and calculability of what the 'right' demands and tactics are, and (of) a comparatively smaller probability of internal conflict" (Offe/Wiesenthal 1980:84), high organizational density among capitalists appears to be explained by *small numbers generally*, plus *a class-specific response to interest heterogeneity through high organizational specialization and fragmentation*. Thus, it is precisely not some "advantage of greater commensurability and calculability" (Offe/Wiesenthal 1980:83) that makes for high organizational density among capitalists, but rather a pattern of organization that *decomposes* the sectoral class interest into a number of less than encompassing, separate *subinterests* - the very pattern that Offe and Wiesenthal would have expected for trade unions. And neither is it "a comparatively smaller probability of internal conflict" (Offe/Wiesenthal 1980:84) but the *elimination of conflicts* through organizational fragmentation from the domain of any one association that seem to account for a larger proportion of capitalists than workers joining interest associations.[9] Far from being "easy to organize", capitalists

---

9   It is by the way precisely the fragmented pattern of capitalist interest organization that makes it so difficult to determine aggregate density ratios for capitalists. Nevertheless, in countries like Britain where there is - unlike in Germany to which Offe and Wiesenthal refer as their only example - no compulsory organization of small (artisanal) firms, one may have doubts as to whether aggregate density among capitalists is indeed (much) higher than among workers. To the extent that the two density ratios differ less than in West Germany - which they should in many countries - the comparatively fragmented pattern of capitalist organization becomes difficult to account for as an organizational technique to raise density. Instead, fragmentation would even more clearly be recognizable as a reflection of high interest heterogeneity. This is in contradic-

seem to be willing to join associations only if they are narrow enough
to cater to their immediate special interests, and if they are small
enough to make for low transaction costs and a strong incentive
against free-riding.

These conclusions still hold up if one takes into account that
membership in the various business associations representing sectoral capitalist interests is not necessarily mutually exclusive, and
that capitalist firms are often members in more than one association.
While the majority of business associations specialize by *product* at
the subsectoral level, some of them, and sometimes in addition, specialize by *function*, e.g., as employers, trade or technical associations.
Multiple membership of firms is common in the latter case but also
occurs in product-differentiated associations, for firms that operate
in more than one product market. The difference to trade unions is
that union members have to subscribe to a collective action, or interest, "package" which they cannot easily modify, whereas the high organizational differentiation of capitalist associations gives individual
firms the choice to select and create their own custom-made
combinations of memberships and - specific - collective involve-
ments. The result is a highly varied and idiosyncratic pattern of associational activity, quite unlike what one would expect if capitalist
interests were indeed as narrow, homogeneous, commensurable and
easy to determine as Offe and Wiesenthal claim. Actually, judging
from observed patterns of associability, capitalist interests appear so
broad, heterogeneous and complex that, to become narrow, homogeneous and simple enough for organization, they must be subdivided into a large number of specialized (sub-) domains. This need
not mean that the interests contained in these domains are necessarily in conflict or incompatible with each other, although they very
well may be; what seems clear, however, is that they are not as easy
to trade off and aggregate as Offe and Wiesenthal suggest and as, in
contradiction of their theory, seems to be the case for labor.[10]

---

tion to a principal assumption of Offe and Wiesenthal's class theory of organizational form.

10 This applies already at the level of the individual firm. Anecdotal evidence on
the internal politics especially of multi-product firms suggests that individual
capitalists have a much harder time developing a consistent and comprehen-

Looking at the *process of organizing* as distinguished from the *pattern of organization*, the empirical data suggest that business associations tend to "find" a larger number of heterogeneous categories of potential members in any specific interest space than trade unions. This is reflected in the fact that organizational and interest-political leaders in the capitalist class tend to cut the *domains* of their organizations more narrowly than their counterparts among labor. *Domain decisions, however, precede optimal size decisions,* and the way Offe and Wiesenthal's optimal size problem poses itself to an established interest association depends crucially on how it has originally demarcated its domain. The reason, that is, why business associations do not *appear* to have an optimal size problem, and why they can *appear* to be straightforward size maximizers, is that they have in the first place defined their domains so narrowly *that even complete organization of their (comparatively very small) potential membership would not overburden their internal process with excessive heterogeneity.* In reality, business associations have "optimized" long before they have begun to "maximize": namely at the point when they decided to limit their organizing activities to a narrowly defined subcategory of interests. Trade unions, on the other hand, in defining their domains more encompassingly, indicate a comparatively high degree of confidence that they will be able to internalize whatever interest diversity may exist in their respective constituency. (Not to mention the fact that trade unions refusing to organize workers within their domain, so as to not exceed their "optimal size", are extremely rarely observed these days - to put it mildly.) From this perspective, and considering domain choice as well as actual organizing behavior, business associations, in contradiction to the class theory of associability, appear to be facing a much stronger dilemma "between size and collective density" (Offe/Wiesenthal 1980:82) than trade unions.

Groups organized in a fragmented pattern of associability frequently, although by no means always, rely on institutionalized inter-organizational links as an alternative way of coordinating en-

sive image of their interests than workers, largely because they have to make more, and more uncertain, strategic choices. This uncertainty may be reflected in conflicting or at least inconsistent commitments in the different product-specific business associations to which such a firm is likely to belong.

compassing collective action. Particularly important in this respect are higher-order associations - especially sectoral or national peak associations - which may strengthen inter-organizational relations by adding a hierarchical dimension to them. In some countries and sectors, a typical difference between capital and labor is that while trade unions are by and large organized in a unitary, encompassing way, on the business side one finds a multitude of small, regional, or product-specific associations which, while independent and autonomous, are joined together in often complex pyramids of higher-order associations.[11] Although inter-organizational coordination through this kind of mechanism can be quite effective, it appears reasonable to regard a "federative" pattern of collective action and organization as less encompassing and more fragmented than one based on unitary organization. A group that, rather than coordinating its activities by internalizing their external effects in a unitary organization, relies for this purpose on inter-organizational diplomacy - breaking up, as it were, a potentially encompassing organization into a set of smaller, more homogeneous subunits that may or may not cooperate with each other - thereby documents the existence of tensions between subinterests that are too strong for an encompassing organization to manage internally. Unless one assumes that the social "meaning" of the distinction between internal and external ways of coordinating collective action differs for capital and labor, it seems legitimate, and indeed compelling, to read the apparent preference of the capitalist class for external coordination as an indication of higher interest heterogeneity or, alternatively, lower organizing capacity.

Organizational Form and Substantive Interests: Unity by Opportunism?

Class theory has been shown to imply that trade unions should be organizationally more fragmented than business associations. This is because of a coincidence of greater heterogeneity of underlying in-

---

11 From which they reserve a formal right to secede (cf. our operational definition of organizational independence, above).

terests with lower organizing capacity. Empirically, however, trade unions turned out to be much less fragmented than their capitalist counterparts - raising the double question of where the theory may have gone so disastrously wrong and, more importantly, how the observed organizational pattern can be accounted for. Two possibilities appear particularly interesting:

- Trade unions are more encompassing not because their interests are less heterogeneous but because their *organizational process is superior* in managing internal diversity. If this was so, Offe and Wiesenthal could still be right with respect to class differences in organizational input, and their mistake would have been to underestimate the integrative capacity of the "dialogical mode".

- Trade unions are more encompassing because their *interest base is simpler* than that of business associations. Even if there were differences in organizational processes between classes, and even if the "dialogical mode" was less conducive to encompassing organization than the monological one - as the authors clearly believe - this would be overridden by the greater simplicity of labor's organizational input. Offe and Wiesenthal would be right on the organizational process; where they would have erred would be in their assessment of the impact of class position on interest variety.

Could it be that the greater encompassingness of trade union organization is due to a superior organizing capacity associated with the "dialogical mode"? While this might "rescue" the theory's assumptions on the differential heterogeneity of class interests, it is clearly not what Marxist class theorists should believe to be possible. And indeed Offe and Wiesenthal are far from being idealistic here. As their optimal size hypothesis makes clear, for them dialogue *presupposes* that the range of admissable arguments and interest perceptions has been narrowed *beforehand* through collective identity-formation and organizational boundary maintenance. *Unity,* for Offe and Wiesenthal, is *built on elimination*. This is confirmed by a quite remarkable passage on the means by which liberal democracies allegedly try to keep trade unions from arriving at unified and undistorted conceptions of their members' interests - namely, by forcibly *increasing unions' internal organizational diversity* through

> the imposition of regulations that make it more difficult for unions to deny access and/or to expel dissident members and *thus* to narrow the spectrum of positions within the membership. Such regulations, commonly advocated in the name of "intra-organizational democracy" or "pluralism", appear, *in the light of the argument we have developed about class-specific distortions of interest perception,* as measures to paralyze *those associational practices which could help to overcome interest distortions or "fetishism".* (Offe/Wiesenthal 1980:103; italics added, W.S.)

Placing legal restrictions on the expulsion of members with deviating interest perceptions, the authors continue in an interestingly euphemistic conceptualization of Leninist organizational *Realpolitik,* is a technique of trade union enemies designed to make it

> more difficult for unions to partially suspend the individualistic orientations of members *in a dialogical process of collective interest articulation.* (Offe/Wiesenthal 1980:103; italics added, W.S.)

There are also empirical indications that, quite in line with Offe and Wiesenthal's skepticism on the unifying power of dialogue inside encompassing organizations, the second explanation for the mismatch between theory and reality is more appropriate, and *that lower interest heterogeneity accounts for a much larger proportion of the greater organizational encompassingness of trade unions than higher organizing capacity.* This conclusion emerges if the business associations that are included in the comparison are limited to those which, either solely or in addition to other activities, act as direct counterparts of trade unions in industrial relations (the so-called "employers' associations"). Of the 55 sectors on which we have data, 23 have more employers' associations than trade unions; in 6 sectors the numbers are equal; and in 26, trade unions outnumber employers' associations.

Differences in national industrial relations systems play an important part and have to be taken into account. For example, in 6 of the 26 sectors where trade unions prevail numerically (all of them in Canada), there are no employers' associations at all as collective bargaining takes place solely at the enterprise level; here, business associability is not more encompassing than trade union organization but in fact non-existing. Of the remaining 20 sectors with fewer employers' associations than trade unions - those sectors, that is, which exhibit a pattern relatively close to that predicted by class theory - three are in Austria with its uniquely compact system of compulsory business associability monopolized by the Bundeskammer der gewerblichen Wirtschaft; five each are in the United Kingdom, the Netherlands and Switzerland with their relatively fragmented trade union structures; and two are in Sweden. In the 23 sectors where, in contradiction of class theory, employers' associations prevail numerically over trade unions, there are on average about two employers' associations to one trade union. This is still low compared to the overall ratio of business associations over trade unions.

In other words, while the evidence on employers' associations by no means conforms with the Offe and Wiesenthal theory, it is considerably more favorable to it. Where the substantive concern of business interest associability is limited to the interaction with labor in the labor market and in industrial relations, the degree of organizational fragmentation varies much less between the two classes, and the organizing capacity of capital - the ability to make firms join comparatively encompassing organizations - is not necessarily much weaker than that of labor. One may note in passing that Offe and Wiesenthal in their paper frequently leave the impression that they treat all business associations as though they were employers' associations - which may be understandable coming from a *class* theory of associability although it can, as we have seen, lead to serious misperceptions.[12]

---

12 On the other hand, precisely because they are so preoccupied with employers' associations, it is remarkable that Offe and Wiesenthal should have overlooked the fact that there are business associations, in some countries at least, which do greatly depend on their members' "willingness to act" - namely, when they

What does the relative degree of symmetry between *employers'*
associations and trade unions, compared to the asymmetry between
all business associations and trade unions, imply for the problem of
heterogeneity *versus* capacity? Employers' associations are business
associations that interact with one out of several "task environments"
facing capitalist firms and the capitalist class. Either exclusively or
together with other functions, employers' associations represent
business interests vis-a-vis the labor market and the industrial relations system regulating it, including those national institutions of
economic and social policy-making that affect the content of employment contracts. Important as the labor market may be for capitalist firms, however, capitalists also have interests relating to product
markets and their regulation through, for example, tariffs, taxes,
standards etc. Although some business associations represent their
members both as employers and producers, or traders, a frequent
pattern is for producer interests to be represented by separate, specialized "trade associations". A sectoral or national system of
employers' associations, being no more than a subset of a typically
much larger sectoral or national system of business associations, thus
covers only a subset of the full range of organized interests of capitalist
firms. By definition, a subset is less internally heterogeneous than the
universe, and therefore *it is easier to organize comprehensively with a*
given organizing capacity. The evidence thus suggests that the comparatively low overall capacity of business to organize comprehensively is a function of comparatively high interest heterogeneity,
indicated by the fact that *if such heterogeneity is reduced, business associ-*
ations do seem to have roughly the same capacity as labor to make their
members form encompassing organizations.

If the high overall fragmentation of business associability is to be
accounted for by comparatively high interest heterogeneity, then the
similarity in the level of encompassingness of employers' associations and trade unions would indicate a similar degree of interest heterogeneity *for these two categories of associations.* From this it should
follow that *the universe of interests that business associations have to cover*

---

impose a lock-out. A successful lock-out presupposes as much internal cohesion in an employers' association as does a successful strike in a trade union.

in any given sector is broader and more complex than the respective interest range on the labor side. Capitalist associations, in other words, would represent not only *different* but, above all, *more* interests than workers, and going by the differences and similarities in organizational fragmentation, such interests as they do represent in addition are those represented by trade associations. (In fact, these interests are being organized and represented even in sectors where there is no need at all to confront trade unions above the individual firm level.[13]) Trade unions, on the other hand, would appear to have an interest base that is much simpler and narrower than that of capital, and this would account for their higher encompassingness. As Offe and Wiesenthal have predicted, low interest heterogeneity results in encompassing organization; but contrary to their theory, interest heterogeneity turns out to be lower, and organizational unity therefore higher, among labor than among capital.

Pursuing further the distinction between trade associations and employers' associations, the problem for business associability which prevents it from taking advantage of encompassing organization - and which Offe and Wiesenthal's class theory seems to have overlooked - appears to be that the members and clients of business associations are not just *buyers of labor* but also *sellers of products*, and that they have collective interests not just in relation to their workers but also to their customers - and, one might add, their suppliers of raw materials, finance and other production inputs. These additional interests, as reflected in their pattern of organization, are more specific, diverse and divisive than labor-market interests. And indeed, there are clearly fewer categories of labor than there are products, and in any given (local) labor market firms producing different products compete for the same category of workers (or at least for workers whose wages are highly interdependent). It is true that different conditions in product markets may reflect also on the interests firms have in industrial relations. Where employers' associations are still more fragmented than trade unions, this could probably often be accounted for by the fact that many business associations are simul-

---

13 While six of the 56 sectors studied have no employers' associations, there is no single sector without a trade association.

taneously trade and employers' associations, with the more centrifugal product-related interests tearing apart organizations that could
be more comprehensive if they were organized only around labor
market interests.

The distinction between employers' and trade associations in-
vokes an important generic difference between two kinds of collective interests of business, *class interests* and *producer interests*. Both
originate in markets. But whereas the axis of interest differentiation
in competitive product markets divides sellers from sellers, labor
markets give rise to a *categoric* cleavage between two groups of actors, capitalists and workers. Employers in labor markets, just as
workers, face a "common enemy" whose interests differ so much
from theirs that they find it comparatively easy to develop a common
identity and policy. Usually, the categoric difference between the two
groups is strong enough to supersede internal diversity by (sub-
)sector or product on the capital side and by skill or occupation on
the labor side. As a consequence, class interests are typically easier to
aggregate than product or occupational interests. Where trade unions have relatively simple organizational structures, this would be
explained by their being essentially organized around class interests
*whereas business associations have in addition to incorporate the more
heterogeneous "producer" interests that originate in product markets.*
Trade union organization can be more compact because the ("class")
interests it exclusively incorporates are less diverse and, consequently, the obstacles to collective interest formation lower. Nothing
quite so compact and simple seems to suffice for capitalists.
Why, then, should it suffice for trade unions? Is it, in other words,
really the case that workers' interests relate exclusively to class and
not to *production* issues (see Figure II)? Without going too much into
detail, it would appear that labor has not always been without organizational equivalents to trade associations - and in fact there still
exist a variety of organizations that, in one way or other, could be
seen as such: professional associations, like those of technicians or
accountants; some craft unions; firm-specific staff associations;
"yellow" or "house unions"; works councils; enterprise unions. What
they have in common is that they do not primarily define the inter

Figure II:

Organizational Types by Interests and Classes

	Capital	Labor
Class Interests **Labor Market**	Employers' Associations	Trade Unions
Producer Interests **Product Market**	Trade Associations	?

ests of their constituents as labor-market based *class* interests but rather in terms of their members' specific contribution to successful production and its match with specific *product markets*. The reason why especially "industrial" or "general" trade unions view such organizations with such suspicion and hostility is that they represent a range of interests which modern unions, striving to organize workers exclusively on the basis of their status as *sellers of labor* and regardless of their occupation, skill, or place of employment, had to submerge or suppress in their long struggle for organizational unity[14] - that is, against a pattern of organization and organizational fragmentation similar to what Figure II shows for capital.

The purge of labor's organized interests of production-related concerns is a fairly recent phenomenon which involves the historical

---

14 A unity which, by the way, is based on extremely simple decision rules which, in their simplicity, remind one strongly of the image that Offe and Wiesenthal have of the internal process of - in their expectation, encompassing - capitalist associations. For example, industrial unions tend to secure their internal cohesion by freezing existing wage structures, thereby avoiding the divisive "moral" problem of a "just" reward for work and skill. Or they settle on a policy of incremental wage equalization through identical or degressive wage increases for higher and lower paid members - although this already, if applied over more than a very short term, normally overtaxes their political cohesion.

defeat not just of "craft" and "yellow" unionism but also of gild-so-
cialist and radical socialist traditions ("workers' control"). In the
course of accepting the rules of the game of "mature", "pluralist"
industrial relations systems under a Taylorist work organization and
a Keynesian economic policy regime, modern trade unions have focused their interest definitions, ideologies, and activities on *distribution* as distinguished from production matters; they have found it
more comfortable politically and organizationally to deal with the
demand side rather than the supply side of the economy; and their
primary policy orientation has turned towards the *macro-* as opposed
to the micro-level of the economy (Przeworski/Wallerstein 1982;
Vidich 1982). One expression is the *de facto* recognition by most trade
unions of managerial prerogative on production issues, especially
product strategy, which lies behind the refusal of trade unions in
many countries to become involved in managerial matters through
"co-determination". Where unions, especially large and encompassing ones, cannot avoid being drawn into production politics, for example in industrial policy, they usually perform poorly, not the least
reason being that they find it difficult to deal with the internal divisions of interest among their members that immediately emerge on
such occasions.

Distribution, of course, is not independent from production; demand and supply are interrelated; and macro-policies are conditional
upon micro-level performance. However, trade unions have more
often than not been careful not to recognize such interrelations in
their ideology. They have preferred to influence production, supply,
and the micro-level, if at all, through distributive, demand and
macro-policies - even while knowing that such instruments were far
from ideal for the purpose. In fact, there can be no doubt that trade
unions and workers - as indicated by the resilience of certain non-
class organizations of workers, as well as by the constant vigilance of
industrial unions against "plant egoism" or "craft syndicalism" - do
have quite significant product- and production-related interests. In
many cases, however, *these are similar to the respective business interests
in the same firm or sector, whereas they differ from the interests of workers
employed in other firms or sectors, or from the interests of workers as con-*

sumers or citizens. Examples of this are industrial subsidies, problems of legal regulation of economic activities, taxation, foreign trade protection, or regional development policies. Trade unions find such issues difficult to take up since they would likely undermine the "class unity" of their members as sellers of labor power. They therefore tend to leave their representation to business, both in relation to the state and to other producer groups. *Seen from this perspective, trade associations function, in important areas of their activities, as though they were vertical associations organizing both labor and capital.* Since the diversity of production-related interests is largely absorbed within their (fragmented) organizational structures, their presence relieves unions of the problem of having to formulate and act upon such interests. *This, in turn, enables them to confine themselves to class interests and, thereby, to build up more encompassing and homogeneous organizations.*

It is at this point that we may briefly return to Offe and Wiesenthal's concept of "opportunism". *For class theory, opportunism involves implicit acceptance of structural subordination through elimination, for organizational convenience, of a range of "systemically unsafe" interests from collective action.* The present analysis has shown that something like that may indeed exist. But the differences are crucial. While Offe and Wiesenthal believe that trade unions reduce their range of organized interests in order to become *like* business associations, it in fact appears that opportunistic trade unionism eliminates interests to become organizationally *different* from, especially *more encompassing* than, business associations. Opportunism, in other words, appears as an attempt precisely *not* to assume the organizational properties of business associability. And while Offe and Wiesenthal believe that opportunism reinforces dependency and subordination by leaving a range of (anti-capitalist) interests *unrepresented*, it seems that in reality dependency and subordination are cemented by leaving specific (production-related and therefore more heterogeneous) interests *to capitalists to represent on their terms.*

Rising Interest Complexity and the Prospects of Class Organization of Workers

If it is true that the comparative organizational unity of modern trade unionism is made possible by tacit delegation of production-related interests to the "trade" interest politics of employers, one might feel tempted to speculate whether this is likely to remain viable in the future. This it would not be if the concentration of labor organizations on class interests was premised on contingent historical circumstances that will, or are already about to, change. For example, the greater simplicity and comprehensiveness of trade unions seems to reflect an experience that structural economic change can either be satisfactorily handled through redistributive "class" politics in a growing economy, or can be prevented by collective worker action without loss of wages and employment. Elimination of production interests from trade union organizational domains also seems to assume that there is no need for trade union intervention in the *qualitative direction* of economic change since this is predetermined by market and technological forces. In social terms, the simple organizational structure of modern trade unions appears to presuppose a functioning external labor market with workers seeing themselves not as members of a specific production unit or sector about whose economic performance they must be concerned, but as independent, mobile sellers of by and large homogeneous labor power.

Today it appears that these and related assumptions are becoming unrealistic (Sorge/Streeck 1988; Streeck 1987). The center of gravity in economic policy is shifting from distribution to *production*, from demand to *supply* management, and from the macro to the *micro*-level. Structural adjustment of firms, industries and economies has taken precedence over issues like the control of inflation or the creation of domestic demand. The high pliability of the new technology has opened new options and alternatives for structural change, making space for alternative concepts of productivity and economic revitalization which are subject to choice and, perhaps, collective-political action. Moreover, internal labor markets are emerging with new structures of skills and qualifications and more workplace-specific human capital, resulting in increased company or sector "patriotism" of workforces and in heightened sensitivity of workers to their firm's or sector's competitive performance. As a consequence of the emerging "situs interests" of a growing part of the modern workforce, trade unions in many countries today are faced with new, more divergent, more specialized and more "qualitative" demands by their members and clients. The result are growing pressures to participate in production- and supply-related policy areas which are difficult to conceptualize in terms of traditional, labor market- and distribution-centered trade union ideology. In many ways, the narrower, more heterogeneous and more specialized concerns of trade union members under the new conditions of *growing entanglement in production issues* would seem to be much more adequately organized in smaller interest domains - like those that are typical of the organization of business interests - than in the comparatively comprehensive structures still typical of trade union organization.

The same development can be described in more abstract terms. Modern trade unionism is premised on the existence of a separate, semi-autonomous socio-economic subsystem of industrial relations that generates rules and entitlements relatively independent from product markets, entrepreneurial production strategies, and technology (Dunlop 1958). The pluralist-functionalist "system of industrial relations", established and "matured" in the era of mass production and steady growth, maintained an institutional boundary between worker interests to be regulated through industrial relations, and production interests that were the domain of management and trade associations. "Modern" industrial relations thus entailed a recognition not only of a right to collective bargaining, but also of managerial prerogative. This "historical compromise" has today become unstable, as a result *not* of labor radicalism but of management demands and production needs for "flexibility". In pursuit of the latter, labor relations are being (re-)integrated into comprehensive production strategies at the company level, pulling more closely together previously separate functions such as marketing, research and development, engineering, work organization, and manpower management (Strauss 1984). The consequence is progressive "dematurity" of industrial relations - to apply a concept introduced to describe changes in industrial organization towards higher innovativeness and flexibility (Abernathy 1978) - related to the emergence of a "post-Fordist" production system (Boyer 1987; Sabel 1982) and characterized by declining differentiation and increasing integration and interdependence between remuneration, working conditions, work motivation, and worker attitudes on the one hand, and the operation and performance of the economic and production system on the other.

A case could be made that in today's economy and polity, the traditional indifference of trade unions to production issues has ceased to be functional for an adequate representation of the interests of workers. If this were so, trade unions would have to learn to involve themselves more directly and intentionally than in the past in production, or "trade", politics. In the course of this they would become immersed in, and infested with, problems and cleavages among their constituents that would be far more diverse and divisive than their traditional preoccupation with class and distribution. As production-related interests having to do with commercial performance in competitive product markets become both more important for their members and more a matter of strategic choice, unions might no longer be able to afford delegating them, as it were by default, to capital and its associations.

While distributive conflicts between capital and labor and the associated problems of demand management are likely to decline in relative significance, the importance of production and work organization has for some time been increasing together with that of supply-side management. With the axis of conflict shifting from class to production interests, trade unions may have to become more similar organizationally to business associations to remain industrially and politically influential. As the interests with which they are confronted by their members and clients change to become more diverse - so as to resemble the heterogeneous interest-political "raw material" that business associations have long been used to - unions might have to adjust their structures. One possibility would be to rely more than in the past on *inter-* instead of *intra-*organizational mechanisms and arrangements of managing interest diversity, with encompassing "industrial" unions turning *de facto,* and later perhaps even *de jure,* into loose federations of workplace and enterprise organizational units. Another, less orderly response would be multi-unionism as is, for example, presently emerging with astonishing speed in Sweden (Lash 1985). In any case, the future may see developing something like a *convergence* between business associations and trade unions with the latter learning from their opponents how a high level of collective action can be achieved in spite of a highly diverse interest structure and highly instrumental, functionally specific, nonideological and idiosyncratic attachments of members to their organizations.

Conclusions

"Labor and capital", according to Offe and Wiesenthal, "show substantial differences with respect to the functioning and performance of their associations. These differences (...) are consequences and manifestations of antagonistic class relations" (1980:72). But the effect of differential location in the class structure on organizational form differs greatly from, and in fact is the reverse of, what class theory expects. Being a privileged social class does not go together with easy generation of consensus *on* common interests or with less interest in common interests. To the contrary, the evidence suggests that a dominant structural position entails the dubious privilege of making decisions that are *difficult* to make and therefore may be *divisive*. A subordinate position, by comparison, may under favorable conditions permit its occupants to concentrate their collective action on a selected range of simple, easily identified objectives and leave aside more complex interests that would divide them. In fact, they may be able to delegate the representation of such interests to the dominant class and thus achieve greater organizational unity at its expense.[15]

An important part of the argument revolves around the concept of opportunism. While for Offe and Wiesenthal this denotes a change

---

15 This is what one could call *the white man's burden theory of interest representation.*

in the organizational process of trade unions that makes them *similar to business associations*, this paper argues that opportunism should be conceived as the *elimination of production-related interests from trade unions' interest base*, in order to make unions organizationally *different* from, and in particular more encompassing than, business associations. There is agreement that opportunism entails a limitation of collective action to interests compatible with "the system"; but whereas for Offe and Wiesenthal this system is *capitalism*, the evidence suggests that it is, more precisely, the established *industrial relations system* of *democratic capitalism*. There is also agreement that opportunism may be a source of institutional instability; but unlike Offe and Wiesenthal, this paper maintains that such instability is likely to be initiated *not by militant trade union members but by management* punctuating, under changed economic conditions, the institutional fence around "industrial relations" and thereby forcing opportunistic unions to choose between two opposite alternatives: being relegated to insignificance under management-controlled "flexibility", or preparing themselves organizationally to invade the domain of managerial prerogative in a market economy.

As opportunities for opportunism recede, workers and their associations will find it increasingly hard to resist entanglement in supply-side interests. The consequences of this for the distribution of power are far from clear and may in fact be of two diametrically opposed kinds. While in some cases assumption of responsibility by trade unions for production matters may entail political subordination to capitalist interests, in others labor may become the driving and guiding force of strategic economic adjustment. But regardless of whether management takes over labor or labor takes over management, functional interpenetration of interest representation and economic decision-making will be accompanied by *disintegration of monolithic class structures of collective action*. The latter will make national-level regulation of aggregate incomes more difficult while at the same time the former will make it less necessary. Problems of symmetry and equity will reemerge in and between the new, narrower, functionally and sectorally more specific arenas of collective action where their resolution will be closely linked to productive performance. With class organization weakening or withering away and other, more complex lines of interest differentiation taking precedence, the important contribution of class politics to social order and social integration may with hindsight be generally recognized, and new, functionally equivalent solutions to the problem of governability are likely to be urgently required.

References

Abernathy, W. J. (1978) *The Productivity Dilemma: Roadblock to Innovation in the Automobile Industry.* Baltimore and London: The John Hopkins University Press

Boyer, R. (1987) *The Eighties: The Search for Alternatives to Fordism. A Very Tentative Assessment.*, ms., Paris: CEPREMAP

Dunlop, J. T. (1958) *Industrial Relations Systems.* Carbondale etc.: Southern Illinois University Press, Ch.1, 'An Industrial Relations System', pp. 1-32

Lash, Scott (1985) 'The End of Neo-Corporatism? The Breakdown of Centralised Bargaining in Sweden', *British Journal of Industrial Relations*, 23: 215-39

Lehmbruch, Gerhard (1979) 'Concluding Remarks: Problems for Future Research on Corporatist Intermediation and Policy-Making', pp. 299-309 in Ph. C. Schmitter and G. Lehmbruch (eds.) *Trends Towards Corporatist Intermediation.* Beverly Hills and London: Sage

Lehmbruch, Gerhard (1984) 'Concertation and the Structure of Corporatist Networks', pp. 60-80 in J. H. Goldthorpe (ed.) *Order and Conflict in Contemporary Capitalism.* Oxford: Clarendon Press

Offe, Claus and Helmut Wiesenthal (1980) 'Two Logics of Collective Action: Theoretical Notes on Social Class and Organizational Form', *Political Power and Social Theory, Vol. 1*, pp. 67-115. Greenwich, Conn.: JAI Press Inc.

Olson, Mancur (1982) *The Rise and Decline of Nations. Economic Growth, Stagflation and Social Rigidities.* New Haven/London: Yale University Press.

Przeworski, Adam and M. Wallerstein (1982) 'Democratic Capitalism at the Crossroads', *Democracy,* July 1982: 52-68

Sabel, Charles F. (1982) *Work and Politics: The Division of Labor in Industry.* New York: Cambridge University Press

Scharpf, Fritz W. (1987) *Inflation und Arbeitslosigkeit in Westeuropa: Eine spieltheoretische Interpretation.* Köln: Max-Planck-Institut für Gesellschaftsforschung, ms.

Schmitter, Philippe C. and Wolfgang Streeck (1981) *The Organization of Business Interests: A Research Design to Study the Associative Action of Business in the Advanced Industrial Societies of Western Europe.* Discussion Paper IIM/LMP 81-13: Wissenschaftszentrum Berlin

Sorge, Arnd und Wolfgang Streeck (1988) 'Industrial Relations and Technical Change: The Case for an Extended Perspective', in R. Hyman and W. Streeck (eds.) *New Technology and Industrial Relations* Oxford: Basil Blackwell

Strauss, G. (1984) 'Industrial Relations: Time of Change', *Industrial Relations,* 23: 1-15

Streeck, Wolfgang (1987) 'The Uncertainties of Management in the Management of Uncertainty: Employers, Labor Relations and Industrial Adjustment in the 1980s', *Work, Employment and Society,* 1: 281-308; and *International Journal of Political Economy,* 17: 57-87

Vidich, A. J. (1982) 'The Moral, Economic and Political Status of Labor in American Society', *Social Research,* 49: 753-9

VII

Can Transaction Cost Economics Explain Trade Associations?*

Marc Schneiberg and J. Rogers Hollingsworth

Oliver Williamson's transaction cost economics (TCE) has sparked renewed interest in how economic activity is governed in capitalist societies. Focusing on the transaction, and insisting that economic institutions can and must be explained in terms of their capacities to regulate exchange relations in an efficient and economic manner, Williamson's work rejects technological, legal, and class analytic approaches and constructs an alternative theory of economic governance via a logic that dimensionalizes transactions, that identifies the mechanisms and institutional arrangements which "harmonize the interfaces" between economic actors, and that uses a comparative assessment of the cost and performance attributes of these arrangements to specify the conditions under which various governance structures form and develop (Williamson 1975, 1981, 1985; Williamson/Ouchi 1981a). What has emerged from

* In writing this paper, we are very indebted to Philippe Schmitter, who more than anyone else has put the study of trade associations on the research agenda of those who are interested in the governance of capitalist societies. We would also like to thank Oliver Williamson, Bo Gustafsson, Masahiko Aoki, Wolfgang Streeck, William Coleman, Wyn Grant, Leon Lindberg, Charles Halaby, David Stark, LaurenEdelman, Ann Miner, Terry Amburgey, Robert Freeland, and the participants in the SCASS conference on "Firms as a Nexus of Treaties" for their comments and support. Errors, omissions, and misrepresentations are, of course, the authors' responsibility.

Williamson's logic is a refined and sophisticated theory of why, where, and when the "visible hand" of informal or formal-bureaucratic modes of governance supplement and/or replace the "invisible hand" of autonomous contracting and the market.

Despite the widespread attention TCE has received, its generality remains substantially unassessed. Facing problems with operationalizing core concepts, and struggling to develop the kinds of data which directly test core propositions, scholarship which empirically examines TCE's capacity to explain the transition from markets to hierarchies is just getting under way. In addition, recent research on the governance of capitalist economies has shown that our analyses must extend beyond markets and hierarchies to consider other governance structures such as various forms of networks and the trade association (for example, Hollingsworth/Lindberg 1985; Streeck/Schmitter 1985). Neither markets nor hierarchies, these forms have not yet been adequately examined in transaction cost terms. Thus, serious questions persist regarding the scope and applicability of TCE.

In an effort to explore and define the limits of TCE, this study focuses on the trade association--one of the important economic institutions of capitalism. Using comparative and historical evidence regarding the rise and development of one form of trade association--the price and production association--we assess five basic features of the transaction cost approach:

1. Its claim that the transaction is the basic unit in analysis of economic governance (Williamson 1985:41);
2. Its assertion that transaction cost economizing is the central force driving governance transformations (Williamson 1985:17);
3. Its argument that non-market governance forms emerge, develop and/or persist when transactions are characterized by uncertainty, frequency, and asset specificity (Williamson 1985:52-63);
4. Its heavy reliance on intra-industry competition as the basis upon which governance forms are selected (Williamson 1985:22-3);

5. Its relegation of power to "a secondary role in the scheme of things" and insistence on a radical separation between the economic and the political (Williamson 1985:123-4).

We do not present either a comprehensive account of trade associations or a general theory of governance. However, our analysis shows that TCE can explain only certain aspects of the "life history" of price and production associations. As we shall see, TCE provides considerable insight into the organizational development of associations. Yet it does not offer much leverage for understanding how, why, and under what conditions price and productions emerge in the first place, and persist over time.

Economic Governance and the Trade Association

Despite its frequent use, little work has been devoted to specifying precisely what is meant by the term "governance." As a first approximation, we define economic governance as the set of practices whereby interdependent economic actors (producers, suppliers, distributors, labor, and state agencies) voluntarily coordinate and/or hierarchically control their activities and interactions. Such practices include--but are not restricted to--negotiating terms of trade and constructing agreements; representing interests; allocating resources and tasks; setting standards; organizing information flows and monitoring compliance; structuring incentives and mobilizing sanctions; resolving conflict; distributing costs and benefits; and managing adaptation to uncertain and changing conditions (for example, Williamson 1975, 1985; Chandler 1977; Pfeffer/Salancik 1978; Ouchi 1980; Daems 1980; Streeck/Schmitter 1985). "Governance structures" are the institutional devices through which economic actors organize these practices and manage inter-organizational relations. The study of governance represents an attempt to understand the motives, dynamics, and conditions that lead to the "choice" of a particular governance structure from a range of possible institutional forms (Williamson/Ouchi 1981a; Daems 1983; Williamson 1985). Thus far, most research on governance has focused on markets and hierarchies, but the trade association is also an important governance form.

Trade associations are a form of regulation in which firms in an industry join together and delegate to a central body the rights and powers to promote common interests, regulate relations within the industry, and order relations between industry members and those whose strategies and activities can decisively affect the industry's fortunes (NICB 1925; Whitney 1934; NAM 1942; Pfeffer/Salancik 1978; Schmitter/Streeck 1981; Staber/Aldrich 1983; Grant/Coleman 1987). While sharing features with other types of business organizations, trade associations generally draw their members from those engaged in the same line of business and address a wide variety of member concerns.

In terms of structure and process, the trade association is neither a market nor a corporate hierarchy. Unlike markets, associations subject economic activity to a form of conscious coordination and central regulation. While the organizational form through which they operate varies, trade associations "internalize" the interactions among previously autonomous firms within deliberately constructed institutional arrangements, and encompass members under some form of inclusive decision-making and authority structure (Streeck/Schmitter 1985).

However, associational governance is not based on property rights, common ownership, and the employment relation. Trade associations neither consolidate ownership nor hire their members. Moreover, associations in most countries are rarely able to intervene directly in firms' internal affairs, dictate firm policies, disband members, or resolve inter-firm disputes via fiat. Instead, the trade association is a more or less voluntary form of collective self-regulation which is based on members' common positions and concerns, and which operates through a process of "structured bargaining" among members, association officers, and important social actors in the external environment (for example, Foth 1930; Galambos 1965; Streeck 1983; Streeck/Schmitter 1985; Schmitter 1986).

Nevertheless, trade associations have emerged in a wide variety of sectors, and have played (and continue to play) an important role in governing economic activity throughout the capitalist world.[1] For example:

1. By developing standard contracts, instituting price-fixing schemes, organizing joint purchases and sales, and by administering and participating in collective bargaining arrangements with labor, trade associations have structured the processes whereby actors construct agreements and establish terms of trade.

2. By creating licensing schemes, and setting standards regarding safety, quality and competition, they have established norms governing market behavior.

3. By operating inspection and testing services, conducting surveys, and disseminating information about inventories, costs, prices, economic trends and political developments; by forming consumer complaint bureaus, instituting arbitration, and routinizing bargaining; and by imposing fines, organizing boycotts, and selectively providing access to markets, political representation and other "categoric goods" (Streeck/Schmitter 1985), associations have played a role in monitoring and enforcing compliance, reducing conflict, and in enhancing members' adaptive capacities.

---

1   For an overview of the structure and function of trade associations, see Schmitter/Streeck 1981. On trade associations in the U.S. see Jones 1922; NICB 1925; Foth 1930; Whitney 1934; NAM 1942; Galambos 1965; Hawley 1966, 1981; Becker 1971; Cuff 1973; Himmelberg 1976; Chandler 1977; Skocpol/Finegold 1982; Staber/Aldrich 1983; Lamoreaux 1985; in the U.K., Hannah 1980; Turner 1988; Davenport-Hines 1988; in Canada, Coleman 1985; in France, Levy-Leboyer 1980; Daviet 1988; in Germany, Marburg 1964; Feldman/Nocken 1975; Kocka 1980; Poensgen 1983; Streeck 1983; Pierenkemper 1988; in Switzerland, Farago 1985; in the Netherlands, de Vroom 1985; van Waarden 1985; in Austria, Marin 1983; Traxler 1985; in Japan, Kikkawa 1988; Miyamoto 1988; in Sweden, Pestoff 1982. For a comparison of the U.S. and U.K., see Schmitter/Brand 1979; Germany and the U.K., Grant/Streeck 1985; Canada and the U.K., Coleman/Grant 1984; Belgium, Canada, France and the U.K., Boddewyn 1985; and for associations in the food processing industries of Canada and Europe, see Coleman 1987; Jacek 1987; and Traxler 1987.

4. And by apportioning territories and market shares, matching buyers and sellers, and operating exchanges in which members pool and distribute profits, research, patents, labor, and surplus output, they have also assumed numerous allocative functions.

Further, associations have engaged in lobbying, joined with state managers in making and administering policy, and have served as vehicles whereby states regulate economies and mobilize support.

It is, of course, rare that any given trade association performs all of these tasks, for the extent to which associations assume governance functions depends on their structural features and administrative capacities. These in turn vary considerably across nations, across sectors and over time (for example, Galambos 1965; Schmitter/Streeck 1981; Coleman/Grant 1984; Grant/Streeck 1985; Jacek 1987). Generally, trade associations are most developed in Western Europe--particularly in Austria and Sweden--where professional staffs, compulsory membership, quasi-public status, multiple funding sources, rights to levy fines and regulate access to markets and political bodies, and formal inter-associational linkages provide associations and their leaders with the autonomy and capacity to set industry targets, shape investment, assign territories, fix prices, punish violators, and thereby displace market governance (Traxler 1985, 1987; Pestoff 1982; Grant 1987). At the other extreme lie U.S. and Canadian associations--competing voluntary organizations which depend on members for support, resources, and staff, which abstain from monopolizing or selectively allocating much of anything, which enjoy little formal authority, and which are thus far less able to displace markets with associational control (Galambos 1965; Schmitter/Brand 1979; Coleman/Grant 1984; Staber/Aldrich 1983; Coleman 1985). Note however that national differences do not exhaust the full range of variation as there are important sectoral and over time differences. Nevertheless, the trade association is a significant and widely used governance form, and qualifies with the market and the corporate hierarchy as one of the most important economic institutions of capitalism.

Transaction Costs Economics and the Trade Association

The transaction cost approach to economic institutions has been presented as a general theory of why, when, and where non-market structures supplement and/or displace the market as the means by which economic activities and interactions are coordinated and governed. Since trade associations represent an important instance of "non-market governance forms," empirical generalizations regarding their life histories can be used to assess the scope and explanatory power of TCE.

Prior research (for example, Chandler 1977; Schmitter/Brand 1979; Hawley 1981; Grant/Coleman 1987; van Waarden 1987; Pierenkemper 1988) has found that firms turn to trade associations

1. in response to intra-industry competition;
2. as a reaction to the market power or organizational efforts of an industry's transaction partners;
3. in anticipation of, in conjunction with and/or in response to state regulation of the industry.

As space is limited, and as we seek to engage fully the empirical and theoretical material, we focus on the first set of processes - the rise and development of the price and production association.

"Ruinous Competition" and the Trade Association

Chronic or sudden overcapacity, particularly in conjunction with high fixed costs and low to medium levels of industrial concentration constitute the principal set of conditions under which firms in an industry find it in their interest to form and reform price and production associations (for example, Whitney 1934; Galambos 1965; Chandler 1977; Feldman/Nocken 1975; Hawley 1981; Lamoreaux 1985; van Waarden 1987; Daviet 1988; Davenport-Hines 1988; Turner 1988). Resulting from postwar demobilization, depression, or foreign competition, overcapacity confronts firms with idle plants, accumulating inventory, and through these the real and/or anticipated threats of sustained price warfare, severe price declines, and business failure. In response to these threats, firms which lack the protection provided by an oligopolistic industry structure frequently seek to control prices, production and investment by forming trade associations.

The use of the price and production association to manage cartel arrangements has occurred in a wide variety of sectors throughout the capitalist world. In the U.S., the railroads were among the first to resort to this measure, but the strategy quickly spread, and by the 1880s, associations "became part of the normal way of doing business in most American industries" (Chandler, 1977:316-17; Galambos 1965; Becker 1971). Like their counterparts in the railroad industry, manufacturing and commercial associations sought to avoid price warfare and mitigate the effects of overcapacity by organizing industry wide price-fixing schemes; by setting production quotas and arranging for members to produce at some fraction of capacity; and by assigning firms the exclusive right to sell their output in a particular locale (Jones 1922; NICB 1925; Whitney 1934; Galambos 1965; Chandler 1977; Becker 1971; Lamoreaux 1985).

Similar associational strategies were pursued in other nations. Beginning in 1880, firms in Japanese industries as diverse as cotton, flour, electrical equipment, paper, cement, pig iron, and coal sought to control price, production, and investment through their associations, many of which were born or reorganized during depressions and which "spread in earnest during the Showa panic" (Kikkawa 1988:7, 21-32). Likewise suffering from the worldwide depressions in the last quarter of the nineteenth century, firms in a number of German industries--notably iron and steel, chemicals, and coal-- whole-heartedly embraced this associational strategy: by 1907 almost 25 percent and by 1938 nearly 50 percent of Germany's industrial output was subject to price and production controls that were devised and managed by trade associations (Kocka 1980:88-89; Feldman/Nocken 1975). The same forces evoked comparable responses in Britain (Hannah 1980; Davenport-Hines 1988; Turner 1988) and in France (Levy-Leboyer 1980; Daviet 1988).

While price and production associations generally emerge as the result of firms' independent efforts, state agencies and state managers have sometimes taken the lead in the construction and development of this institutional form. During World War I, for example, the American state promoted the formation of associations in a number of industries as a part of the war effort (NICB 1925; Foth 1930; Cuff 1973); and during the Early New Deal, comparable actions were undertaken in an attempt to facilitate economic recovery (Whitney 1934; Hawley 1966; Himmelberg 1976; Skocpol/Finegold 1982). Similar policies have been pursued by other states, particularly in "late developing" nations such as Japan and Germany, where state actors routinely fostered the construction of associations as an integral component of their war-making and economic development programs (Marburg 1964; Feldman/Nocken 1975; Caves/Uekusa 1976; Magaziner/Hout 1980; Miyamoto 1988).

In all of these countries, industry members and/or state agencies became convinced that their interests were no longer served by the unqualified operation of the market, and sought to supplement and even displace the market governance of competitive relations with associational modes of control. As noted earlier, the historical record regarding the use of these non-market forms constitutes a basis upon which TCE can be empirically assessed.

The Applicability of Transaction Cost Economics

The life history of the price and production association can be understood in terms of three stages: *initial emergence*, organizational *development*, and ongoing *reproduction* or death. Initial emergence refers to the shift from market or hierarchical governance to collective self-regulation, and often involves the rise of "dinner-clubs" and the formation of "gentleman's agreements." Organizational development refers to the fortification of the association's governance capacities in response to problems of cheating, entry and defection, and involves firms' efforts to make the association capable of enforcing price, production and/or investment agreements. These efforts can produce substantial changes in the organizational form through which self-regulation occurs. Ongoing reproduction or death refers to the association's ultimate prospects, and includes the extent to which the association displaces—or is displaced by—alternative governance forms in the longer term.

The correspondence between this analytic scheme and the actual trajectory of associational development is, of course, variable. Well developed forms sometimes emerge from the outset, and some associations disband or persist without a great deal of organizational development. Nevertheless, many associations do exhibit three empirically distinct developmental stages, and all confront problems of controlling markets, containing defection and ensuring the ongoing maintenance of operations. More importantly, this scheme allows us to consider separately the different forces at work at different points in an association's life history, and thus permits a more nuanced assessment of TCE.

Initial Emergence: Explaining the rise of non-market governance forms first requires a theory of genesis, or at the very least, some specification of the motives which lead actors to transform institutional arrangements. While TCE is largely functionalist in character, it does suggest that economic actors are motivated by interests in transaction cost economizing. Moreover, competition looms large in the model, and while TCE is not a theory of strategic choice, it implies that actors turn to non-market forms in order to gain competitive advantage.

The formation of price and production associations does represent a competitive strategy. However, the motives involved here have little to do with enhancing efficiency or with reducing the costs of establishing, monitoring, and governing exchange relations. Instead, the main purpose and intended effects of these forms are to fix prices, limit output and more generally facilitate and regulate conscious, coordinated efforts to control competition, stabilize profits, and shield members from the adverse consequences of untrammelled market competition. In essence, price and production associations are created for strategic and distributional purposes: they are formed in an attempt by firms to protect and enhance their market positions, shift the burden of adjustment onto their transaction partners, and extract from these partners a form of rent. By rejecting "monopoly" in favor of efficiency purposes, and by putting aside the possibility that some governance transformations are driven by purely distributional concerns, TCE leaves us without an account of the motives which prompt firms to abandon markets in favor of associational control.

Explaining governance transformations also presupposes a specification of the "object" of governance, that is, an account of the types of activities and relationships that are coordinated and regulated by governance structures. In this respect, TCE is quite clear: The transaction is the basic unit of analysis. Vertical integration, internal labor markets and so on all represent alternatives to the market governance of the transfer of goods and services between suppliers and consumers, managers and workers, and investors and firms. Further, such explanations require an enumeration of the conditions under which non-market governance forms emerge. Here again, TCE is very clear: They emerge when transactions are characterized by uncertainty, frequency, and asset specificity. Under these conditions, managing transactions by market contracts becomes costly, and actors face powerful incentives to supplement or displace market governance with non-market institutions.

The rise of price and production associations poses problems for both of these claims. First, the construction of these associations represents a process in which similarly placed firms create agreements amongst themselves in order to organize, stabilize and govern relations within the industry, i.e., horizontal relations among non-transacting competitors. To be sure, these agreements are designed to influence the terms of trade between industry members and their transaction partners. Yet unlike vertically integrated firms, internal labor markets, or other forms of associational governance, price and production associations do not subject the behavior of the industry's transaction partners to administrative controls, coordinate the activities of the transacting parties, or regulate directly the transfer of resources between industry members and their exchange partners. Instead, they are concerned with intra-industry competition, confine their efforts to one side of the market, generally the selling side, and are principally designed to stabilize terms of trade indirectly by co-

production and/or investment. For example, amendments to Japan's Anti-Monopoly Law allow Japanese associations to form cartels which, among other things, regulate investment and capacity, set export price floors, and allocate production among member firms (Magaziner/Hout 1980). Moreover, states in many of these countries have promoted the formation of associations in "strategic" sectors, and have provided firms in these industries with powerful incentives for undertaking these efforts. The Swedish state, for example, funded organizational efforts among agricultural firms throughout the 1930s and 1940s as a part of its attempt to establish as system of quasi-public price regulation associations (Pestoff 1982). Furthermore, state actors in some of these nations have gone as far as legally compelling firms to create price and production associations, as was the case, for example, in Germany during the two World Wars (Marburg 1964; Feldman/Nocken 1975). In all of these countries, state policy has had a salutary effect on the formation of price and production associations.

In contrast, the American state has displayed an exceptional enmity toward price and production associations since the early twentieth century (for example, NICB 1925; Foth 1930; Whitney 1934; Galambos 1965; Hawley 1966; Cuff 1973; Himmelberg 1976; Chandler 1977; Schmitter/Brand 1979; Keller 1980, 1981; Skocpol/Finegold 1982; Lamoreaux 1985). While state agencies have at times promoted the construction of associations, such efforts were temporary, short-lived expedients; emerged as responses to tremendous economic or political upheavals such as war and the Great Depression; and represented radical departures from the policy of consistently abstaining from encouraging associational formation. In fact, the American state has vigorously opposed the formation of price and production associations. Committed to liberal principles, and actively pursuing anti-trust policies, the courts, the Federal Trade Commission, the Justice Department and the U.S. Congress have produced a legal and political environment which is quite hostile to the price and production association, and which has led American business to avoid studiously even the hint of an attempt to control competition via associative behavior. Thus, state policy in the

U.S. has functioned to suppress the formation of price and production associations in all but a few sectors.

In sum, the transaction cost approach provides little leverage for explaining the initial emergence of price and production associations. First, the shift from markets to collective self-regulation of competition via associations is driven not by transaction cost economizing, but rather by strategic and distributional concerns. Moreover, this governance form is created to regulate non-contractual relations among competitors; and its emergence hinges less on transactional characteristics than it does on industry-level characteristics. Further, state policy - a factor bracketed by TCE's separation of economics and politics - plays a central role in generating variation in the extent and rate of associational formation.

Organizational Development: The construction of agreements regarding price, production and so on does not exhaust the life history of the price and production association. As noted previously, the creation of associations exposes industry members to new kinds of problems, subjects firms to new kinds of pressures, and spurs a process of organizational development. In particular, newly formed associations are frequently forced to (1) deal with members who cheat on their agreements; (2) contend with new entrants; and (3) modify prices, market shares and production quotas when business conditions change (for example, Galambos 1965; Chandler 1977; Lamoreaux 1985; Kikkawa 1988). To resolve these problems, firms have sought to fortify their associations' governance capacities, have delegated rights and powers to full-time professional staffs, and have instituted a variety of bureaucratic controls. In some cases, associations have gone as far as forming selling "syndicates" which purchase members' output, sell it at a fixed price and distribute the proceeds according to a quota system; in other cases, associations have organized "money pools" which tax overproducers and subsidize firms which produced below quota; and it is hardly unusual for associations to seek state aid, either in the form of protective tariffs, and/or of laws which ban new entry, make membership compulsory and which grant associations rights to regulate investment (Jones 1922; NICB 1925; Chandler 1977; Kocka 1980; Levy-Leboyer 1980;

Streeck/Schmitter 1985; Jacek 1987; Daviet 1988; Pierenkemper 1988 Turner 1988).

TCE is quite well-placed to explain these developments. To begin with, the initial formation of the price and production association is a process whereby like firms create exchange relations amongst themselves. It is a contracting operation in which firms agree to perform in a particular way--to maintain a minimum price, produce at a certain percentage of capacity, restrict sales to a particular locale, and so on--in exchange for a commitment from other firms to perform in the same or similar manner. Moreover, the organizational innovations that emerge as associations become institutionalized represent vehicles through which these newly-created exchange relations are monitored, regulated and maintained. For example, inspection services, reporting requirements and information-gathering departments serve important surveillance functions and enable associations to monitor the extent to which members comply with agreements and sustain contractual commitments. Similarly, structural features such as money pools, selling syndicates and special departments charged with levying fines and organizing boycotts all operate to provide the association with the means to enforce contracts, ensure that members abide by the terms of their agreements, and selectively punish cheaters. Further, forecasting services, grievance procedures, patent stockpiles, and compulsory membership allow the association to manage changes in business conditions, contain conflict among the transacting parties, and prevent outsiders from disrupting the transactional nexus. In short, the structural features connected with the development of the association constitute devices whereby members manage inter-firm agreements, subject intra-industry transactions to administrative controls, and regulate directly the exchange relations they have created amongst themselves. For this aspect of the price and production association's life history, TCE's claim that the transaction is the basic unit of analysis is clearly warranted.

The record regarding the structural reform of the price and production association also confirms TCE's claims concerning the problems, forces and motives which prompt actors to supplement or displace contractual relations with more developed, hierarchical and authoritative forms of control. First, the emergence of associations transforms the problem of regulating competition into a problem of contracting, and subjects participants to pressures and difficulties of a transaction cost nature. As seen above, newly formed associations frequently have to contend with defection and free-riding. On the one hand, association members often try to gain short-term advantages by producing above quota, selling below the fixed price, or by otherwise reneging on their contractual commitments. On the other hand, outsiders seek to profit from artificial scarcity and high prices by entering the market, refusing to join the association, and by selling output just below the cartel price. Both of these strategies represent instances of "self-interest seeking with guile" which expose associations to the hazards of opportunism, and which make negotiating, expanding and maintaining the nexus of inter-firm agreements extremely difficult. Such difficulties are often compounded by the fact that the limits on rationality prevent associations from monitoring compliance, keeping track of new entrants, and anticipating changes in market conditions that could render inter-firm agreements maladaptive. Moreover, the process of organizing and maintaining a price and production association often involves significant transaction costs. Firms have to communicate to each other their intentions and understandings of the situation; negotiate and renegotiate the terms under which they will cooperate; provide one another with assurances that they will abide by their agreements; and monitor and enforce compliance. These operations can consume a great deal of time and resources, especially where the limits of bounded rationality are reached and incentives for opportunism are present. In sum, many associations find that bounded rationality and opportunism produce serious contracting problems, generate substantial transaction costs, and undermine the efficacy of collective self-regulation.

Furthermore, associations deliberately institute the types of organizational innovations discussed above in order to resolve these problems, that is, to overcome the difficulties and reduce the costs involved in making, regulating and adjusting intra-industry transactions. By forming inspection departments, developing forecasting services, and delegating surveillance functions to a full-time professional staff, associations and their members seek to enhance their information processing capabilities, and thereby to economize on bounded rationality. Further, firms solicit state assistance, attempt to make membership compulsory, institute grievance procedures, organize selling syndicates, money pools and the like in an attempt to contain intra-industry conflict and safeguard members against the hazards of opportunism. More generally, firms centralize association operations, create specialized governance structures, and delegate rights, resources and powers to full-time association officers in order to reduce transaction costs. By reorganizing the association in this manner, firms not only simplify the tasks of incorporating new members, managing adaptation to changing conditions and maintaining the integrity of the transactional nexus, but they also relieve themselves of the burden of having to maintain separate contractual relations with each and every other member of the association. Put simply, the organizational development of the price and production association is driven by transaction cost economizing.

Finally, the historical record indicates that TCE correctly specifies some of the conditions under which firms embark on a path of structural reform. Uncertainty clearly plays an important role. Market turbulence, sudden and unanticipated declines in demand, and/or rapid changes in the composition of the industry generate renewed pressures for price competition; strain associations' forecasting, regulatory and adaptive capacities; and thereby prod members to introduce organizational innovations (for example, Chandler 1977; Lamoreaux 1985; Pierenkemper 1988). The frequency of transactions--or more properly, the duration of the inter-firm agreements--also appears to affect the likelihood of organizational development. Where overcapacity is a chronic problem, firms face the prospect of having to maintain the association over a long period of time, and thus experience powerful pressures for creating specialized governance structures and hiring full-time association staffs (for example, Galambos 1965; Van Waarden 1987). Further, asset specificity contributes to structural reform, although the ability to redeploy assets may have contradictory effects. On the one hand, high asset specificity may have a "lock in" affect and produce incentives for organizational development. On the other hand, low levels of asset specificity make it easier for outsiders to enter the market, a problem that plays a major role in prompting firms' efforts to fortify their associations' governance capacities (for example, Lamoreaux 1985; Kikkawa 1988).

Nevertheless, a full specification of the conditions under which organizational development takes place requires us to go beyond TCE's particular formulations, as the structural reform of the price and production association frequently hinges on the characteristics of the industry involved. The level of fixed costs, for example, plays an extremely important role in promoting associational development (for example, Becker 1971; Chandler 1977; Lamoreaux 1985). As fixed costs increase, firms experience intense pressures to keep their plants "running full," more frequently succumb to the price cutting temptation, and find that highly centralized and well-developed associations are required to maintain the transactional nexus. Also affecting the likelihood of structural reform are the size and number of firms in the industry (for example, Galambos 1965; Feldman/Nocken 1975; Streeck/Schmitter 1985; Turner 1988). Where firms are large and few in number, they are generally able to maintain associational discipline via informal and decentralized means. But where firms are small and numerous, transaction costs increase, informal associations prove unable to monitor or enforce compliance, and firms turn to more formalized and centralized associational forms. Finally, the costs and difficulties involved in regulating inter-industry transactions increases as members are divided by "rival projects" such as ethnicity or region, when there is substantial project heterogeneity, or when firms in an industry use different processes or confront different costs and constraints (for example, Galambos 1965; Feldman/Nocken 1975; Schmitter 1986; Van Waarden 1987). In short, the magnitude of contracting problems, the costs of governing intra-industry transactions, and the extent to which firms fortify their associations' capacities are largely determined by industry level characteristics which lie outside of TCE's present formulations.

Overall, the evidence regarding the organizational development of the price and production association confirms TCE's core claims and insights. Once associations are in place, intra-industry transactions become important, and members find themselves exposed to problems of contracting, that is, to limits, pressures and constraints that figure centrally in the transaction cost approach. Moreover, these difficulties produce interests in resolving contracting problems and in reducing transaction costs, interests which lead firms to transform the organizational structure of the association and institute devices which regulate intra-industry exchange relations. Further, TCE does specify some of the conditions under which firms fortify associations, although the model must be extended to incorporate the role that industry level factors play in generating transactional difficulties and precipitating structural reform.

Reproduction or death: The last processes to be considered involve the factors and forces which promote or undermine the longer-term survival of the price and production association. Of particular interest here is the extent to which the collective self regulation of competition displaces--or is displaced by--alternative governance forms.

TCE presents two kinds of arguments regarding the conditions under which governance forms are reproduced. The first argument maintains that the reproduciblity of governance forms hinges on their transaction cost consequences, that is, on whether or not they provide actors with more opportunities to economize on transaction costs than do alternative governance forms. When firms achieve a more efficient or "discriminating" match between governance structures and underlying transactions, they can realize considerable cost savings. These savings, in turn, allow firms to outperform their less efficiently organized rivals, and to increase their chances of survival in the competitive process. Over "intervals of five to ten years," such competitive processes effectively "perform a sort between more and less efficient modes and ... shift resources in favor of the former" (Williamson, 1985:22-23). In short, governance forms survive because they are "fitter," i.e., more efficient ways of regulating transactions than alternative forms, and are thus better able to withstand the selection processes involved in economic competition.

A second argument emerges from a series of comments regarding the history of American railroad cartels (Williamson, 1985:159-160, 277-279). According to these comments, the railroad cartels were disbanded first, because they encountered severe auditing limits and thus could not determine whether or not members had complied with agreements; and second, because they were unable to localize discipline, selectively punish opportunism, and overcome powerful incentives to cheat. Implied here is the more general claim that the survival of collective self-regulation hinges on the extent to which the association is able to monitor and enforce inter-firm agreements.

The historical record regarding the reproduction or death of the price and production association poses serious problems for both of these formulations. To begin with, competition is not a constant. It is a variable, an endogenous factor or constraint that is an object of struggle and strategic behavior. In fact, price and production associations in some countries have sometimes been quite successful in reducing and even eliminating competition for long periods of time (for example, Feldman/Nocken 1975; Keller 1981; Grant 1985; Pestoff 1987; Kikkawa 1988). Thus, our models cannot simply assume that competitive pressures sort out governance forms, even in the long run.

Furthermore, while the evidence supports TCE's claim that the survival of the price and production depends on its capacities to enforce inter-agreements, these capacities are directly and fundamentally determined by political factors.

More specifically, comparative analysis indicates that the extent to which associations can forge agreements within an industry, impose discipline on members, cope with the problem of new entrants, and displace market governance ultimately depends on state structures and state policies--that is, on factors largely ignored by TCE.

As noted above, the American state has strenuously opposed the regulation of competition by price and production associations (Naylor 1921; Jones 1922; NICB 1925; Foth 1930; Whitney 1934; NAM 1942; Galambos 1965; Hawley 1966, 1981; Cuff 1973; Himmelberg

1976; Chandler 1977; Schmitter/Brand 1979; Keller 1980, 1981; Skocpol/Finegold 1982; Lamoreaux 1985). Courts and regulators refused to make cartel agreements legally binding; state and federal legislatures passed anti-trust laws, including the 1890 Sherman Act that declared illegal "every contract, combination...or conspiracy, in restraint of trade;" and the Supreme Court rendered decisions from 1895 to 1925 which dissolved associations, fined members, and which placed cartel practices (output limits, price fixing, market division) and their instruments (joint selling, boycotts, pools, exclusion) under a ban of law. While, federal agencies have at times advocated associational forms of governance--notably the War Industries Board during World War I, Hoover's policies within the Commerce Department in the 1920s and the NRA in the early New Deal--departmental rivalries, separation of powers and other structural features of the U.S. political system prevented these agencies from achieving more than partial, short-term successes. Overall, with a few exceptions - for example, insurance, agriculture, and professional sports - the structure and policy of the American state have generally functioned to support liberal principles, and to deprive associations of the rights, resources and capacities needed to organize effective cartels.

Since the American state barred associations from making price and production agreements, from enforcing discipline, and from erecting barriers to entry, American business began in the 1890s to search for other means of controlling competition. Firms in highly fragmented sectors such as lumber and cotton experimented with scaled-down associations which eschewed central direction in favor of product standardization, uniform cost accounting and "open price" schemes which sought to stabilize competitive relations indirectly by eliminating "waste," by restricting competition to price, and by providing firms with the data needed to make independently price and output decisions that would reduce overcapacity and the likelihood of price warfare (Jones 1922; NICB 1925; Whitney 1934; Galambos 1965; Hawley 1981). Firms in more concentrated sectors--such as railroads, petroleum, and steel—abandoned price and production associations; turned to alternative institutional arrangements for managing competitive relations including the trust, the holding company and the horizontal merger; and ultimately achieved some degree of stability via the price leadership afforded by oligopolistic structures (Chandler 1977; Keller 1980; Lamoreaux 1985). In both cases, the American state's hostility toward the collective self-regulation of competition rendered the price and production association non-reproducible, and precipitated a shift toward alternative governance forms.

In contrast, British state policy before World War II tolerated price and production associations and effectively slowed the pace of corporate consolidation (Schmitter/Brand 1979; Hannah 1980; Keller 1980, 1981; Turner 1988). While British courts sometimes decided against attempts to impose cartel provisions on members, they imposed no general ban on cartel agreements, vigorously defended the freedom of contract, and consistently ruled that contracts among associations and third parties were binding even when they involved restraints on trade. Moreover, there were no British anti-trust statutes until the 1948 and 1956 Restrictive Practices Acts. In France too, the state was far less opposed to cartel associations than was the case in the U.S., and there were even instances when state-owned enterprises joined associations (Keller 1980, 1981; Daviet 1987).

Yet it was Japan and a few continental countries that departed most dramatically from liberal principles and the U.S. anti-trust tradition. In Germany, government support of price and production associations before World War II "[resulted in a] degree of cartelization unmatched elsewhere" (Keller, 1981:61; cf. Marburg 1964; Feldman/Nocken 1975; Keller 1980; Kocka 1980; Poensgen 1983). Courts and legislatures sustained boycotts and rebates, held that price, production and market sharing agreements were legally binding and in the public interest, and thereby placed the power of the state firmly and squarely behind associational governance. Further, state agencies actively promoted cartels and occasionally compelled non-members to join associations. In fact, it was not until 1957 that the German government imposed a general ban on cartels. Passed partly in response to Allied pressures, the 1957 Cartel Law limits firms' abilities to form associations; yet it contains exceptions, and has sometimes been used to support quotas, syndicates, and rationalization cartels.

Like its German counterpart, the Japanese state actively sustained the collective self-regulation of competition before the end of World War II, particularly in the 1930s when the passage of supporting legislation prompted and even compelled firms in a large number of industries to form or reorganize price and production associations (Kikkawa 1988; Miyamoto 1988). While this practice was curtailed when the Allies imposed on Japan the Antimonopoly Act of 1947--an act which prohibited cartel agreements and which banned associations from limiting entry, restricting member activities and so on--the Diet and the Ministries have since weakened this statute significantly by passing laws that permit whole classes of price and production associations and by supporting the use of hundreds of rationalization, depression, export, import and small business cartels (Caves/Uekusa 1976; Magaziner and Hout 1980). State policies have also promoted the reproduction of price and production associations in Switzerland, the Netherlands, Sweden, and Austria. By granting associations rights to compel participation and regulate members' investment decisions, the state in these countries has effectively promoted the long term use of the price and production association (Pestoff 1982; Traxler 1985; Jacek 1987; Farago 1987; van Waarden 1987).

In sum, comparative historical analysis reveals that state policy toward economic governance plays an important role in determining the extent to which price and production associations (1) persist over time, and (2) displace or are displaced by alternative governance forms. Where governments opposed the collective self-regulation of competition, the price and production association proved non-reproducible, and firms either turned to weaker forms of associational control or sought to control competition through trusts, holding companies, horizontal mergers and oligopolistic structures. But where governments supported this regulatory mode, associations' long-term survival prospects were dramatically enhanced; firms turned more slowly to and relied less heavily on the horizontal merger, and opted instead to supplement and even displace market governance of competitive relations via centrally regulated associational behavior. Thus, TCE's failure to incorporate the state into its analysis leaves it unable to account for the cross-national, cross-sectoral and over-time variations in the reproductive histories of the price and production association.

Conclusion

Can transaction cost economics explain trade associations?

Focusing on one associational form, our analysis indicates (1) that different factors and forces operate at varying points in the price and production association's life history, and (2) that TCE's applicability and explanatory power critically depends on the aspect or phase of this life history that is under consideration. With regard to the organizational development of the association, the evidence largely confirms TCE's core concepts and propositions. The transaction is the basic unit of analysis; bounded rationality and opportunism expose association members to problems of contracting; and the structural reforms of the associations are driven by an interest in transaction cost economizing. Furthermore, TCE correctly specifies some of the factors which promote structural reform, although the model must be extended to describe fully the conditions under which these reforms are undertaken. Above all, firms create more developed and hierarchical forms when transaction costs are high, and when prior forms prove incapable of managing adaptation to changing circumstances and selectively punishing opportunism. Thus, our analysis shows that TCE has provided us with a set of variables and propositions that explanations of associational development can only ignore at great peril.

However, our analysis also demonstrates that TCE cannot explain either the initial emergence or the ongoing reproduction of the price and production association. Firms create these associations for strategic and distributional purposes, that is, to enhance their market power and shift the risks and burdens of adjustment onto their exchange partners. Moreover, while firms mobilize this associative strategy in order to regulate relations in which they find themselves vulnerable to the strategic behavior of others, the relations at issue do not involve prior transfers of goods and services, and the extent to which firms find themselves vulnerable does not depend on the nature or properties of exchange relations. Instead, the principle object of the price and production association is to regulate horizontal relations among non-transacting competitors, and the shift from markets to collective self regulation is far more sensitive to industry and political factors than it is to characteristics of transactions. Finally, state policy toward economic governance - a factor ignored by TCE - plays a far more important role that competition and transaction cost economizing in determining whether or not price and production associations displace alternative forms and persist over the long run. Thus, TCE's core concepts and propositions do not account for the rise and reproduction of price and production associations.

While further research is required, our analysis indicates that TCE's ability to explain trade associations is limited. Strategic considerations often dominate associative behavior; non-transactional relations figure centrally in associational governance; and the state plays a fundamental role in determining the extent to which transactional and non-transactional relations can be subjected to collective self regulation. Note, however, that we do not conclude that TCE should be rejected. The considerable insight it provides into certain aspects of the trade association's life history; the fact that the study of governance is still in its adolescence; and the ongoing refinement of the transaction cost framework militate against such a hasty conclusion. Instead, we conclude that a complete account of the rise, development and persistence of the trade association requires us to retain many of TCE's core concepts and insights, and incorporate its claims within a more general theory of the factors, forces, motives, and contextual conditions that underlie governance structures and their transformation.

References

Becker, William H. (1971) 'American Wholesale Hardware Trade Association, 1870-1900', *Business History Review*,45: 179-200.

Boddewyn, J. J. (1985) 'Advertising Self-Regulation: Organizational Structures in Belgium, Canada, France and the United Kingdom', pp.1-43 in Wolfgang Streeck and Philippe C. Schmitter (eds.) *Private Interest Government*. Beverly Hills: Sage Publications.

Caves, Richard and Masu Uekusa (1976) 'Industrial Organization', pp. 459-523 in Hugh Patrick and Henry Rosovsky (eds.) *Asia's New Giant*. Washington, D.C.: The Brookings Institute.

Chandler, Alfred D., Jr. (1962) *Strategy and Structure*. Cambridge, MA: MIT Press.

Chandler, Alfred D., Jr. (1977) *The Visible Hand*. Cambridge, MA: Harvard University Press.

Chandler, Alfred D., Jr. (1980) 'The United States: Seedbed of Managerial Capitalism', pp. 9-40 in Alfred D. Chandler, Jr. and Herman Daems (eds.) *Managerial Hierarchies*. Cambridge, MA: Harvard University Press.

Coleman, William D. (1985) 'Analyzing the Associative Action of Business: Policy Advocacy and Policy Participation', *Canadian Public Administration*, 28: 413-33.

Coleman, William D. (1987) 'Agricultural Policy and the Associations of the Food Processing Industry', pp.151-165 in Wyn Grant (ed.) *Business Interests, Organizational Development and Private Interest Government*. Berlin: Walter de Gruyter.

Coleman, William D. and Wyn Grant (1984) 'Business Associations and Public Policy: A Comparison of Organizational Development in Britain and Canada', *Journal of Public Policy*, 3: 209-235.

Coleman, William D. and Wyn Grant (1988) 'The Organizational Cohesion and Political Access of Business: A Study of Comprehensive Associations', *European Journal of Political Research* 16:467-487

Cuff, Robert D. (1973) *The War Industries Board: Business- Government Relations During World War I*. Baltimore: The Johns Hopkins University Press.

Daems, Herman (1980) 'The Rise of the Modern Industrial Enterprise: A New Perspective', pp. 202-223 in Alfred D. Chandler, Jr. and Herman Daems (eds.) *Managerial Hierarchies*. Cambridge, MA: Harvard University Press.

Daems, Herman (1983) 'The Determinants of the Hierarchical Organization of Industry', pp. 35-53 in Arthur Francis, Jeremy Turk and Paul Willman (eds.) *Power, Efficiency and Institutions*. London: Heinemann Educational Books.

Davenport-Hines, R. P. T (1988) 'Trade associations and the Modernization Crisis of British Industry, 1910-35', pp. 205-226 in Hiroaki Yamazaki and Matao Miyamoto (eds.) *Trade Associations in Business History*. Tokyo: Tokyo University Press.

Daviet, Jean-Pierre (1988) 'Trade Associations or Agreements and Controlled Competition in France, 1830-1939', pp. 269-295 in Hiroaki Yamazaki and Matao Miyamoto (eds.) *Trade Associations in Business History*. Tokyo: Tokyo University Press.

de Vroom, Burt (1985) 'Quality Regulation in the Dutch Pharmaceutical Industry: Conditions for Private Regulation by Business Interest Associations', pp. 128-149 in Wolfgang Streeck and Philippe C. Schmitter (eds.) *Private Interest Government*. Beverly Hills: Sage Publications.

Farago, Peter (1985) 'Regulating Milk Markets: Corporatist Arrangements in the Swiss Dairy Industry', pp. 168-181 in Wolfgang Streeck and Philippe C. Schmitter (eds.) *Private Interest Government*. Beverly Hills: Sage Publications.

Farago, Peter (1987) 'Retail Pressure and the Collective Reactions of the Food Processing Industry', pp. 166-179 in Wyn Grant (ed.) *Business Interests, Organizational Development and Private Interest Government*. Berlin: Walter de Gruyter.

Feldman, Gerald and Ulrich Nocken (1975) 'Trade Associations and Economic Power: Interest Group Development in the German Iron and Steel and Machine Building Industries, 1900-1933', *Business History Review*, 49: 413-445.

Foth, Joseph Henry (1930) *Trade Associations: Their Service to Industry.* New York: Ronald Press Company.

Galambos, Louis (1965) *Competition and Cooperation: The Emergence of a National Trade Association.* Baltimore: John Hopkins Press.

Granovetter, Mark (1985) 'Economic Action and Social Structure: A Theory of Embeddedness', *American Journal of Sociology*, 91: 481-510.

Grant, Wyn (1985) 'Private Arganizations as Agents of Public Policy: the Case of Milk Marketing in Britain', pp. 182-196 in Wolfgang Streeck and Philippe C. Schmitter (eds.) *Private Interest Government.* Beverly Hills: Sage Publications.

Grant, Wyn (1987) 'Introduction', pp. 1-17 in Wyn Grant (ed.) *Business Interests, Organizational Development and Private Interest Government.* Berlin: Walter de Gruyter.

Grant, Wyn and William D. Coleman (1987) 'Conclusions', pp. 208-227 in Wyn Grant (ed.) *Business Interests, Organizational Development and Private Interest Government.* Berlin: de Gruyter.

Grant, Wyn and Wolfgang Streeck (1985) 'Large Firms and the Representation of Business Interests in the UK and West German Construction Industry', pp. 145-173 in A. Cawson (ed.) *Organized Interests and the State.* London: Sage.

Hannah, Leslie (1980) 'Visible and Invisible Hands in Great Britain', pp. 41-76 in Alfred D. Chandler, Jr. and Herman Daems (eds.) *Managerial Hierarchies.* Cambridge, MA: Harvard Press.

Hawley, Ellis (1966) *The New Deal and the Problem of Monopoly.* Princeton: Princeton University Press.

Hawley, Ellis (1981) 'Three Facets of Hooverian Associationalism: Lumber, Aviation, and Movies, 1921-1930', pp. 95-123 in Thomas K. McGraw (ed.) *Regulation in Perspective*. Cambridge, MA: Harvard University Press.

Himmelberg, Robert F. (1976) *The Origins of the National Recovery Administration: Business, Government and the Trade Association Issue, 1921-1933*. New York: Fordham University Press.

Hollingsworth, J. Rogers and Leon Lindberg (1985) 'The Governance of the American Economy: The Role of Markets, Clans, Hierarchies, and Associative Behavior', pp. 221-254 in Wolfgang Streeck and Philippe C. Schmitter (eds.) *Private Interest Government*. Beverly Hills: Sage Publications.

Jacek, Henry J. (1987) 'Business Interest Associations as Private Interest Governments', pp. 34-62 in Wyn Grant (ed.) *Business Interests, Organizational Development and Private Interest Government*. Berlin: Walter de Gruyter.

Jones, Franklin D. (1922) *Trade Association Activities and the Law: A Discussion of the Legal and Economic Aspects of Collective Action through Trade Associations*. New York: McGraw Hill.

Keller, Morton (1980) 'Regulation of Large Enterprise: United States Experience in Comparative Perspective', pp. 161-181 in Alfred D. Chandler, Jr. and Herman Daems (eds.) *Managerial Hierarchies*. Cambridge, MA: Harvard University Press.

Keller, Morton (1981) 'The Pluralist State: American Economic Regulation in Comparative Perspective, 1900-1930', pp. 56-94 in Thomas K. McGraw (ed.) *Regulation in Perspective*. Cambridge, MA: Harvard University Press.

Kikkawa, Takeo (1988) 'Functions of Japanese Trade Associations before World War II: The Case of Cartel Organizations', pp. 53-83 in Hiroaki Yamazaki and Matao Miyamoto (eds.) *Trade Associations in Business History*. Tokyo: Tokyo University Press.

Kocka, Jurgen (1980) 'The Rise of the Modern Industrial Enterprise in Germany', pp.77-116 in Alfred D. Chandler, Jr. and Herman Daems (eds.) *Managerial Hierarchies*. Cambridge, MA: Harvard University Press.

Lamoreaux, Naiomi R. (1985) *The Great Merger Movement in American Business, 1895-1904*. Cambridge: Cambridge University Press.

Lehmbruch, Gerhard (1977) 'Liberal Corporatism and Party Government', *Comparative Political Studies*, 10: 91-126.

Levy-Leboyer, Maurice (1980) 'The Large Corporation in Modern France', pp. 117-160 in Alfred D. Chandler, Jr. and Herman Daems (eds.) *Managerial Hierarchies*. Cambridge, MA: Harvard University Press.

Magaziner, Ira and Thomas Hout (1980) *Japanese Industrial Policy*. Berkeley: University of California Press.

Marburg, Theodore (1964) 'Government and Business in Germany: Public policy toward cartels', *Business History Review*, 38: 78-101.

Marin, Bernd (1983) 'Organizing Interests by Interest Associations: Associational Prerequisites of Cooperation in Austria', *International Political Science Review*, 4: 197-216.

Miyamoto, Matao (1988) 'The Development of Business Associations in Pre-War Japan', pp. 1-45 in Hiroaki Yamazaki and Matao Miyamoto (eds.) *Trade Associations in Business History*. Tokyo: Tokyo University Press.

National Association of Manufacturers (1942) 'Review of T.N.E.C. Monograph No. 18: Trade Association Survey', pp. 260-273 in John Scoville and Noel Sargent (compilers) *Fact and Fancy in the T.N.E.C. Monographs*. NAM.

National Industrial Conference Board (1925) *Trade Associations, Their Economic Significance and Legal Status*. New York: National Industrial Conference Board, Inc.

Naylor, Emmett Hay (1921) *Trade Associations, Their Organization and Management*. New York: The Ronald Press Company.

Ouchi, William G. (1980) 'Markets, Bureaucracies and Clans', *Administrative Science Quarterly*, 25: 129-141.

Perrow, Charles (1981) 'Markets, Hierarchies and Hegemony', pp. 371-386 in Andrew H. Van de Ven and William F. Joyce (eds.) *Perspectives on Organizational Design and Behavior*. New York: Wiley.

Pestoff, Victor (1982) *The Organization of Business Interests in the Swedish Food Processing Industry*. Paper presented at the Organization of Business Interests conference, Wroxton, St. Mary, Banbury, Oxfordshire.

Pestoff, Victor (1987) 'The Effect of State Institutions on Associative Action in the Food Processing Industry', pp. 91-116 in Wyn Grant (ed.) *Business Interests, Organizational Development and Private Interest Government*. Berlin: Walter de Gruyter.

Pfeffer, Jeffrey and Gerald R. Salancik (1978) *The External Control of Organizations*. New York: Harper and Row.

Pierenkemper, Toni (1988) 'Trade Associations in Germany in the Late Nineteenth and Early Twentieth Century', pp. 233-261 in Hiroaki Yamazaki and Matao Miyamoto (eds.) *Trade Associations in Business History*. Tokyo: Tokyo University Press.

Poensgen, Otto H. (1983) 'Between Markets and Hierarchies', pp. 54-80 in Arthur Francis, Jeremy Turk and Paul Willman (eds.) *Power, Efficiency and Institutions*. London: Heinemann Educational Books.

Schmitter, Philippe C and Wolfgang Streeck (1981) *The Organization of Business Interests: A Research Design to Study the Associative Action of Business in the Advanced Industrial Societies of Western Europe*. Discussion Paper IIM/LMP 81-13, Berlin: Wisenschaftszentrum.

Schmitter, Philippe C. (1986) 'Neo-corporatism and the State', pp. 32-62 in Wyn Grant (ed.) *The Political Economy of Corporatism*. London: Macmillian.

Schmitter, Philippe C. and Donald Brand (1979) *Organizing Capitalists in the United States: The Advantages and Disadvantages of Exceptionalism.* Unpublished paper presented before the American Political Science Association.

Skocpol, Theda and Kenneth Finegold (1982) 'State Capacity and Economic Intervention in the early New Deal', *Political Science Quarterly,* 92: 255-278.

Staber, Udo and Howard Aldrich (1983) 'Trade Association Stability and Public Policy', pp. 163-178 in R. H. Hall and R.E. Quinn (eds.) *Organizational Theory and Public Policy.* London: Sage.

Streeck, Wolfgang (1983) 'Between Pluralism and Corporatism: German Business Associations and the State', *Journal of Public Policy,* 3: 265-284.

Streeck, Wolfgang and Philippe C. Schmitter (1985) 'Community, Market, State -- and Associations? The Prospective Contribution of Interest Governance to Social Order', pp. 1-29 in Wolfgang Streeck and Philippe C. Schmitter (eds.) *Private Interest Government.* Beverly Hills: Sage Publications.

Traxler, Franz (1985) 'Prerequisites, Problem Solving Capacity and Limits of Neo-Corporatist Regulation: A Case Study of Private Interest Government and Economic Performance in Austria', pp. 150-167 in Wolfgang Streeck and Philippe C. Schmitter (eds.) *Private Interest Government.* Beverly Hills: Sage Publications.

Traxler, Franz (1987) 'Patterns of associative action', pp. 18-33 in Wyn Grant (ed.) *Business Interests, Organizational Development and Private Interest Government.* Berlin: de Gruyter.

Turner, John (1988) 'Servants of Two Masters: British Trade Associations in the First Half of the Twentieth Century', pp. 173-198 in Hiroaki Yamazaki and Matao Miyamoto (eds.) *Trade Associations in Business History.* Tokyo: Tokyo University Press.

van Waarden, Frans (1985) 'Varieties of Collective Self-Regulation of Business: The Example of the Dutch Dairy Industry', pp. 197-220 in Wolfgang Streeck and Philippe C. Schmitter (eds.) *Private Interest Government*. Beverly Hills: Sage Publications.

van Waarden, Frans (1987) 'Sector Structure, Interests and Associative Action in the Food Processing Industry', pp. 63-92 in Wyn Grant (ed.) *Business Interests, Organizational Development and Private Interest Government*. Berlin: Walter de Gruyter.

Whitney, Simon N. (1934) *Trade Associations and Industrial Control, A Critique of the N.R.A.* New York: Central Book Co.

Williamson, Oliver and William G. Ouchi (1981a) 'The Markets and Hierarchies and Visible Hand Perspectives', pp. 347-370 in Andrew H. Van de Ven and William F. Joyce (eds.) *Perspectives on Organizational Design and Behavior*. New York: Wiley.

Williamson, Oliver and William G. Ouchi (1981b) 'A rejoinder', pp. 387-390 in Andrew H. Van de Ven and William F. Joyce (eds.) *Perspectives on Organizational Design and Behavior*. New York: Wiley.

Williamson, Oliver E. (1975) *Markets and Hierarchies: Analysis and Antitrust Implications*. New York: Free Press

Williamson, Oliver E. (1981) 'The Economics of Organization: The Transaction Cost Approach', *American Journal of Sociology*, 87: 548-77.

Williamson, Oliver E. (1985) *The Economic Institutions of Capitalism*. New York: Free Press.

Young, Brigitta, Leon Lindberg and J. Rogers Hollingsworth (forthcoming) 'The Governance of the American Dairy Industry: From Regional Dominance to Regional Cleavage', in Henry Jacek and William D. Coleman (eds.) *Regionalism, Business Interest Associations and Public Policy*. Berlin, New York: Walter de Gruyter.

VIII

The Institutional Control of Organized Interest Intermediation

A Political-Economic Perspective

Franz Lehner

The heavy influence of special interest groups on public policy constitutes a strong challenge to the governability of western democracies and to the efficiency of government interventions in the economy. To solve this problem, devices of a stronger control of organized interest intermediation have to be developed and implemented. The search for such devices and the investigation into their feasibility is an interesting and important task for research in the social sciences. Drawing on ideas from public choice theory and the research on liberal corporatism, this article will outline an avenue to such research. The article focusses on the establishment of institutional mechanisms that limit the influence of special interest groups and advance a stronger impact of general interests. The argument put forth here is based on ideas from research on liberal corporatism, especially by Gerhard Lehmbruch, and attempts to further develop these ideas by applying the tools of public choice theory. Some examples from industrial policy and banking regulation will be used to illustrate the argument.

The Institutional Control of Interest Intermediation: An Outline of the Problem

In a growing number of studies in political science and economics, it is argued that the pluralist interest structures of the advanced capitalist societies produce severe problems of legitimacy, stability, and efficiency in economic and social policy. More precisely, it is argued that these structures are associated with imbalanced interest intermediation as well as with disproportionally high power and influence of special groups. Consequently, social and economic policy reflects, for the most part, the particular interests of special groups and neglects more general interests. This results in public policy with an often low legitimacy and a correspondingly low capacity for a stable accomodation of distributive conflict. Moreover, public policy is often inefficient and inhibits growth, employment and, innovation.

Some of these studies associate this situation with a general tendency, or even an inevitable development, of modern democracies. Prominent examples of this line of argument are James Buchanan's book, *The Limits of Liberty* (Buchanan 1975) and Mancur Olson's book *The Rise and Decline of Nations* (Olson 1982), as well as a large part of the literature on "governability" in political science (see e.g. Crozier/Huntington/ Watanuki 1975).

In Buchanan's (1975) view, the problems of legitimacy and efficiency of public policy in modern democracies result from the fact that public goods are produced and distributed on the basis of non-unanimity rules. If decisions concerning the allocation of public goods are made unanimously, the allocation will be efficient in terms of the preferences of the members of the concerned society. Deviations from unanimity create inefficiencies and reduce the legitimacy of collective decisions. This causes strong incentives to form majority coalitions which influence decisions on the allocations of public goods. As the resulting allocation of public goods is inefficient, strong incentives for the loosing groups to form a new majority coalition are built up. The ultimate result of this condition is a process of changing majorities, which tends to increase the production of public goods at the expense of market allocation. Driven by changing majorities, the scope of government tends to expand without producing a stable allocation of public goods and a stable accommodation of distributive conflict.

Buchanan's solution to this problem is a radical reform of the constitutional basis of politics and market allocation. He suggests a redefinition and redistribution of property rights by an unanimous contractual agreement to all members of society. Such a rearrangement would create a socially accepted distribution of property rights and, thus, would create a new and improved basis for market allocation. Consequently, government interventions in the economy and the production of public goods could be drastically reduced.

As I have demonstrated elsewhere (Lehner 1983a), this solution is theoretically intriguing, but practically unfeasible. Given the pluralist interest structures of modern democracies, a consensual redefinition of property rights can hardly be reached. Moreover, any new distribution of property rights would soon be obsolete because a high amount of technical, economic and social transition also changes the meaning and relevance of property rights. Frequent adjustments of property rights by consensual agreement would be necessary.

Although Buchanan's proposal is practically unfeasible, it does however suggest institutional devices that may lead to practicable solutions. If we accept Buchanans diagnosis that much of the inefficiency and expansion of public policy is created by ongoing distributive conflicts and instable political majorities, we have to search for arrangements that lead to a better accomodation of distributive conflict, to an encompassing interest intermediation and to widely accepted policy choices. Moreover, we should search for contractual mechanisms that reduce the load on public policy and allow for an accomodation of distributive conflicts without government intervention. We will further discuss this later in this article.

A different approach to the explanation of the inefficiency of government interventions in the economy is offered by Olson (1982). Based on his *Logic of Collective Action* (Olson 1965), he argues that small special interest groups can be organized more easily and more effectively than larger general interest groups. In modern democracies, there is therefore a strong and increasing influence of distributive coalitions formed by special interests that are narrow in scope, and represent a rather small part of a nation's population and resources. Encompassing coalitions with a broad scope representing a large part of a nations population and resources are much less frequently formed and brought effectively into operation.

As Olson (1982) demonstrates, encompassing coalitions representing a large part of a nation's population and resources have strong incentives to press for economically efficient policies. Due to their share in a nations population and resources, encompassing coalitions have to cover a large proportion of social costs of inefficient policies. Due to their size, benefits accrueing from the effectuation of their special interests are broadly distributed. As a result, encompassing coalitions often face situations in which their share of social costs in public policies outranges the benefits accrued from the effectuation of special interests. This case motivates encompassing coalitions to enhance policies that on one hand adjust to their interests, but on the other are economically efficient.

For small coalitions with a narrow scope, the contrary is the case. Effectuating their special interests at the expense of inefficient policies, these coalitions can gain concentrated benefits while they only have to cover a small proportion of the social costs of inefficient policies. Consequently, economic policy dominated by special interest groups and distributive coalitions with narrow scope are likely to be protective, static and inefficient. This results in low growth, wealth and innovation.

Olson's theory offers a coherent and stringent theoretical explanation of organized interest intermediation with an impact on public policy. It is based on a systematic analysis of the interest structures of modern democracies, as well as the conditions of organization and effectuation of social economic interests. Olson (1982), however, translates his systematic argument into a historical one. He assumes that the longer societies exist in a condition of stable boundaries and unlimited democracy with freedom of organization, the more special interest groups and distributive coalitions with narrow scope will be accummulated by these societies. As is indicated in the title of Olson's book, this assumption implies that societies tend to decline economically as the period of unlimited democracy in the society expands over time. Obviously, this is a deterministic view of the economic development of modern democracies which contains little or no suggestions for a solution of the concerned problems. Olson's hypotheses on the structure of interest intermediation and the size of distributive coalitions, however, offer such suggestions. This will be further discussed below.

Interesting suggestions are also offered by studies based on the theory of liberal corporatism which demonstrate that different institutional arrangements account for different patterns of interest intermediation. This involves differences in power and influence of special interest groups as well as different policy capacities. Moreover, they demonstrate that there are institutional devices available to overcome problems of legitimacy, stability and efficiency of public policy accrueing from the pluralist interest structures of modern capitalist societies. (cf. Czada 1983; Lehmbruch 1984; Lehmbruch/Schmitter 1982; Schmitter 1981; Schmitter/Lehmbruch 1979).

This line of argument contributes much to the development of an institutional theory of interest intermediation and policy-making. It in turn replaces the originally simple developmental approach of the theory of liberal corporatism by a more sophisticated structural approach. The basic assumption of this approach is that different institutional structures contain different capacities. They are assumed to institutionally integrate pluralist interest structures and to institutionally control and restrict, the power and influence of special interests. This opens an interesting avenue for the analysis of the relationship between political institutions, interest intermediation, and public policy. Following this approach, we ought to investigate the extent to which the institutional integration of interest intermediation is capable of compensating negative effects of pluralist interest structures on public policy-making and economic development.

Political Structures and Public Policy:
Empirical Evidence

In accordance with the theory of corporatism and with Olson's hypotheses on the structure of interest intermediation, as well as the size of distributive coalitions, we may theoretically expect that an institutional integration enhances the formation of encompassing distributive coalitions. Furthermore, a more comprehensive interest intermediation is encouraged, the power and influence of special interest groups being thus reduced. This should result in more widely accepted policies and a more stable accomodation of distributive conflict. It should further result in more efficient economic and social policies and consequently, in better economic performance.

Empirical studies on different areas of economic and social policy provide some support for this argument. They underline the relevance of institutional arrangements. However, the available empirical evidence is only partially in accordance with our theoretical expectations. Institutional integration increases the performance in some policy areas and with respect to some economic indicators. It also results in relatively low performance in other areas. More precisely, we find that countries with an institutionally integrated interest intermediation perform comparatively well with respect to the management of distributive conflict and the securing of employment. As far as performance, growth, inflation, and innovation is concerned, there are no clear differences between countries with different institutional structures. Also, the evidence concerning fiscal performance contradicts our theoretical expectations. (Lehner 1987, 1988; Lehner/Nordhause-Janz 1988; Paloheimo 1984; Schmidt 1988).

This ambiguity in the relationship between institutional arrangements, interest intermediation, and economic performance can be explained if we consider that different institutional arrangements are not only associated with different capacities to integrate and control interest intermediation, but also with different restrictions and costs concerning policy-making. A high institutional integration, for example, often requires a considerable consensus among a smaller or larger number of interest groups. Thus, it is associated with high transaction-costs in terms of time, opportunities and other efforts. This may considerably restrict the number of acceptable policy-choices and the capacity of public policy, to flexibly adjust to changing conditions. In contrast, a low integration is associated with considerable problems concerning the power and influence of special interest groups. However, it may also allow for a flexible adjustment of public policy to changing conditions. These and other effects of institutional arrangements on the formation of public policy may be illustrated in a number of different examples.

A first example are the structures of liberal corporatism. These policy structures are characterized by a strong dominant stable coalition of the peak associations of capital, labour, and government. These structures are well designed to accomodate distributive conflict by means of income policies. Low strike activity and and low unemployment in the concerned countries demonstrate the high capacity of corporatist structures to accommodate distributive conflict. At the same time, however, these countries are also characterized by a considerable fiscal expansion with a comparatively high level of public outlays, taxation and public debts. This case suggests that corporatist arrangements, characterized by stable coalitions with limited access and participation, on the one hand, allow for purposive policies concerning income, while on the other the costs of income policies and the accommodation of distributive conflict on government are burdened. (cf. Lehner 1987, 1988).

According to Olson (1986), we may expect that corporatist arrangements contain considerable rigidities resulting from the stability and exclusiveness of the relevant coalitions. The relatively high level of fiscal expansion provides some support for this conjecture. Some more support is received if we consider industrial policy in Austria. In the past years, Austria has had considerable difficulties in managing structural change in its industry. In many cases, corporatist structures have protected non-profitable industries by means of nationalization. Industrial modernization has proceeded and still proceeds at a rather low rate. Contrary to this, Sweden has managed industrial innovation well within its corporatist structures. Furthermore, Swedish industry secures a high level of competitiveness (cf. Katzenstein 1985).

Industrial policy in Sweden thus shows little signs of institutional rigidity which may be associated with corporatism, whereas, these rigidities are strongly effective in the Austrian case. These differences may hardly be explained by differences in the institutional structures of interest intermediation. Rather, they may be associated with economic conditions, namely the profitability and competiveness of industry and the way in which these conditions affect interest intermediation within corporatist structures.

In cases of large industries with low profitability and competiveness, the labour side usually has a strong interest in securing jobs in these industries. If these industries are sufficiently large, parts of the capital side (such as related business or financial institutions) may also have economic interests to secure the survival of these industries. In addition, the capital side has, within corporatist structures, a strong political interest in avoiding distributive conflict resulting from larger job losses and, thus, in securing industries with low profitability and competitiveness. Similarly, government has a political interest in avoiding larger job losses and related distributive conflicts. In such a situation, corporatist structures enhance protectionist strategies whose costs are covered by public expenses and, thereby, dispersed among the public-at-large. This is, to some extent, the case in Austria.

A different case exists if industries are profitable and competitive. In this situation, incentives for labor and capital pressing for government interventions are low. Jobs are secure and distributive conflicts can be solved or avoided by an agreed distribution of profits. Moreover, chances are high that growth allows for growing labour income and growing profits. Since there is no pressure from the concerned interest groups and no politically relevant distributive problem, government has no reason to intervene in a protectionist fashion. Rather, government as well as labor and capital, may have strong interests in providing for public policies enhancing growth, innovation, and competiveness in industry. This is, by-and-large, the case in Sweden.

By comparing Sweden and Austria, we may hardly hold that corporatist arrangements generally contain considerable rigidities. With good reasons, however, we may suggest that within corporatist arrangements rigidities and protectionist policies are likely to take place, if in the economy as a whole, or in significant parts of it, problems of profitability and competitiveness occur. If however, the economy as a whole along with its significant parts are in profitable and competitive condition, the integrated and exclusive structures of liberal corporatism enhance economically efficient policies. This is because they reduce the power and influence of special interests groups in the making of economic policy. (cf. Katzenstein 1984).

In this context, it is interesting to consider briefly the case of Japan. Japan has in the post-war period experienced a high rate of economic growth and innovation. Starting from the situation of scarcity in terms of capital, modern technology, and raw material after the war, it has meanwhile become one of the worlds leading industrial nations. This development is the result of a cohesive and elaborated policy of industrial modernization. This policy combines a number of different instruments. They include the support of private financing of innovation and export by means of regulation of financial markets, the support of competition on domestic markets and a strong protection against foreign competition, the building-up of a qualified education and science structure, as well as the provision of information and consulting services. (cf. Alten 1981; Rothwell/Zegveld 1981; Sato 1980)

Interestingly enough, within this policy, public financing of research and development in the private sector does not play an important role. Public financing only amounts to less than a third of gross expenditures on research and development. However, in most other OECD-countries, including the United States, the United Kingdom, France, Italy, and West Germany, public finances cover more than 40 % of gross expenditures on research and development. Moreover, a large part of public spending for research and developement is allocated to higher education and academic research. (OECD 1985).

In Japan, economic policy is embedded in an institutional arrangement that is characterized by a strong cooperation of governement, namely the Ministry of International Trade and Industry, and big enterprises in the modern industries. Similarly to corporatist arrangements, direct participation of socio-economic interests in economic policy-making is exclusively limited to a small number of large organizations in the private sector. Contrary to corporatist arrangements, there is no direct participation of labor in economic policy-making. The Japanese case is, therefore, sometimes considered as corporatism without labour. (Czada 1983; Lehmbruch 1984; Pempel/Tsunekawa 1979).

This classification is, however, misleading. Although direct participation in economic policy-making is limited to a small number of large organizations in the private sector, economic policy relies on a much more encompassing accomodation of distributive conflict and the formation of a far-reaching consensus in society. Distributive problems between capital and labour are, to a large extent, accomodated within the private sector by policies of the large companies. Moreover, economic policy, that is the policy of industrial modernization, is shaped in a way that also benefits much of business and industry, not directly participating in policy-making. Finally, strategies of persuasion and socialization produce and maintain value structures and attitudes in society that secure a far-reaching consensus on industrial modernisation. (Lehner 1987).

Considering this fundamental features of economic policy-making in Japan, we may associate the relevant institutional arrangement with a case of concordance rather than corporatism. Policy-making is based on the formation and maintainance of a large encompassing coalition among socio-economic interests. This coalition, however, is not formed on the basis of equal participation and voluntary agreement among socio-economic interests and political actors. Rather, it has a hierarchical structure. It is strongly dominated and led by big business and the Ministry of International Trade and Industry, it also relies on persuasive action of the leading actors.

This arrangement secures an encompassing interest aggregation on the one hand, while on the other reducing the transaction costs of interest intermediation and decision-making. Thus, it allows for a purposive and cohesive economic policy while still securing a high degree of societal consensus on or acceptance of economic policy.

An interesting contrast to the Japanese case is Switzerland. Like Japan, Switzerland is characterized by an encompassing coalition among socio-economic interests and a strategy of forming a wide consensus on public policy. Contrary to Japan, however, policy-making is not based on the dominance of big business or any other large interest group or peak association. Rather, it is based on consensual bargaining of a large number of interest groups and political actors. Whereas Japan has an encompassing, but hierarchical policy structure, the arrangement in Switzerland is one of pluralist participation, but encompassing bargaining. As a result of these features of consociational democracy, policy-making in Switzerland requires difficult negotiations of government. A large number of different interests will participate, and extensive compromising is needed to reach decisions that are widely accepted. Therefore, policy-making is usually associated with high transaction costs in terms of time and opportunity. (cf. Lehner 1983b, 1984).

These differences in the institutional arrangements strongly affect economic policy. Japan is a case of active, purposive, and cohesive political strategy which strives to advance modernization and to steer economic development. Switzerland is the opposite case, namely one of a liberal economic policy with a low amount of government intervention in the economy, and with attempts at purposely steering economic development. This is not only marked by a generally low amount of government activity and spending, but also by the absence of any developed industrial policy. In Switzerland, industrial modernization is, for the most part, a matter of the private sector, not of government. (Katzenstein 1984, 1985; Lehner 1986, 1987).

A good example for the different style of economic policy in the two countries is the regulation of banking. Japan has a credit-based financial system with administered prices that are used as an important instrument in industrial policy. Banking regulation attempts to channel funds into key industries and to secure a high provision of risk-capital by means of differential regulation and a system of compartmentalized prices guarantees the regulatory support of parcelling out corporate debts, tax arrangements, the legal prevention of bancruptcies, and other devices. Additional measures, such as regulations that facilitate foreign loans but inhibit foreign investments, or the control of the import and export of capital, supplement this strategy. Banking regulation and supplementary financial policies, thus, are a major instrument of industrial modernization policy. (cf. Zysman 1983).

In Switzerland, a credit-based system exists that is strongly dominated by banks with a strong influence on industry. Banking regulation is confined to minimum to secure deposits, to inhibit government control of deposits, and to maintain competition. Moreover, banking regulation is, to a considerable amount, delegated to nongovernmental or quasi-nongovernmental institution. Finally, there is almost no macro-economic component in banking regulation. Banking regulation is, therefore, not an effective tool for government interventions. Rather, it is the type of banking regulation that accomodates a liberal economic policy in a system with a low capacity of active and purposeful policy.

The case of Switzerland demonstrates that encompassing interest intermediation and policy-making, based on bargaining and consensus among a large number of interest groups and actors, is associated with high transaction costs that strongly limit the capacities for active and purposive interventions. In the case of Japan, a limited participation in policy-making and a hierarchical structure of the relevant institutional arrangements drastically reduce transaction costs and secures capacities for active and purposive policy. Activities in the private sector to accomodate distributive conflict and a wider distribution of the profits from policy nevertheless secure a sufficient consensus. Consensus, however, can only be reached as long as the interests of the dominating groups are sufficiently connected to these of other groups and as long as there exists a commonly accepted concept for economic policy and economic development. In contrast, consociational decision-making in Switzerland is but a formal bargaining mechanism and does not rely on substantial consensus.

Another interesting comparison with Japan is France. Similar to Japan, government, too, plays a leading role in economic policy and industrial modernization. Like Japan, France also uses banking regulation as an important instrument of industrial policy and has established a credit-based financial system with administered prices. This strategy is even more strongly developed in France than in Japan. French policy uses similar devices of compartmentalized prices, guarantees, control of capital import and export towards financial markets as does Japan. In addition, the government in France has acquired a strong control over banks by means of public ownership or public representation on boards. Moreover, the French government, especially the ministry of finance, undertakes strong activites as a financial intermediary and has established parastate institutions to operate in financial markets. Finally, unlike Japan, France makes strong use of subventions to channel capital into key industries.

There is, however, with respect to industrial policy and the utilization of banking regulation for that policy, a crucial difference between Japan and France. The difference concerns the cohesion of industrial policy and its role in economic policy. Whereas Japan has a highly cohesive industrial policy and subordinates all economic policy to a strategy of industrial modernization, the policy of industrial modernization in France is much less cohesive and not all economic policy is systematically oriented at industrial modernization. On the contrary, there exist competing economic policies protecting industries with low competiveness and low innovation. (Hayward 1982; Rothwell/Zegveld 1981; Zysman 1984)

This crucial difference with respect to economic policy may be explained by important differences in the relevant institutional arrangements. France has a very strong and powerful administration, a strongly interlocked elite structure, but a pluralist and little integrated interest intermediation. Moreover, there is little encompassing interest intermediation and policy-making, but much segmented policy-making. As a result, there is a strong need to provide for compensating benefits for a variety of socio-economic groups, which are negatively affected by industrial modernization. In addition, many groups have sufficient power to press for special interest policies. Consequently, in France there exist diverging or even competing economic policies rather than a cohesive strategy for economic development.

The comparison of France and Japan demonstrates again that there exists a rather strong relationship between institutional arrangements and public policy. More support for this hypothesis could be received if industrial policy in countries with pluralist structures, such as the United Kingdom or the United States, were also considered (see Lehner 1987).

Institutional Arrangements and Interest Intermediation: A Theoretical Approach

Analyzing policy-making in different institutional arrangements, one can well demonstrate the relevance and impact of these arrangements. It is much more difficult, however, to provide for a systematic explanation of this impact. Available theories often consist of only a set of rather unsophisticated hypotheses which are not systematically connected, and are often only vaguely formulated. The theory of liberal corporatism is a good example of this state of affairs. It consists of a large number of hypotheses and empirical generalizations concerning the development of corporatist structures, the conditions of their operation, and the impact of different degrees of corporatism regarding the regulation of distributive conflict and the concertation of social or economic policies. Yet, it still lacks a consistent theory based on a set of fundamental assumptions. (cf. Czada 1983; Katzenstein 1984; Lehmbruch 1984; Lehmbruch/Schmitter 1982; Schmitter 1981; Schmitter/Lehmbruch 1979).

A much more systematic theory is provided by Olson (1982). Based on his "Logic of Collective Action" (Olson 1965), he formulates a number of hypotheses on the behavior of interest groups with a different share in a nation's population and resources. Applying these hypotheses, he then derives conjectures regarding the impact of interest intermediation on economic development. Olson's theory, however, is narrow in scope because it only considers the relationship between the size of interest groups, that is their share in a nations population and resources, and their related incentives to press for efficient economic policies. It neglects institutional structures and other important conditions of interest intermediation. Therefore, it can only partially explain the cases we have discussed in the second part of this article. (Lehner 1983b, 1987, 1988).

Nevertheless, Oson's theory provides an interesting basis for further theoretical analysis of the relationship between the structure of interest intermediation and economic policy. In a recent article, Olson develops his hypotheses on the behavior of encompassing interest organizations (Olson 1986). He argues that the internal structure of encompassing organizations often reduces their capacity to support efficient policies. This is because the parts of organizations always have a smaller share of a nation's population and resources than the organization as a whole. This implies that the parts of an organization have less incentives than the organization as a whole to use their influence in favour of efficient policies. In those cases where some parts of an organization either have some autonomy, or have a considerable amount of influence on the decision-making of the organization as a whole, the organization's capacity to act in favour of efficient policies is reduced.

Generalizing, we may advance the following hypothesis: The larger either the autonomy or the influence of existing sub-organizations on the organizational decision-making, the less capacity an encompassing organization has to act in favour of efficient policies.

Such a situation exists in countries with so-called "medium corporatism" in the scaling of Czada (1983) and Lehmbruch (1984). These are countries with a broad scope of collective bargaining, but only sectoral participation. Countries with "medium corporatism" are for example Belgium, Denmark and West Germany. In contrast, countries with "strong corporatism", especially Sweden and Austria, are characterized not only by a broad scope of bargaining, but also by comprehensive interest intermediation and a tripartite coordination of policy-making in the public and private sector. In both types of countries, labor and capital form encompassing organizations, but they differ in their degree of centralization. In "medium corporatism" the organization of labor and capital is less centralized. The sectoral parts of the labor movement and business-associations have a considerable autonomy vis-à-vis the organization as a whole and a considerable influence on its activities. This makes, as experience in the Federal Republic of Germany demonstrates, the establishement of an effective concertation of policies difficult.

Moreover, the type of situation given in "medium corporatism" enhances, as Olson (1986) argues, the formation of sectoral cartels of labour and business. These sectoral cartels secure higher profits and wages than would exist in a more comprehensive situation. This results in inefficient wage policies which are associated with higher unemployment than would exist in a condition of efficient wage policies. With respect to employment, countries with "medium corporatism" therefore, often perform less than those with "strong corporatism". Empirical data support this argument (cf. Lehner 1987, 1988).

In this context, Switzerland again constitutes an interesting case. Consociational decision-making in Switzerland is a highly encompassing arrangement of interest intermediation. It is, however, not based on encompassing organizations of interests. Labour unions, business associations, parties, and other relevant organizations are, on the contrary, strongly decentralized. There is a considerable sectoral decentralization, but more important is the fragmentation of interest organization along federal lines. Within the decentralized federal system of Switzerland, the interest organizations in the different cantons possess a high autonomy and power vis-à-vis their national organizations. Indeed, as far as interest organization is concerned, Switzerland has a highly pluralist and segmented structure. This structure is, however, overlayed by conditions and procedures of interest intermediation and policy-making that are factually based on a close-to-unanimity rule. These proceedures, not the organization of interests itself, provide for an encompassing interest intermediation. They are especially effective in imposing strong restrictions on the power of interest organizations and the formation of distributive coalitions with narrow scope. (cf. Lehner 1984; Lehner/Homann 1987).

The case of Switzerland demonstrates that a decentralized and fragmented structure of interest organization is not necessarily associated with high power of special interests and inefficient policy. Comprehensive procedures enforcing the formation of encompassing distributive coalitions may have similar effects as does an encompassing organization of interests. This is not a new and surprising insight, but may be theoretically explained.

According to Buchanan and Tullock (1962), the efficiency of collective decisions may be analyzed in terms of two kinds of costs involved. One type is decision costs. This includes effort, time, and losses in opportunity that have to be invested to reach a decision. The other type is externalities, which are costs imposed on members of the collectivity who have no adequate return from the decision. The two kinds of costs vary differently with the relative number of members of a collectivity who have to agree on collective decisions: decision costs increase as this number increases, whereas externalities decrease at the same time. If an unanimity rule is applied, externalities are zero and transaction costs extremely high. Theoretically, there is a required majority below unanimity at which the sum of decision costs and externalities, that is the total transaction costs, reach an optimum.

As consociational democracy in Switzerland operates under a close-to-unanimity rule, it is capable of minimizing externalities, but involves high decision costs. Policy decisions, therefore, as they are highly fitted to different socio-economic interests are insofar efficient. But high decision costs reduce efficiency to a higher or lower degree. As will be discussed later, the extent to which decisions costs reduce efficiency, however, depends upon the type of policy performed.

The theoretical argument applied to the Swiss case may be generalized and used to analyze the transaction costs involved in different types of encompassing interest intermediation and policy-making. Decision rules and other conditions determining required majorities obviously affect the size of distributive coalitions in terms of the number of participating interest groups and their share of a nation's population and resources. If rules and conditions contain or imply high majority requirements they force societal interests to form large and encompassing coalitions.

Such coalitions may be formed by a small number of large and encompassing organizations, or by a large number of smaller special interest groups, or by a mixed constellation. These different ways of forming an encompassing coalition determines its transaction costs. A coalition of few large organizations involves much lower decision costs than does a coalition of a large number of small special interest groups. At the same time, a coalition of few large organizations is more likely to produce considerable externalities than is a coalition of a large number of small special interest groups.

This may, however, not be the case, if the large organizations are composed of sub-organizations, with a considerable autonomy and influence on the organizations behaviour. Such a coalition is similar to a coalition of a large number of small special interest groups. Also, it is associated with high decision costs, but low externalities.

The side cost of the argument just outlined is obvious. Less obvious, however, is that a coalition of few large organisations is more likely to produce considerable externalities than is a coalition of a large number of small special interest groups. There are two reasons for this. First, a situation in which a large number of different policy interests have to be agreed on contains much more mutual checks and balances. Furthermore, decisions can only be made at a low common denominator, that is, at the level of rather broad and general interests. A few large organizations may find an agreement that better fits the special interests of the participating interests. Second, large organizations representing a considerable share of a nation's population and resources also have considerable political power. A coalition of such organizations gains enough power to externalize the costs of the commonly agreed policy to non-participating groups.

A good example for the externalization of costs by encompassing coalitions formed by large organizations is neo-corporatism in Sweden, Norway and Austria. During most of the post-war period, these countries economically exceeded the average performing OECD-countries. They have been especially successful in managing distributive conflict and securing employment by means of income policy and active labour market policy. They have, however, performed badly with respect to fiscal expansion measured in terms of public outlays, public debts, and taxation.

Encompassing coalitions formed by large centralized organizations and the low decision-costs associated with this arrangement secure high capacities for active income and labour market policies which are at the roots of the economic success in these countries. At the same time, firstly, this arrangement, according to our argument, is associated with a considerable concentration of political power by a few large organizations. And secondly, these organizations enjoy the considerable capacity to externalize some of the costs of the income and labour market policies they commonly agreed on beforehand. More specifically, the costs of these policies are financed by the public budget, rather than by contributions from employers and labour, as it is the case in other countries. Costs are thus partially externalized to interest groups that are not included in neo-corporatist policy-making. A consequence of this strategy is fiscal expansion in the public sector.

Such a strategy is hardly possible in an arrangement where a large number of different interests participate in encompassing coalitions, such as is found in the type of consociational decision-making. Indeed, Switzerland performs extremely well with respect to the fiscal expansion of the public sector. Public outlays and debts, as well as taxation are far below the level reached in all other OECD-countries. The reason is that consociational decision-making hardly allows for the externalization of public policy costs. However, the price for this is, as we have discussed earlier in this article, extremely low capacities for active and purposeful interventions into economic developments.

An interesting mix of consociational decision-making and neo-corporatism is found in Japan. It is consociational insofar as it relies on extensive social, cultural and economic strategies to base economic policy on a wide societal consensus. At the same time, it contains strong elements of corporatism because only a few large organizations participate directly in policy-making. Obviously, this type of arrangement is associated with externalities which are lower than in the case of neo-corporatism, as well as with decision-costs which are lower than in the case of consociational decision-making. It thus contains considerable capacities for active and purposeful policies, yet this type of arrangements limits the externalization of costs of these policies.

At this point, it is important to briefly discuss the extent to which decision-costs reduce policy efficiency. When we speak of high decision-costs, we are essentially referring to situations where decisions take a long time and require high efforts, in terms of bargaining and compromising. High efforts in terms of bargaining and compromising, imply that decision-making is usually inflexible, the range of possible decisions is small, and that the selectivity of decision-making is low. Consequently, in arrangements associated with high decision-costs it is usally difficult to agree on active and purposeful policies to selectively intervene in economic developments. Moreover, it is usually difficult to adjust policy-making rapidly to changing socio-economic conditions.

This, however, does not imply that arrangements associated with high decision-costs generally have low capacities to manage economic policy. On the contrary, inclusive participation and extensive bargaining enhance policies that are based on widely shared general interests and gain a high stability over time. Arrangements associated with high decision-costs are thus well designed to decide and effectuate long-dated structural policies.

Long-dated structural policies are appropriate to secure economic performance in a condition of a well-developed competitive economy and favourable economic structures. In this condition, high decision-costs do not negatively affect the efficiency of economic policy, but rather advance it. Market forces are capable of securing a favourable economic development in terms of growth, employment, and innovation. Also, economic policy may be confined to create and maintain functionable market conditions. This is why Switzerland reaches a high economic performance, although economic policy is embedded in an arrangement associated with high decision-costs.

In particular cases, market forces are not capable of securing a sufficiently high rate of growth, employment, or innovation. Nor are they able to develop competitive industries and business. This frequently occurs in an economic environment characterized by scarcity of capital, raw material, and modern technology, as well as by a lack of competitive business and industry, or unfavourable economic structures (e.g. a dominance of old industries or industries with low competitiveness). In such situations, active and purposeful policies may be capable of providing for a faster and better economic development than would occur under a pure market regime. If this is the case, arrangements associated with high decision-costs negatively affect the efficiency of economic policy, and arrangements with lower decision-costs may provide for better policy performance. Japan serves is a good example for this situation.

Generally speaking, we assume that different institutional arrangements are associated with different constellations concerning decision-costs and externalities. Thus, they contain specific capacities and restrictions with respect to policy-making. For any given institutional arrangement there exists a larger or smaller set of policies which can be effectively performed within this arrangement. Whether this allows for efficient economic policy or not, depends upon the degree to which one or more of the policies in that set are appropriate to the relevant economic conditions. When we analyze the relationship between institutional arrangements, public policies and economic performance, we are thus concerned with the relationship between institutionally determined policy-capacities on one side and certain economic conditions on the other.

Conclusion

In this article, I have outlined a theoretical approach to analyzing the capacity of different institutional arrangements to provide for efficient economic policy and high economic performance. The approach is one in terms of decision-costs, and externalities associated with different institutional arrangements. This approach may be further developed by considering transaction costs, their different components and the factors determining them in more detail. The hope is that a further development of this approach will lead to a rather simple, but fruitful theory.

254 Franz Lehner

References

Alten, G.C. (1981) 'Industrial Policy and Innovation in Japan' in Charles Carter (ed.) *Industrial Policy and Innovation*. London: Heinemann.

Buchanan, James M. (1975) *The Limits of Liberty*. Chicago: University of Chicago Press.

Buchanan, James M. and G. Tullock (1962) *The Calculus of Consent*. Ann Arbor: University of Michigan Press.

Crozier, Michel, S. Peter Huntington and J. Watanuki (1975) *The Crisis of Democracy*. New York: New York University Press.

Czada, Roland (1983) 'Konsensbedingungen und Auswirkungen neokorporatistischer Politikentwicklung', *Journal für Sozialforschung*, 23: 421-39.

Hayward, Jack (1982) 'Mobilising Private Interests in the Service of Public Ambitions: The Salient Element in the Dual French Policy Style?', in J. Richardson (ed.) *Policy Styles in Western Europe*. London: George Allan & Unwin.

Katzenstein, Peter J. (1984) *Corporatism and Change*. Ithaca-London: Cornell University Press.

Katzenstein, Peter J. (1985) *Small States in World Markets*. Ithaca-London: Cornell University Press.

Lehmbruch, Gerhard, (1984) 'Concertation and the Structure of Corporatist Networks', in J. Goldthorpe (ed.) *Order and Conflict in Contemporary Capitalism*. Oxford: Clarendon Press.

Lehmbruch, Gerhard and Philippe C. Schmitter (eds.)(1982) *Patterns of Corporatist Policy-Making*. Beverly-Hills-London: Sage.

Lehner, Franz (1983a) 'The Vanishing of Spontaneity: Socio-Economic Conditions of the Welfare State', *European Journal of Political Research*, 11: 437-444.

Lehner, Franz (1983b) 'Pressure Politics and Economic Growth: Olsons Theory and the Swiss Experience', in D.C. Mueller (ed.) *The Political Economy of Growth*. New Haven-London: Yale University Press.

Lehner, Franz (1984) 'Consociational Democracy in Switzerland: A Political-Economic Explanation and Some Empirical Evidence', *European Journal of Political Research*, 12: 25-42.

Lehner, Franz (1986) 'Strukturen und Strategien der Technologiepolitik. Eine vergleichende Analyse', in Hans-Hermann Hartwich (Hg.) *Politik und die Macht der Technik*. Opladen: Westdeutscher Verlag

Lehner, Franz (1987) 'Interest Intermediation, Institutional Structures and Public Policy', pp. 54-82 in Keman, Hans, Heikki Paloheimo, and Paul F. Whiteley(eds.), *Coping with the Economic Crisis*, London, Beverly Hills: Sage

Lehner, Franz (1988) 'The Political Economy of Distributive Conflict', pp. 54-96 in Francis G. Castles, Franz Lehner and Manfred G. Schmidt (eds.) *Managing Mixed Economies*. Berlin-New York: Walter de Gruyter.

Lehner, Franz and B. Homann (1987) 'Consociational Decision-Making and Party Government in Switzerland', in R.S. Katz (ed.) *Party Governments: European and American Experiences*. Berlin-New York: Walter de Gruyter.

Lehner, Franz and Jürgen Nordhause-Janz (1988) 'Die Politische Ökonomie gesellschaftlicher Verteilungskonflikte: Möglichkeiten, Grenzen und Defizite staatlicher Wirtschaftspolitik', pp. 38-60 in Manfred G. Schmidt (ed.) *Staatstätigkeit*. Opladen: Westdeutscher Verlag.

OECD (1985) *Science and Technology Indicators*. Paris: OECD-publications.

Olson, Mancur (1965) *The Logic of Collective Action*. Cambridge: Harvard University Press.

Olson, Mancur (1982) *The Rise and Decline of Nations*. New Haven-London: Yale University Press.

Olson, Mancur (1986) 'A Theory of the Incentives Facing Political Organizations', *International Political Science Review*, 7:165-189

Paloheimo, Heikki (1984) 'Distributive Struggle and Economic Development in the 1970's', *European Journal of Political Research*, 12: 171-89.

Pempel, T.J. and K. Tsunekawa (1979) 'Corporatism Without Labour? The Japanese Anomaly', in P.C. Schmitter and G. Lehmbruch (eds.)(1979) *Trends Towards Corporatist Intermediation*. Beverly Hills-London: Sage.

Rothwell, Ray and Walter Zegveld (1981) *Industrial Innovation and Public Policy: Preparing for the 1980s and the 1990s*. London: Frances Pinter.

Sato, Kazuo (ed.) (1980) *Industry and Business in Japan*. New York: Sharpe.

Schmidt, Manfred G. (1988) 'The Politics of Labour Market Policy: Structural and Political Determinants of Rates of Unemployment in Industrial Nations', pp. 4-53 in Francis G. Castles, Franz Lehner and Manfred G. Schmidt (eds.) *Managing Mixed Economies*. Berlin-New York: Walter de Gruyter.

Schmitter, Philippe C. (1981) 'Interest Intermediation and Regime Governability in Western Europe and North America', pp. 287-330 in S. Berger (ed.) *Organizing Interests in Western Europe*. New York: Cambridge University Press.

Schmitter, Philippe C. and Gerhard Lehmbruch (eds.)(1979) *Trends Towards Corporatist Intermediation*. Beverly Hills-London: Sage.

Zysman, John (1984) *Governments, Markets, and Growth*. Ithaca-London: Cornell University Press.

IX

Interest Groups, Self-Interest, and the Institutionalization of Political Action[*]

Roland M. Czada

Institutions often constrain choices. Simultaneously they provide advantages through routinization and opportunities for strategic interaction. The individual and social benefits of interactional rules and collective organizations have been emphasized in this volume. Another view prevails however, which focuses on the losses of wealth and freedom due to unrestricted growth, stickiness, and economic malfeasance of institutions. The idea of modern man being entrapped by institutions is common to many grand theories of society and politics. One can find it in Marx's critique of capitalism, as well as in Weber's theory of rationalization, when he considers the irrational and illiberal features of the "iron cage" of bureaucracy.

In contrast to many social theories, economists have often propagated an optimistic view of open societies with competitive politics and free economic markets. Nowadays, however, some of their concepts tend to remind us of somewhat aged social theories of decline. Mancur Olson (1982), who predicts social rigidities and economic losses through an increase of monopolistic narrow interest groups,

[*]   I wish to thank Berndt Keller, Karin Tritt, and Frans van Waarden for their critical comments on earlier versions of this chapter.

represents a most notable approach of this school of thought. Applying the economic paradigm to the explanation of political choices offers new insights, yet simultaneously marks the limitations of the neoclassical approach. In particular, the belief in mutually beneficial voluntary exchanges, leading to economic equilibria and social welfare, has been shaken, and the quest for efficient institutions of capitalism has come to the fore.

Rational actors in institutional settings

The institutionalization of action still poses unresolved problems for theoretical formulation. In a macro-to-micro perspective, rules appear to be functional, because they guide actors through otherwise uncertain environments, and restrict socially harmful individual passions. In an individualist rational choice approach, however, institutionalization has been discussed as a *public goods problem*. From this perspective, it may seem inconceiveable that individuals could be organized on a voluntary basis for the purpose of rule-building - rules that impose duties, obligations, and roles on them.

Individualist social theories rely on the assumption that social states are no more than *aggregates* of individual choices - though they have different notions on the mechanisms of aggregation. The Public Choice School concentrates on problems of *collective decision-making*. Game theory emphasizes *strategic interaction* between individuals. Both approaches imply that collective or social states emerge from the transitory coupling of individual rational choices. This constitutes a market-like aggregative process which is conceived as highly adaptive and open for social change. Thus, public choice and game theories do not provide an appropriate understanding of rigid, highly regulated social systems. A perspective of political control must be added to the utilitarian notion of rational choice, if the formation and existence of societal order is to be theoretically grasped. I will start from the assumption that a theory of order that is able to avoid falling into mere functionalism or metaphysical explanations has to take collective action as its point of departure. Collective action necessarily involves the formation and maintenance of social regulations. Collective action as I will show, is essentially political; it usually involves the power to accumulate and redistribute resources from and among individuals.

What does the step from classic Social Choice Analysis to the Logic of Collective Action entail? Olson (1982) combined the individualist approach with an *associational* concept of "social closure". According to him, freedom of association favors powerful associational monopolies with narrowly defined interests. This ends up in a downward spiral in which the rationally motivated social closure of interests causes social rigitities and economic decline. Thus he assumes a positive linear relationship of associational power, monopolistic regulations, and economic losses. In contrast, public choice and game theories tend to locate individual action in *atomistic* egalitarian social ecologies, and thus discover basic social rules of reciprocity at best (e.g. Axelrod 1984).

The aim of this chapter is to explain collective choices pertaining to institutionalization. While tackling this, the one-directional micro-to-macro perspective of choice will be turned round. This, however, is not to abandon the idea of self-interest as being a major source of action. It will be shown that attributes of macro-structures - e.g. the institutionally determined *costs of lobbying vs. corporatist concertation*, associational *powers*, or the *relieving properties of interactional rules* - influence actor's choices as they refer to these structures. Often choices do not strategically depend on certain other actors' choices directly, but on rational expectations of how "impersonal" social rules or structures affect them and, additionally, determine one's own pay-offs from these choices. Public policy-making aimed at regulating social aggregates would be a case in point.

To found or restructure an organization involves another kind of choice than just to accept or utilize its rules. The latter intends to avoid sanctions or to exchange goods and services directly, or through networks of *generalized exchange* (cf. Marin 1990). The former is to prepare or strengthen an actor for future transactions. This however appears to be essentially political. Institutional political choices determine an actor's future position among other actors within an organizational domain and in interorganizational networks. In the following section the contrast of compensatory mutual *exchanges* between *complementary interests* on the one hand and the *political association* or *distributive conflict* of *parallel interests* on the other requires elaboration in order to establish the notion of political choice.

Game theory and the problem of institutionalization

Among the most elaborated individualist explanations of rule formation one finds Axelrod's (1984) game-theoretical work on the "Evolution of Cooperation". Doing without corporate actors, Axelrod explains the social expansion of a cooperative individual strategy - *"Tit for Tat"* - within a greater social population. "Tit for Tat" is a simple rule of reciprocity. It means to cooperate first, but to answer other's defections with punishment, i.e. counter-defection.

In Axelrod's concept, cooperation occurs between two actors at a time. A cooperative order, then, is an accumulation of bipartite cooperative acts. In terms of individual pay-offs, "Tit for Tat" proved to be the most successful of 64 strategies in a computer-aided experiment of iterated *Prisoner's Dilemma* games. Cooperation on this reciprocal basis was more rewarding than any other rule of strategic interaction. Thus, the pursuit of individual interests can help to spread a rule of reciprocity that could be considered as a prelude to cooperative social order. Axelrod himself discusses bipartite compensatory exchanges as possible sources of social rules, i.e. more or less explicit arrangements involving not only individuals but also collectivities.

To establish a cooperative rule, however, requires a learning-process in the course of which individuals must recognize that the restraining of their immediate interests or passions will generate positive pay-offs for them in the long run. Cooperation appears to be unstable, due to continuous temptations to betray the good will of others. Once established, a cooperative order based on Tit for Tat is also highly vulnerable to "invaders", who "travel around" and exploit the general trust involved in a cooperative rule. The problem of "invaders" could easily be solved by a public register or a penal authority for instance. Axelrod (1984:109 pp.) recommends this and several other measures to cope with the problem, for instance: extend the "shadow of the future", change pay-off-structures, or teach the people to cooperate. Thus, he acknowledges the necessity of an authority that enables institutions to undertake these measures.

Axelrod's approach indicates the social benefits of a government. However, it does not explain how governance emerges. Game theory can handle the evolution of a basic rule of reciprocity, but the establishment of authoritative institutions does not fit into the game theoretical approach. Introducing a particular actor who is authorized to enforce social rules would break up the paradigm of voluntary, discourse-free, costless exchanges between atomized and equally strong actors.[2]

In Axelrod's view, cooperation evolves from unhappy experiences with conflict. Actors punishing each other have to bear losses and thus come out worse than those following a cooperative norm. This is why Tit for Tat can develop into a *collectively stable strategy*. However, it resolves an iterated prisoner's dilemma only when the actors are *equally dependent* on each other, and thus possess *equal forces* to punish. If an actor was able to compel cooperation from others, Tit for Tat would obviously lose its significance. The same holds for game theory in general: Hierarchies enable one-sided solutions imposed by one actor and thus, diminish interactional dilemmas.

To assume that societal order is being derived from *power dependencies* is certainly realistic. Domination, however, should not be confused with a rule-system based on mutually beneficial exchanges. Otherwise a notion of politics would remain that resembles a marketplace which everybody could leave as a satisfied "customer".

Political associations and the formation of power

In social life and in the reality of politics we find actors of unequal strength. Power dependencies are derived from unevenly distributed charismatic, financial, dynastic, or informational resources. These can be organized in order to increase one's power position, to win

---

2   Of course, these assumptions can be applied loosely. However, if economists account for real-world phenomena such as power-dependencies, normative behavior, ideological discourse, and transaction-costs, their argument hardly becomes more realistic (cf. Elster 1986).

legitimacy, or to withstand external opposition. Generally this requires some form of associational action. Individuals often act as parts - members or leaders - of groups in order to improve their position vis à vis competitors. This is an essential feature of political action. "Organized groups are structures of power, and therefore within the scope of political inquiry" (Latham 1952:17).

The capacity and power of corporate actors to act, e.g. labor unions or business associations, depends on *group sizes*, organizational *resources*, and not least on their ability to *disrupt* the productive basis of society. Putting aside these important structural aspects, however, one can say that the essential power-base of corporate actors evolves from the *pooling* of individual resources (Coleman 1986) and the consequential conversion of individual competences into organizational authority. Structures of authority enable inter-organizational relations on the leadership level and contribute to the solution of internal distributive conflicts.

How to employ the dues and gains from membership can be decided in a more discursive, oligarchic, or autocratic manner. However, some sort of agency is needed to organize decision-making and implement decisions. Processes of consensus mobilization, social control, and bureaucratization determine the autonomy and political power of corporate actors. They cannot be understood from an exchange paradigm as employed by game-theoretical analysis. This might be one reason why "Axelrod's ... model has been taken up by biologists more enthusiastically than by social scientists" (McLean 1987:147).

Game-theoretical exchange-models of interaction imply exogenously given, single, *complementary* interests of two actors involved at a time. Now, *mutual* complementary interests and *joint* interests can be viewed as quite different sources of cooperation. Max Weber distinguished "the rational free exchange on a market, a case of agreement which constitutes a compromise of opposed but complementary interests", from: "the pure voluntary association based on (parallel, R.C.) self-interests, a case of agreement as to a long-run course of action oriented purely to the promotion of specific ulterior interests, economic or other, of its members" (Weber 1968:41).

Cooperative behavior is either based on the "rationally motivated mutal compensation of interests, or on a similarly motivated union-ization of interests" (ibid).[3] Moreover, one has to distinguish between *complementary* and *parallel* interests, and distinguish both of these from *conflicting* interests. Politial and economic actors can face each other as potential *exchange-partners, associates,* or *competitors*. In reality, the recourse to these patterns of behavior is open to strategic choices. One can find them in highly volatile mixtures, depending on actors' goals, available resources, changing environments, and power-dependencies. Mechanisms of exchange and competition - the *"invisible hand"* of markets or process of *"creative destruction"* as Schumpeter called it - have been investigated by economists for a long time. How they interact with *"protectionist"* interest associations is still an open question which is heavily disputed by politicians and academic experts. The association of convergent interests appears to be much more a theoretical problem than explaining relations of ex-change or competition.

Markets can be understood without the notion of an actor, since a process occuring "behind the backs" of men translates their individ-ual choices into social choices and, in this manner, determines the macro-level consequences of individual actions. In contrast, interest associations supersede the transitory coupling of atomized actors. They try to influence or organize self-regulatory social processes. As far as the formal association of parallel interests is concerned, a pro-portion of agreement and an "organ" - authority or executive body - is required in order to maintain and manage an association (with re-gard to its internal, as well as external relations). This is the point at which *politics* as a force of *social integration* comes into play.

This line of reasoning leads back to Olson's theory of collective action. Its core argument points to *social closure* evoked by pre-dominant narrow interest associations. In his view, narrow interest

---

3   New translation of Weber (1972:21). Weber explicitly contrasted the compensation of interests (Interessenausgleich) with the unionization of interests (Interessenverbindung).

groups are based on collusion among their members. Using the term
"collusion", Olson emphazises the social harmfulness and par-
ticularism of such groups. According to him, *collusive action* creates
social powers and regulates social exchanges. Eventually it fosters
social rigidities and standardization, and thus reduces the opportunities of choice between alternative paths of action.

Wrestlers in a china shop

Olson demonstrates that the conditions for organizing interests vary
by group size: there is little incentive to join large interest-orga-
nizations, because they act independently from an individual's contribution. In small groups, however, individual membership might
decide upon the supply of a collective good. Thus, the organization
of small groups is encouraged by their member's individual interests,
whereas large groups suffer from opportunism and free-riding.
These arguments refute the pluralist belief in symmetrical organization and representation. In Weber's (1968:344 pp.) terms, this would
mean that *monopolistic* groups - based on social closure - can be organized more easily than *propagandistic* expansionist ones, and hence
will eventually dominate society and politics.

Monopolistic group action "may provoke a corresponding reaction on the part of those against whom it is directed" (ibid:342). This
holds even more so, when negatively afflicted groups have narrowly
defined interests and are small in size. For small groups can easily
associate and oppose monopolistic policies. The question arises as to
the extent that competition among small special-interest groups
contributes to allocative efficiency. Distributional coalitions that nul-
lify or offset the effects of others, and thereby increase the efficiency
and income of the society, are conceivable. Olson (1982:46 pp.) views
them as an exception proving the rule. In this section I will discuss
how special interest groups typically interact with each other.
Thinking of narrow interest groups as "wrestlers struggling over the
contents of a china shop", Olson emphasizes the zero-sum character
of distributional fights for shares of a shrinking national product. Yet
in the long run, he predicts, the emergence of a rigid distributional

order and the stickiness of wages, prices, and social structures will result from such struggles.

Olson does not consider that powerful "narrow" interest groups, by competing for their shares of the social product, usually attenuate each other's associational power. For example, as far as economic competition between cartels is concerned, one can observe rivalries of concrete and asphalt interests in the Austrian road construction sector (Marin 1986). There, associational monopolies fought against each other eventually to the advantage of the society as a whole. Now one could engage in an experiment of thought, and argue that all road construction interests would probably merge into a super-cartel sooner or later. Prices of road-construction would rise then, and both the concrete and asphalt interests could profit, whereas the general interest in useful and reasonably priced roads would suffer. Such mergers, however, increase the size and divisiveness of organizations, which no longer represent narrow interests. A road-construction cartel will eventually be threatened by persisting conflicts between subgroups of concrete and asphalt firms. More-over, there are other special-interest groups in society which are strongly in favor of the construction of many excellent roads with a given budget. A car producers' association would certainly not accept the dead-weight-losses from collusive action on the part of road constructors, since this interferes with their specific interests in individual transport and marketing of cars. This shows that groups with narrowly defined interests cannot be further monopolized in larger and larger organizational units, because they compete with each other. In particular, organizational problems tend to increase as the level of inclusion increases. At least, Olson's theory itself rejects the idea of an autonomous trend towards highly centralized trans-sectoral encompassing associations.

In distributional struggles no one can gain without others losing. This generates resentment and political divisiveness. It restricts en-during or stable political choices, and can make societies un-governable (Olson 1982:47). Not all relations between special in-terest-groups, however, are distributional struggles in this sense. Overlapping interests in high prices of road-construction show that asphalt and concrete associations have an incentive to cooperate. Simple turn-taking, or any agreement on a quota of concrete and asphaltic roads to be built, would probably stabilize their inter-relationship. This scenario resembles Fritz W. Scharpf's (this volume) game-theoretical analysis of "Battle of the Sexes" constellations, where players have common and opposed interests at the same time. In a two-actors view, turn-taking is a way of rational *"problem solving"* that appears to be fair and optimal. According to Scharpf (p. 71), this is the "socially most desirable decision style", since it affords both actors the highest joint outcome. In the context of interest-politics of narrowly defined groups and economic cartels, however, this kind of agreement can be most harmful for the society as a whole.[4]

The enforcement of rules

To establish a multitude of associational orders causes severe problems when the relations between associations are concerned. These problems are due to distributional conflicts which, like collusive associations themselves, result from self-interest in the face of scarce resources in society.

Assuming a car-manufacturing association, whose members suffer from inefficiencies caused by a road-construction cartel, we approach a "zero-sum" constellation. One could also consider conflicts between a farmer's association and a cartel of farm-machinery manufacturers, between publishing-houses and a cartel of paper-mills, between car manufacturers and the rolled steel industry, and so forth. Sooner or later, distributional conflicts will arise between such groups which can hardly be solved through turn-taking or mutually beneficial exchanges. Otherwise we would have cartels of cartels of cartels..., with ultimately one cartel encompassing the whole economy. This, however, is an absurd idea in the face of distributional conflict over scarce resources. The only way for

---

4 "Problem-Solving" hardly solves problems that are caused by its possible negative external effects. Even state actors in a segmented polity can solve their interactional dilemmas at the expense of third parties. Thus, in a two actors model of politics - statist or societal - turn-taking does not provide a general solution to political conflicts over scarce resources.

antagonistic groups to "cooperate" in order to escape from "zero-sum" distributional struggles are either to introduce compensatory side-payments, or to establish hierarchical power-dependencies between them. Compensations of groups for their losses from other's monopolistic actions will hardly be voluntary. Both compensatory transfers between social groups and the enforcement of rules regulating their inter-relations appear to be typical tasks of governments. However, a government enforcing compensatory transfers cannot emerge from a voluntary contract. As soon as one adds features of social closure and group action to individualistic contract theories of state formation, it becomes evident that strong groups have no reason to agree on the establishment of a sanctioning power that eventually constrains their freedom of action.[5] On the contrary, monopolistic associations will probably urge on the universalization of rules protecting their priviledged status.

One should assume that the concentration and centralization of social power and ensuing translation into a legitimate political authority have emerged from monopolistic interests and differentials of group power in the face of distributional conflict. This is what Max Weber argued in "Economy and Society":

> "In spite of their continued competition against one another, jointly acting competitors form an "interest group" toward outsiders; there is a growing tendency to set up some kind of association with rational regulations; if the monopolistic interests persist, the time comes when the competitors, or another group whom they can influence (for example a political community) establish a legal order that limits competition through formal monopolies. From then on certain persons are available as "organs" to protect the monopolistic practices, if need be, with force. An interest group has become a "corporate body", and the particpants

---

5   Generally, utilitarian contract theories (see Brennan and Buchanan 1985 for instance) provide for ex-post rationalizations of statehood and political order. Though logically correct, they cannot explain how the state of a social contract practically emerges. To establish societal order, whether it is being imposed or freely agreed upon, requires collective organization first. Theories of order involving collective action therefore have to embody a concept of political control of social organizations.

are "privileged members" (Rechtsgemeinschaft). Such closure, as we want to call it, is an ever-recurring process; it is
the source of property in land as well as of all guild and
other group monopolies". (Weber 1968:343, see also Weber
1972:201).

Weber shows that rule-formation and the propagation of a legal order are concomitants of rationally motivated *social closure* through
monopolistic groups. Monopolistic interests in rule-formation aim at
the strenghtening of power. Therefore, striving for power is a motor
for the building of economic and political structures. Simultaneously,
such structures guide the use of power and moreover, make social
transactions calculable. Now, the *ordering potential of group-power* is
completely neglected in Olson's Theory of Collective Action. On the
contrary, emphasis is laid on the notion that it is entirely destructive
to social life and particularly to economic markets.

Weber conceives of social closure and the accumulation of power
as one particular source - among others - of rational organization and
the formation of law. This view contrasts sharply with Olson's scenario of an ever-increasing downward spiral in which growing
numbers of narrow-interest associations, rigid distributional structures, and economic decline reinforce each other. In the following, I
will discuss possible correlations of social closure, regulatory
powers, and economic efficiency.

Reality provides for an intricate, often positive relationship between "rigid" formalization and substantive rationality.[6] In a Weberian tradition, effectiveness has always been considered as a concomitant of institutional regulation. This can be assumed for reasons,
like the "predictability", "routinization", and "lower frictions" of institutionalized social interactions (Weber 1972:561 pp.). Here one
comes close to some ideas of *Transaction Cost Economics* (Williamson
1985, cf. Schneiberg and Hollingsworth, this volume). Transaction
cost-saving properties of organizations have also been neglected in
Olson's theory. To consider them would certainly modify the sce-

---

6   March and Olsen (1989) with their appraisal of standard operating proceedures
    and garbage can solutions stand close to this Weberian argument (cf. Johan
    Olsen's contribution in this volume, Weber 1972).

nario of economic decline as it results from interest groups' organizational action.

Williamson (1975) discovered that in many instances industrial organization reduces the costs of economic transactions. This applies to transactions which are *frequent*, highly *asset-specific*, and threatened by *uncertainty* (Williamson 1985;52). Under these circumstances, the allocative efficiency of organizational rules is superior to that of exchanges on markets. Williamson's work deals exclusively with micro-economic institutions: contractual relationships and corporate hierarchies. Others extended this approach to additional forms of institutional coordination, namely *"clans"* (Ouchi 1980) and *associations* (Lindberg and Hollingsworth 1985). Frequency, uncertainty, and the involvement of human assets characterize many kinds of social relations, and probably all kinds of political relations. These issues could also be understood in terms of transaction costs (North 1981, cf. Lehner, this volume, Schneiberg and Hollingsworth, this volume).

Transaction Cost Economics attribute cost-saving properties to non-market institutional rules of coordination - regardless of how they once emerged. Contrasting views on the efficiency of markets and organizations are due to the application of different time-horizons. In the short run, bipartite exchanges on spot markets minimize the costs of actual transactions, but leave future transactions in uncertainty. This impedes investments, and thus limits the development of productivity. Institutionalization, in contrast, widens the time-horizon of action and stabilizes rational expectations of individuals. Institutions make decisions more calculable, and enable actors to build complex long-term strategies. Such an *investment in future transactions*, however, poses *collective goods problems* as have been mentioned above. Thus, leaving out the dimension of associational power, Transaction Cost Economics cannot explain how institutions emerge (cf. Schneiberg and Hollingsworth, this volume, p. 223). However, it can explain why the *political* regulation of markets does not necessarily result in economic decline. Yet the question remains: how is the tendency towards overregulation eventually checked? Obviously, rigid organization and the disorganized transitory coupling of actors are both apt to cause losses of wealth. Accordingly, how can appropriate levels of formalization be determined by actors, wanting to *minimize frictions* and *maximize certainty* in organizational settings?

Of course, selection through competitive social environments as emphasized by Schneiberg and Hollingworth (this volume, p. 218) may be an effective way to prevent ever increasing organizational rigidities. However, in politics - defined as the strife for power-share (Weber 1965) - actors seek to evade adaptive pressures from turbulent environments. In contrast to economic markets, survival of the fittest does not necessarily mean that the most efficient organization survives, but rather the most powerful one. Thus, one has to ask about the relations between associational power and the efficiency of policies. As will be shown below, the political power of associations depends on many factors: organizational size, complexity of tasks, inter-organizational networks, social embeddedness, and not the least on economic resources. The scarcity of the latter determines organizational efforts, and thus gives an incentive to calculate the costs and benefits of interest-politics. In a competitive polity, this will eventually weaken the tendency towards social closure in a declining economy. The pluralist group-school and most of its critics emphasized the associational benefits from interest politics, but ignored the transaction-costs which associations have to defray for the pursuit of monopolistic goals. To consider them, sheds some new light on the pluralist paradigm.

The regulation of competitive pluralism

In the following sections I will discuss two major points favoring social openness. The first argument is an extension of Transaction Cost Economics. It emphasizes the costs of competitive group-politics and economies of scale of associations. The second points to the rationally motivated openness of individual actors as it emanates from their multiple preferences and overlapping membership.

In institutional economics of the Olsonian type, actors do not consider transaction costs. Rational Choice Theories generally assume that men choose in a sudden, timeless, logical operation - without calculating the costs of information and the institutional obstacles to the realization of their choices. *Transaction Cost Economics* (Williamson 1975, 1985) and *Economic Theories of Regulation* (Becker 1983, 1986) however suggest that the costs of institutional arrangements will probably affect actor's choices. Hence these theories link individual choices to structural attributes and performance characteristics of organizations.

Interest intermediation - *pluralist pressure-politics* as well as *corporatist networking* - raises enormous costs in terms of information, mobilization and persuasion, decision-making, implementation, and bureaucracy (cf. Lehner, this volume). Thus, Becker's (1986) *"pressure-cost"* label could easily be extended to *general costs of interest politics*. His basic argument is that "Olson's condemnation of special interest groups is excessive, because competition among these groups contributes to the survival of policies that raise output" (Becker 1986:102). One should keep in mind that Olson himself predicts an ever-increasing number of special interest-groups competing with each other for shares of the national product. Now, Becker found that the costs of competitive interest politics are related to the *"dead-weight" losses resulting from it*. "Dead-weight" losses are incurred by the costs of lobbying, various restraints of transactions, the costs of collecting taxes and distributing subsidies, etc.

Becker (1986) demonstrated with the aid of a formal two-group model that regulations or subsidies reducing social outputs stimulate more countervailing pressures from cost-bearers than those increasing social outputs![7] This is mainly because the potential compensation of cost-bearers decreases owing to the dead-weight losses of cartelization and redistributive schemes. For example: compensating groups suffering from other's monopoly status is only possible if monopolistic associations provide regulations to their members, enabling them to increase their productive efficiency - technical norms would be a case in point. Apart from compensatory problems, dead-weight losses diminish the cost-benefit relation of beneficiaries:

---

7   In the following, only well-organized special-interest groups are considered. Therefore cost-bearers are not equated with tax-payers, as in Becker's model, but rather with special-interest groups that suffer from inefficiencies caused by distributional coalitions.

they get less for constant or even increasing costs of lobbying. This is partly due to the growing opposition of cost-bearers; their engagement pays more when their losses increase.

Becker's model assumes democratic governments which collect taxes and distribute subsidies. If one accounts for organizational costs of governmental redistribution and associational lobbying, then it follows that favorably affected groups tend to engage more for output-raising policies than unfavorably affected groups will be apt to oppose. On the other hand, policies that reduce output will encourage unfavorably affected groups to fight against and raise the marginal pressure costs of favorably affected groups.[8] Hence, in the long run, a few distributional coalitions cannot easily obtain very large subsidies.

After all, it is important to note that the activities of interest groups depend on their "individual" costs and expected benefits. Becker's concept provides a formalized model of pluralism that does not necessarily balance political powers (as in the traditional, normative pluralist hypothesis) but equilibrates the "price" of competitive policy-making. In contrast to economic markets, however, this "price" rises with an increase in competition. The more narrow-interest groups struggle against each other, the higher their individual "war-expenses" will be - as well as the "burdens of war" for a general public. One could think of Olson's wrestlers in a china shop, who expend all their energy, and yet only push up the price of china.

This is by no means meant to support Bentley's (1967) mechanistic view of competitive equilibrium in the pluralist politics of distributional conflict. In contrast, our view points to the cost/benefit

---

8   Likewise "an increase in the dead-weight costs of taxation encourages pressures by tax-payers because they are then harmed more by tax-payments. Similarly an increase in the dead-weight costs of subsidies discourages pressure by recipients because they then benefit less from subsidies received" (Becker 1986:101). This can explain variations in tax revolts among western industrialized countries. The more taxes wear off owing to inefficient administrations and politically determined misallocations, the less resources are available to compensate tax payers for their individual losses; and the smaller are the benefits for subsidized groups in relation to their costs of lobbying.

calculations of political actors. In democratic states, rising marginal costs of socially destructive interest-politics mark the limits of an excessively unbalanced growth of narrow interest groups.

The regulation of corporatist networks

It has been shown that inefficiencies of pluralist politics will eventually be checked by rising "prices" which single actors have to pay for competitive lobbying. This *invisible-hand mechanism* can, and under favorable historical conditions[9] will be discerned and influenced by the corporate actors involved. Assuming overlapping membership as well as the intersection of organizational goals, narrow interest groups could eventually overcome their rivalries in order to profit from the scale-economies and increased calculability of broader coalitions.[10] Here one comes close to the conception of *corporatist networks* (Lehmbruch 1984:74). These can be viewed as rationally motivated institutional arrangements to limit the potential threats and uncertainties of pluralist lobbying and ongoing distributional struggles. As a matter of fact, neo-corporatist institutions in industrial relations systems of Sweden, Austria, Germany, and the Netherlands have their origin in unhappy, costly experiences with conflict during the 1920s and 30s.

Once established, encompassing associations and corporatist networks are always threatened by internal conflict and the opposition of sub-groups (cf. Olson 1986). This is particularly true in periods of social and technological change. At the same time, single actors have to calculate the potential risks and benefits of breaking up

---

9   Examples of these conditions would be the specific economic problems of small countries suffering from turbulences of world markets, associational structures and historically determined state regulations, which enable or even force political actors to overcome or confine excessive distributional struggles (cf. Czada 1989).

10 In a game theoretical approach this would mean that distributional conflicts lose their zero-sum character. It is questionable however, whether antagonistic interest associations conciously choose a cooperative rule in order to raise their *future* pay-offs from an increased social output. On could also conceive strong organizational interests in saving *actual* costs of conflict, e.g. rich unions with considerable strike funds as in Sweden or Germany would then be more cooperative than those who have nothing to lose.

274 *Roland M. Czada*

their membership. Lack of information about alternatives, moving costs, and personal ties generally tend to support the status quo ante of "group solidarity" (Hechter 1987). This explanation of institutional persistence adds to an exchange hypothesis, which emphazises direct material rewards from corporatist cooperation and thus, implies a notion of *commutative* market-like justice between the parties involved.[11] It can also explain why corporatist networks tend to resist continuing temptations of participants to exploit each other in relationships of direct exchange. Even if an actor overreaches others in a single issue, this does not set off a chain of defection as suggested by "Tit for Tat" in order to enforce cooperation. The *distributive* justice of political associations and networks cannot be based on a rule of "Tit for Tat". Often "unequal" *political transfers* rather than market-like exchanges are necessary to stabilize institutions. Political transfers are apt to reduce uncertainties or elevated risks which would eventually raise transaction-costs and dead-weight losses of interest intermediation.

The competition among special-interest groups for political influence, as well as the encompassing organization of more general interests or corporatist networks, can all help to prevent excessive "dead-weight" losses from interest intermediation. The operational mechanisms however are different in both cases. Despite their internal cleavages, *encompassing associations* dispose of considerable economic resources and political power. More than narrow-interest groups, they are able to change their social and political environment in a systematic manner. The shaping of the Swedish welfare state by corporatist policies of unions and employers' associations is a case in point. Indeed, this may result in a "robbers' coalition" of large encompassing groups against the state budget (Lehner, this volume). Positive economic adjustments and economic welfare would eventually suffer from such practices. In open world markets however corporatist associations have no incentive to support national policies that slow down economic productivity. Due to their large size, they must

---

11 Hayek (1969:185) employs the analytical distinction of "commutative" and "distributive" justice; as for the corporatist exchange hypothesis, see Lehmbruch (1984, and this volume).

account for the social and economic effects of their policies on society as a whole, since these will eventually hurt their own members (Olson 1982:48).

Both pluralist competition and organized intermediation of interests typically support policies that raise output. One can, therefore, easily explain why "corporatist" Sweden, "paternalist" Japan, and "consociationalist" Switzerland- despite differences of structures of interest intermediation - do not suffer from economic regulations; and one can also explain why "pluralist" countries like the USA do not suffer from laissez-faire[12]. Of course, empirical structures and practices of interest intermediation and thus their effectiveness vary across countries. This is due to different national institutional configurations including parliaments, bureaucracies, and associational systems. Also distributions of power in given institutional settings vary. Additionally, national economies are burdened with different problems stemming from their size, openness, industrial structure, ethnic or religious cleavages, paths of industrialization, etc.. Corporatism, for example, appears to have been stimulated by centralized bureaucracies in small countries with highly centralized class based associations and open economies (Katzenstein 1985, Czada 1987, 1988, Weir/Scocpol 1985, Lehmbruch, this volume). Lehner (this volume) suggests that the nature of economic problems affect the appropriateness of certain institutional solutions.

In principle, *pluralism* and *corporatism* should provide *efficient* - though not necessarily democratic or just - allocative mechanisms. Only *sectoralism*, the rigid compartmentalization of narrow sectoral interests, generates endless disagreement, blockages, and socially

---

12 These countries are among the richest capitalist nations (in terms of GDP per capita), albeit they differ considerably when distributive issues are concerned. In our context however, the *structure* of interest intermediation and its effects on *productive* efficiency is in the fore. The *distribution* of wealth depends on state policies and the *relative power* of interest groups which are not discussed here. Of course, these are bound to structural aspects of interest systems (cf. Schmidt 1987, Czada 1987). In reality, however, one finds similar methods of social coordination with different power relations and participants: for instance one can find corporatism with (Sweden) or without labor (Japan) and pluralist structures with strong and well organized (Australia) labor unions or with disorganized labor (USA).

suboptimal outcomes. Hence, Olson might be right in pointing to sectarian unionism and to the British industrial relations crisis in order to substantiate his theoretical argument. However, the sectoralist structure of British industrial relations neither comes close to competitive pluralism like in the USA nor to trans-sectoral corporatism like in Sweden or Austria (cf. Czada 1983). British unions have rejected efforts of conservative governments to abolish closed shop regulations, picketing, or their close ties with the Labour Party. They have also resisted any attempts on the part of Labour governments to establish a Social Contract between the state and both sides of industry. This might be due to the highly antibureaucratic solidarity norms of union members.[13] Without bureaucratic formalization however, large groups cannot realize the scale-economies of associational action.

Scale-economies of associational action

To understand corporatism one has to scrutinize large _encompassing_ organizations, since these are the essential units of corporatist networks. In our context, encompassingness can be partly explained by scale-economies of associational action. I have argued that the cost/benefit relations of interest-politics are part of rational corporate actors' calculations - whether they enagage in pressure politics or corporatist networks. In this context, encompassing organizations can be viewed as _joint ventures_, economizing interest politics in fields where overlapping interests of otherwise narrowly defined groups are concerned. A peak association representing the common interest of its member associations in spite of the latter's persisting special interests would be a case in point. The federation of corporate actors depends on scale-economies similar to those of associations of individuals.

Indeed, small interest groups appear to be more efficient due to the size effects of free riding. However, they are handicapped at the

---

13 I owe this argument to Mary Douglas who, in a personal communication, called British unions _sectarian_, since their cultural attitude of personal solidarity paired with isolation from their wider social environment supresses any kind of formalization and inclusiveness of problem-solving.

same time "because small groups may not be able to take advantage of scale economies in the production of pressure" (Becker 1983:395). This argument would imply an advantage for large groups, as long as they are homogenous with respect of a specific interest. Scale economies of association allow for low membership dues and a wide range of selective incentives - like information hotlines, news-magazines, assurance schemes, emergency services, and many others. This makes it rather attractive to join, and thus facilitates the solution of free-rider problems. For example, a car driver's association with millions of members can be a very powerful political actor. Related interest associations of the manufacturers of cars, public transport systems, or road constructors would have to burden their fewer members with enormous dues, in order to keep with the financial resources of mass associations. The scale-economies of associations become even more politically important when one considers their potential to mobilize votes in democratic elections.

The importance of scale effects and administrative skills increase with an organization's involvement in politics. This holds true especially for the case of interest intermediation in corporatist systems. There, governments and state bureaucracies foster privileged relations with larger groups, for these are usually well-equipped with administrative skills and expertise, not to forget resources to obtain legitimacy. This is clearly shown by the Swedish system of interest intermediation. Participation in governmental commissions, executive committees, advisory bodies, hearings, and remiss-procedures is a costly matter. Quantitative data on the participation of Swedish interest groups in government show that only organizations with sufficient employment of qualified personnel including academic experts can effectively participate in legislation and government (Peterson 1977, cf. Lehmbruch, this volume). Thus, high costs of expertise and influence prevent formally open access and communication structures from being impaired by mass political participation.

Surveys have shown that politicians and leading board-officers consider representatives of well-organized large groups as most useful negotiating partners, to whom they try to give privileged access (Peterson 1977, Rothstein 1988). In turn, participation offers opportunities to compensate organizations for losses from governmental regulations. In this way, the large Swedish umbrella associations are stabilized by their participation in government, and are efficient in controlling free-riding as well as in taking advantage of scale economies of interest intermediation. Compared to Olson's "logic", this example demonstrates an effective and stable alternative of a more inclusive type of societal interest intermediation (Lehner 1987).

However, there is another integrative mechanism of interorganizational relations working on an individual level. Rothstein (1988:252) reports on group representatives of Swedish public agencies developing a "sort of psychological incorporation". They increased their understanding of other interests in society and eventually felt as if they were "sitting between two chairs". Now, similar aspects of interest politics have been investigated by the pluralist "group-school" under the headings of *"overlapping membership"*, individual *"cross-pressures"*, and *"fellow-travelling"*. These will be subject of the following paragraphs.

Beyond a simple world of homogeneous actors

Rational choice theories often view individuals as rather uninfluenced monads pursuing one indivisible purpose. This holds for many game theoretical models as well as for Olson's theory of collective action. The latter is based on a concept of *"narrow interest organizations"*, each of them representing one singular interest shared identically by all members. Consequently, internal disagreement is restricted to problems of how much of a collective good should be produced and at what cost, in terms of individual membership-fees. Even large "encompassing" associations - whose emergence remains obscure in Olson's theory - are treated as not having any problems with internal cohesion and "voice", but only with regard to threats of "exit" and "free-riding" (cf. Hirschman 1970). Thus, problems of organizational governance and bureaucratization appear to be minimized due to the *"monological"* (Offe and Wiesenthal 1980) conception of interest associations.

It is certainly not realistic to assume one-purpose "narrow-interest" associations, each of them representing a unique goal that is derived from one identical singular preference of each individual member. Individuals have manifold interests, and thus can belong to many groups in society. Realism, however, is not the only yardstick for a credible theory. One should therefore ask, whether this assumption prejudices the theory's central argument in such a way that its findings have to be taken as methodological artifacts. I will discuss this question by contrasting the pluralist concept of group-politics with Olson's (1965) economic theory of associations.

There is a widespread belief that Olson's "Logic of Collective Action" has defeated the whole theory of pluralism. Indeed, it has demonstrated that there is not - and will not be - a symmetrically organized society. In one respect, however, pluralists have been more realistic than Olson. The elder pluralist "group-school" (Bentley, Truman) as well as their later variants (Dahl, Lindblom) assumed individual *"cross-pressures"* and *"overlapping membership"* as being essential elements of group-politics. I would even go further and claim that "overlapping membership" has become a most important feature of political action in highly differentiated, *"post-modern"* societies. An increasing number of individual and corporate actors experience preference-conflicts when faced with the social multiplicity and complexity of highly industrialized countries.[14] For example: a unionized chemical worker who likes fishing down the river on Sundays and works in a chemical plant upriver during the week will probably experience a conflict of interest, if his union opposes sharper environmental regulations; and similar "cross-pressures" would also affect a shareholder of this firm, living somewhere along the river bank. Thus, overlapping preferences constitute integrative

---

14 Multiple interests of individuals not only disperse *across* groups with the effect of overlapping membership; likewise individual motives to associate can differ considerably *within* groups. That is because associations accomplish more than one task and provide for many services which usually attract their members in different mixtures (Keller 1988). Mixed motives to associate contribute to *associational heterogeneity*. Their effect on inter-organizational politics and policy-making usually adds to overlapping membership as an *integrative* force of associational systems.

forces, which often accentuate a more general interest on the level of individual actors[15].

> "As Arthur Bentley has put it: 'To say that a man belongs to two groups of men which are clashing with each other; to say that he reflects two seemingly irreconcilable aspects of the social life; to say that he is reasoning on a question of public policy, these all are but to state the same fact in three forms'. The phenomenon of the overlapping membership of social groups is thus a fundamental fact whose importance for the process of group politics, through its impact on the internal politics of interest groups, can scarcely be exaggerated." (Truman 1951:158).

The *pluralist "group-school"* provided for other elements that are worth considering in a concept of political choice and associational action. Among them, one finds the notion of *"fellow travellers"*. These sympathize with or completely share the goals of an interest group, without being due-paying members or "free-riders" of its organization. Nevertheless, "the loyalty of such "members" may be important to the successful achievement of a group's claims. Those in the dues-paying category differ from their "fellow-travellers", it is true, but both "may in varying degrees experience the conflicts of overlapping membership"(ibid.). "Fellow-travelling" stands for a *rationally motivated open-mindedness* that counteracts social closure and rigid structures. This also explains why group-politics, contrary to Olson's theory, does not necessarily result in "zero-sum" distributional struggles. Pluralism is based on loosely coupled networks of narrow-interest groups who compete against one another despite their continuing overlapping interests. Usually, this

---

15 Overlapping membership appears to be a social correlate of the individual *"multiple-self"* (Elster 1985). Multiple selves are often mediated through multiple social belongings. When many people experience them as contradictory and are "forced" to *"preference-falsification"*, i.e. to hide their latent preferences, sudden outbursts of public denomination can occur and *destabilize* societies. (See for instance Timur Kurans (1989, 1990) theory of revolutions, which is based on only two preferences or, as one could also say, belongings: public and private.) Therefore, in repressive societies, the intergrative effects of overlapping membership can rapidly change into desintegration, depending on social and political circumstances.

sort of coupling prevents intransigent divisiveness, institutional scle-rosis, or economic decline.[16]

Overlapping membership can be interpreted as a means of inte-gration, as has long been done by the pluralist "group-school". How-ever it also implies areas of conflict between organizations. I will substantiate the argument that overlapping membership has an im-pact on organizational structures and competitive external relations behavior of interest groups by presenting an example from the US-nuclear-power sector. In this case, one finds a few associational ac-tors with strong and specific interests in nuclear power operations. Despite their small size they have considerable problems of collective action that could only be solved with the aid of overlapping social networks.

Social networks and political action in the US nuclear power sector

In the US nuclear power sector one finds less than a handful of busi-ness associatons with very strong and very specific economic inter-ests in nuclear power operations. The associational structure over-laps with a multitude of contractual relationships between firms (e.g. electric utilities) and with rather informal social networks of manu-facturers, utilities, regulatory bodies, national laboratories, and the nuclear navy in fields of research, professional training, and techni-cal development. We are dealing with *small* overlapping narrow-in-

---

16 All the more in democratic systems with freedom of association, social closure does not establish such rigid and impermeable, and often mental, borders be-tween groups as one finds in medieval guilds or indian castes. These were based on a considerable extent of coercion. Besides, they did not represent nar-row interests but general ideological orientations which subdivided society in closed layers. Guilds and castes fully determined the lives of their members, and did not allow for overlapping membership. Nevertheless Olson (1982:157) calls them distributional coalitions, comparable to pluralist groups in modern western civilizations. Such historical examples fail to meet the essentials of voluntary association in modern societies. Guilds and castes did not allow for individual autonomy as it is required for rational individual choices. Though, ironically, Olson's rather unrealistic premise of one singular exogeneous indi-vidual preference being identical for all members of a group comes close to them.

terest groups faced by obstacles to cooperation in a sometimes hostile political environment.

US nuclear-power business interests are organized in a multitude of organizations, among which are the *"Atomic Industrial Forum"* (AIF), the *"American Nuclear Energy Council"* (ANEC), the *"Nuclear Utility Management and Resources Council"* (NUMARC), the *"Institute of Nuclear Power Operations"* (INPO), and others. Why is this small sector so heterogeneously organized, notwithstanding the fact that all actors strongly support nuclear power? My suggested answer points to conflicting interests in and between specific regulatory fields of the sector, and to heterogeneous political and administrative target structures. Taking all organizations involved as a promotional network, one finds rather different and even volatile preference orders within subsets of the network.

NUMARC deals with regulatory questions exclusively. Within this association, electric utilities operating nuclear power plants try to work out and implement a coherent strategy vis à vis the Nuclear Regulatory Commission (NRC). Other members, namely manufacturers and architect-engineers merely have observer status in NUMARC. This prevents possible conflicts of interests when state regulations are concerned: Manufacturers would probably support statutory regulations that prescribe expensive safety equipment, because it is their business to sell such equipment. Public utilities, on the other hand, try to negotiate compromises regarding such questions with the Nuclear Regulatory Commission. Among the utilities, one finds rather different views regarding the operation of nuclear power plants. Safety standards range from exemplary operations to the inefficient "black sheep" of the industry. Conflicts often arise when safety problems are concerend that can be solved by alternative technical or organizational measures. To reconcile possible conflicts and prevent non-compliance on the part of its members, NUMARC works on the basis of an 80 percent majority rule among its core membership of public utilitites.

Only the "Atomic Industrial Forum" is a registered lobbying association, representing the sector's very general interests in supportive legislation. However, this compels the AIF to be cautious regarding special issues such as safety regulations, licensing, standardization, etc. Coping with the sector's internal conflicts requires a complex design of organizations, based on high degrees of overlapping membership. Actors' choices within the sector's representational structure are determined by *cross-pressures*.

Individuals and corporate actors do have many, often contradictory and fluctuating preferences. This is why US-nuclear interests are not concentrated in one association: Manufacturers *sell* and utilities *buy* nuclear plants. Some utilities have none or only a few nuclear operations, while others rely heavily on nuclear energy. Architect-engineering firms don't like standardized reactor designs, whereas some manufacturers and utilities urge for standardization. Outside of these core-groups one finds professional associations, networks, and clans of private and public investors, assurance companies, research laboratories, and many other small special interest groups. Their preferences depend on different perceptions, rule systems, and sets of strategies. Due to their loyalty to the core groups, some of those, who are not due-paying members can be conceived of as "Fellow Travellers" of nuclear business associations. How important they are as *interlocutors* or *"relais"* (Crozier) will be demonstrated in the following paragraphs.

During the eighties, after the *nuclear accidents in Three Mile Island* and *Chernobyl*, the main preoccupation of US nuclear power business executives was to improve safety standards of nuclear operations. They had to agree on a strategy that could demonstrate their efforts in order to regain the support of investors, insurance companies, politicians, and not least the general public. The establishment of new corporate actors, like INPO in 1979 and NUMARC in 1987, was an attempt to create a structure with well-defined tasks and boundaries that should enhance cooperation among the utilities and with regulatory authorities. This large-scale reorganization of trade-associations and the overall sectoral network with Congress and the administrations could hardly be viewed as a political exchange. Only economically powerful, big companies and politically influential *"fellow travellers"* succeeded in reorganizing the representational structure and pressing the sector's "black sheep" into an agreement for this purpose. Exchange requires mututal compensation of the actors involved. INPO, however, has even disparaged several of its members before the public, in mass media, and political circles because of their safety problems.

INPO is an association whose ratings of safety and performance of nuclear power plants serve as a basis for the insurance rates of their members. Thus, INPO holds considerable leverage over individual companies. The system is based on agreement with private insurance carriers and is covered by special state legislation.[17] Together with NUMARC, INPO is part of a network that pools resources in order to produce and distribute expertise and services for the nuclear power sector. This network goes beyond the state of mutual supportive relations that governed the sector during the supportive period from the fifties to the mid-seventies. Prior to the "crisis-era", individual companies often relied on bipartite "deals" with executive agencies. This practice of compromising state regulatory functions led to the widespread opinion that the former *Atomic Energy Commission* was a "captured" agency. At the end of the eighties, however, the reorganized industry itself provided for a public good - namely nuclear safety. However, some of its members have long resisted the strategy of self-regulation. The former *clan-like network* aggregating rather general interests of the nuclear power sector had to be converted into a sort of hierarchical associational order. This required an institutionalization of action that has succeeded due to the severe political and economic crises suffered by the nuclear sector (Campbell 1988, 1989). Nevertheless, internal cleavages between sub-groups and former institutional structures determined the choice and the implementation of a new organizational structure. In the following, I will show the important role of social ties for the success of organizational reform. Major initiatives and the unification

---

17 According to the Price-Anderson Act passed in 1957, the government was committed to insure the difference between the amount of insurance available from private insurers and a $560 million limit for a single accident. In the 1980s the Price-Anderson Act was amended, making the industry's limits of liability and insurance rates depend on the performance and safety ratings provided by INPO for individual plants.

of action took place in a rather loosely coupled overlapping social network.

As an early reaction to "Three-Mile-Island" the "Institute of Nuclear Power Operations" was founded, evolving from the "Three Mile Island Ad Hoc Oversight Committee" at the end of 1979. This association set out to raise the economic efficiency and safety performance of nuclear power plants. Nearly half of its professional staff was recruited from the Nuclear Navy, as for instance INPO-Director Zech Pate, a former collaborator of Admiral Hyman Rickover. Rickover, the "father of the Nuclear Navy", had informally participated in the foundation of INPO together with Admirals Watkins (later the Secretary of the Department of Energy) and Carr (for many years commissioner and later Chairman of the Nuclear Regulatory Commission). It is said that the president of a major utility, who was also a former naval officer and leading member of the Three Mile Island Ad Hoc Oversight Committee, asked Rickover for his support in establishing INPO as a self-regulatory body, saying, "we need someone who can run INPO like you run the Navy". Rickover had widespread contacts with state administrations, National Laboratories, and parts of the manufacturing industry which built the first commercial power reactors for the US-Navy's submarines (Duncan 1990). After the accident at Three Mile Island, Rickover was an official advisor for nuclear safety and policy under President Carter, who himself had once been a naval cadet in the Rickover-Group. From then on, until his demission by President Reagan, Rickover had his office in the Department of Energy.

This case demonstrates the *"strength of weak ties"* (Granovetter). Their importance has already been emphasized in Truman's (1952) notion of *"fellow-travellers"*. Pluralists assumed that the varying degrees and complex overlappings of group-affiliations play an important role in group-politics and, generally, determine political action. The INPO case also shows the possible influence of state officials on the formation and activities of interest groups. Although the NRC consorts with INPO in a discrete manner, cooperative relations between state and group actors generally have been a domain of personal contacts. These, however, grew from specific meeting points of state and society, namely the Nuclear Navy and National Laboratories. Overlapping social networks of individuals also appear to have been a major cause for unitary action in the US nuclear power sector. At least this was true for the specific crisis situation investigated here.[18]

The question arises, why US nuclear power associations in a situation of distress "invested" in the organization of nuclear safety rather than expanding their previous pressure politics and lobbying? Olson's theory would lead us to expect the latter alternative, all the more since the core actors' interest and trust in nuclear power have remained unbroken. My suggested answer is that due to the increasing anti-nuclear opposition, competitive lobbying would have cost much more than during the 1950s and '60s. Simultaneously, its benefit became highly uncertain. Thus, investing in economic performance and higher safety standards was the only promising way to reduce the pressure of opposing parties, among them an increasing number of environmental groups,[19] parts of the financial sector, and of the energy policy community.

Our analysis has discerned two attributes of macro-structures influencing institutional choices: the *extent of uncertainty* in a given situation and the *expected cost/benefit relations of alternative paths of action*. Of course, actors often cannot or, if they possess superior power, need not calculate the transactional savings of organizational efforts in advance. Therefore Transaction Cost Economics hardly predicts the *initial emergence* and *growth* of interest associations. However, associations whose expenses on organization, expertise, and lobbying rise due to transactional losses will probably modify

---

18 Campbell (1986) reports about a clan-like network that helped to promote nuclear power during its formative period in the '50s. The question arises as to the extent that such unifying networks arise from traditions of social affiliation in scattered institutional structures. Of course, social networks can also be created or used as instruments for the purpose of actual state policies. Our analysis reveals, however, that during the eighties the networks of state-officials and business representatives as well as private associations were not exposed to any official interventions from state administrations such as the NRC.

19 One should hold in mind that environmental groups, particularly those living in the neighborhood of nuclear sites, are seen as special interest groups by the nuclear establishment.

their organizational strategy. This holds particularly when opposing groups seriously attack their power-position.

Olson's associational actor is based on certainty, because his theory does not consider preference conflicts, strategic dilemmas, or informational problems. In this view, even large encompassing organizations experience certainty in regard to their goals and strategies. However, there are obviously other types of voluntary associations which are based on high degrees of uncertainty and complex relations between their members. They provide complex goods by serving their members with controversial and transient solutions to intricate collective problems. Olson focuses on the first type, and conceives the second - politically the much more interesting one - as a logical absurdity. Admittingly, he does considers *"encompassing"*, heterogeneous large groups (Olson 1986), but they merely account for public welfare because of their size: by encompassing huge parts of society they cannot externalize the social costs of their group actions (cf. Lehner, this volume). This argument, however, does not apply to small groups serving public interests in nuclear safety, like INPO in the US nuclear sector. Even more important: the "encompassingness" of organizations is not a constituent part of Olson's theory. In fact, "encompassingness" is introduced as an ad-hoc argument in order to cope with reality. According to his basic argument such groups should not even exist.

Integrating the concepts of *cross-pressures, overlapping membership*, and *uncertainty* would soften the sharp contrast in Olson's theory between small and encompassing organizations. For these features belong to both small and large groups. This is clearly shown by the small networks of manufacturers and operators of US nuclear power plants. Their capacity to act is not determined by size, but by the *complexity* of purposes, means, and strategies of organizations. In addition to distinguishing "organizational size" in terms of the number of members, one should also consider "size" in terms of interest differentiation and the complexity of tasks. Groups with few members can involve even more complex tasks and a higher degree of structural complexity than groups with many members.[20] *Rising complexity*, however, tends to constitute motives for structural change. As tasks and distributional characteristics within the nuclear power sector became more complex, actors within the policy community urged for new specialized associations. The scope of tasks within nuclear associations narrowed as the number of associations increased. Contrary to Olson's theory, the new network of highly exclusive interest associations serves public interests in nuclear safety more than the former informal and somewhat inclusive clan-structure!

Conclusion

This chapter dealt with strategies of collective action pertaining to institutionalization. We found that the basic principles of political - in contrast to economic - action cannot be reduced to a logic of complementary mutual exchange. A theory of social order based on the *association* of individuals is certainly more realistic than models of bipartite exchanges in an *atomistic* society. This is not to deny the explanatory power of theories of rational choice and strategic interaction. Their premises and paradigmatic ideas of reciprocal action, however, are not adequate to the particular logic of political choice. The latter assumes that actors would try to escape dilemmas of strategic choice by involving others in associations and networks, or by establishing one-sided power-dependencies. Thus they strengthen themselves for future transactions. In doing so, actors hurt the premises of rational choice theories: - equal powers to reward or punish, - exogeneous preferences and discourse-free exchanges, - no

---

20 Although interest heterogeneity and the complexity of tasks are normally higher in large groups, size does not fully determine the dependency of collective action upon formal organization as Offe and Wiesenthal (1980) suggest. One should rather think of "size" as a twofold, output and product related, concept. On the one hand, associational problems depend on the volume and complexity of *organizational "products"* like nuclear monitoring, wage-contracts, or technical norms. Simultaneously, there is an *input related dimension of size*, the number and homogeneity of membership, which affects the production of associational goods. It would be wrong, however, to assume a linear positive relationship between these different measures of organizational "size".

costs of decison-making and transactions, - consequential action that is ambiguous in regard to individual *re*-actions, but guided by a well-defined and generally known reward-pattern. An approach based on this premises could hardly deal with some of the most important features of politics: *power-dependency; uncertainty, changing reward-structures; costly transactions;* efforts of *collective organization* and resulting *institutional rigidities; discourse* and *social affiliations,* as well as *ideological commitments.*

Political actors interested in strengthening their power position in the face of distributional conflict have an incentive to build or join coalitions. Thus, characteristic problems of associational order and (inter)organizational relations arise. The ubiquity of powerful corporate actors would let us expect social closure, structural rigidity, and ever-increasing individual committments.

Social closure and ridigties of political representation and income-distribution have been held responsible for declining economies by many economists and politicians. In reality, however, the flexibility and adaptibility of institutions varies considerably across nations; and it is still an open question: how markets and interest associations interact, and how economic welfare is affected by these forms of governance. This chapter should have shed some light on a specific facet of this issue. Starting with Olson's "stagnation hypothesis", I have tried to explain why social rigidities are much less ubiquitous in democratic systems than predicted, or, in other words, why economies that are dominated by pluralist or corporatist group politics can be efficient in the long run. Of course one could present further explanations dealing with factors such as cultural attitudes, consensual orientations, associational hierarchies, smallness of countries, traditions of a strong administrative state, openness of the legislative process and of administrations, etc. Generally, those explanations pertain to national paths of institutionalization (cf. Katzenstein 1984, 1985, Weir/Skocpol 1985, Czada 1987, Lehmbruch, this volume). Historical explanations are certainly correct, but not fully statisfying when confronted with such deductive nomological theories as Mancur Olson's "Rise and Decline of Nations".

Three principle mechanisms have been identified that counter-poise social rigidities and economic decline. In general, they encourage actors to choose strategies resulting in social openness and the universalisation, as well as the efficiency of social order. In particular, however, their concrete operations depend on institutional and cultural prerequisites, and do not solve the manifold problems of economic governance in an equally efficient manner. Hence, their effectiveness may vary across countries with different institutions, social cleavages, and economic problems.

- *Competitive relations between groups.* These can and will probably be regulated in order to reduce the risks of distributional struggles and the costs of competitive lobbying. However, in the face of scarce resources, the possibilities of cartellization are also limited. Many groups suffering from distributional coalitions are rather small and well-organized. Hence, they can easily oppose the collusive action of others. Generally, one can say that in a competitive political environment and at a constant level of associability, interest groups which raise social output meet less opposition, and therefore have less problems strenghtening their position in society than harmful Olsonian distributional coalitions. Moreover, the example of U.S. nuclear interest-associations has shown that group size is an insufficient indicator of associability. One has to account for the historically determined complexity of preference-structures and of applied technologies, as well as for environmental turbulences and scales of conflict in societal sectors.

- *Scale-economies of associations.* It has been shown that group politics, even of small special interest groups, raises costs of organization, expertise, bargaining, and lobbying. Large groups can afford an effective management and a rich supply of selective services on the basis of low membership dues. Thus, scale-economies of associations provide for an inherent solution of the free-rider problem. This is particularly true when individual risks are involved that can be averted through membership. Moreover, scale-economies contribute to the professionalization, opportunitites of strategic interaction, and efficiency of associational management. The example of US-nuclear interest associations shows that autonomous associational bureaucracies can enlarge the somewhat restricted world-views of special-interest groups. Whether groups can profit from associational scale-economies, however, depends on the scale of internal conflict, ideological commitments,[21] and on external threats in specific historical constellations.

- *Overlapping membership and the social embeddedness of political action.* Individuals have multiple, often conflicting preferences which they share with different social groups. Theories starting from exogeneous *singular* preferences of individuals, as for instance Olson's "stagnation hypothesis", necessarily arrive at a perception of narrow interest groups interacting in a socially destructive manner. In contrast, overlapping membership as emphasized by pluralist theory mitigates social conflict. It causes individual cross-pressures and can foster a rationally motivated open-mindedness towards various interests in society. Besides, multiple preferences encourage "fellow-travelling" (Truman 1951:158) that can be thought of as a counterpart to free-riding. Fellow-travellers support goals of organizations without belonging to the dues-paying members. Expanding this argument leads to a concept of "social embeddedness" which stresses the link between institutions, interests, and values such as: sociability, approval, loyalty, compromise, justice, and status (Granovetter 1985). How "overlapping membership" and "fellow-travelling" affect

---

21 Ideological commitments influence the costs of unitary action. They can reduce the transaction-costs of organizational order (North 1981), or, if sectarian solidarity norms prevail, restrict internal bureaucratization and inter-group coordination (cf. footnote 10).

national or sectoral policies depends on the recruitment, structure, and placement of elites in national systems.[22]

According to our analysis, there is still some truth in the pluralist belief that group politics promote allocative efficiency and economic wealth. One apparently has to separate this argument from the normative assumptions of the pluralist theory of democracy. Pluralism does not fully support democracy, since freedom of association does not provide for the symmetrical organization and representation of interests in a society (Olson 1965). However, this does not render the whole theory of pluralism worthless. A bias of representation does not necessarily effect the *allocative principles* of competitive group-politics; though it can fundamentally change the distribution of its *actual outcomes*. So far, the analysis revealed an elitist organized pluralism which is economically efficient.

In particular, the Olsonian critique has failed to respond to pluralist assumptions about the social nature and multiplicity of individual interests. Rising levels of welfare and social differentiation helped enlarge the wants and preferences of individuals. The concomitant increase of overlapping membership favors a kind of openness and "fellow-travelling" contrasting sharply with Olsons's implicit premise of single exogeneously given individual interests, being exclusively organized in monopolistic special interest associations. Rational choice theories commonly assume unitary actors choosing on the basis of one preference.[23] Actually, one can find an ethic of absolute ends followed by politicians and political parties. This, however, tends to diminish opportunities for political choice and, in allowing no compromises, bears premodern features of narrow-mindedness and irrationality.

---

22 To illustrate: the Swiss body of militia officers penetrates the command posts of political and economic organizations; in Austria, Sweden, and Norway one finds close ties of economic experts of unions and employers' associations caused by the small numbers of economic faculties in small countries. The role of the U.S. nuclear navy for the civilian nuclear power operations described in this chapter would also be a case in point.

23 In game theory, the "Battle of the Sexes" constellation represents an exception. There two actors have one overlapping, common preference and one exclusive, opposing preference each (Scharpf, this volume, p. 64).

In his essay "Politics as a Vocation", Max Weber (1965) emphasized that struggling for one ultimate end lacks rationality, since the eventual costs of means and side-effects of such struggles can hardly be calculated. The pursuit of a singular end tends to blind political actors to the manifold social consequences of their action and tempt them into the use of bad means. Both blindness and temptation sap their abilities for strategic interaction. Rational actors have to account for the burdens of their means and consider a multiplicity of side-effects which may eventually hurt their own interests. Wrestling in a china shop - according to Olson (1982:44) the essence of group politics - is certainly not the best way to acquire more pieces of china (and especially to keep them). In situations that are characterized by high levels of mutual dependency of individuals and social groups, the ethic of singular absolute ends has self-destroying consequences. This is particularly true when propertied social groups bear a risk of losing. All the more, they will calculate the mode and costs of distributional conflict in advance. Therefore, in today's welfare states, the poor cost/benefit relation of distributive struggles and the rationally motivated openness and sociability of men usually prevent more economic damage than Olson's stagnation hypothesis would let us expect.

References

Arrow Kenneth J. (1963) *Social Choice and Individual Values* (rev. Edition of 1951). New York: Wiley.

Axelrod, Robert (1984) *The Evolution of Cooperation*. New-York: Basic Books.

Becker, Gary (1983) 'A Theory of Competition among Pressure Groups for Political Influence', *Quarterly Journal of Economics* 98: 329-347.

Becker, Gary (1986) 'Public Policies, Pressure Groups and Dead Weight Costs', pp. 85-105 in George W. Stigler (ed.), *Chicago Studies in Political Economy*. Chicago: Univ. of Chicago Press.

Bentley, Arthur F. (1967) 'The Process of Government'. Cambridge. Mass.: Harvard University Press (first published in 1908 by the Univ. of Chicago Press).

Brennan, Geoffrey and James M. Buchanan (1985) *The Reason of Rules*. Cambridge: Cambridge University Press.

Buchanan, James M. (1954) 'Individual choice in voting and the market', *Journal of Political Economy* 62: 334-343.

Buchanan, James M. (1975) *The Limits of Liberty: Between Anarchy and Leviathan*. Chicago: Chicago University Press.

Campbell, John L. (1988) *Collapse of an Industry. Nuclear Power and the Contradictions of U.S. Policy*. Ithaca and London: Cornell Univ. Press.

Campbell, John L. (1989) 'Corporations, Collective Organization, and the Industry Response to the Accident at Three Mile Island', *Social Science Quarterly* 70: 650 - 666.

Coleman, James S. (1986) *Individual Interests and Collective Action*. New York: Cambridge University Press.

Crouch, Colin (1982) *Trade Unions: The Logic of Collective Action*. London: Fontana.

Czada, Roland (1983) 'Konsensbedingungen und Auswirkungen neokorporatistischer Politikentwicklung', *Journal für Sozialforschung* 23: 421-440.

Czada Roland M. (1987) 'The impact of interest politics on flexible adjustment policies', pp. 20-53 in Hans Keman, Heikki Paloheimo and Paul F. Whiteley (eds.) *Coping with the Economic Crisis. Alternative Responses to Economic Recession in Advanced Industrial Societies*. London: Sage.

Elster, Jon (ed.) (1985) *The Multiple Self*. Cambridge, Mass.: Cambridge University Press.

Elster, Jon (ed.) (1986) *Rational Choice*. New York: New York University Press.

Etzioni, Amitai (1968) *The Active Society. A Theory of Societal and Political Processes*. New York: The Free Press.

Granovetter, Mark (1985) 'Economic Action and Social Structures: The Problem of Embeddedness', *American Journal of Sociology* 91: 481 - 510.

Hayek, Friedrich August v. (1969) *Freiburger Studien - Gesammelte Aufsätze*. Tübingen: Mohr-Siebeck.

Hechter, Michael (1987) *Priciples of Group Solidarity*. Berkeley and London: University of California Press.

Hechter, Michael, Karl-Dieter Opp, and Reinhard Wippler (eds.) (1990) *Social Institutions: Their Emergence, Maintenance, and Effects*. New York and Berlin: Aldine.

Hirschman, Albert O. (1970) *Exit, Voice and Loyalty. Responses to Decline in Firms, Organizations and States*. Cambridge, Mass.: Harvard University Press.

Hollingsworth, J. Rogers and Leon Lindberg (1985) 'The governance of the American Economy: The role of markets, clans, hierarchies, and associative behavior', pp. 221-254 in Wolfgang Streeck and Philippe C. Schmitter (eds.) *Private Interest Government*. Beverly Hills: Sage Publications.

Katzenstein, Peter (1984) *Corporatism and Change*. Ithaca, N.Y., London: Cornell University Press.

Katzenstein, Peter (1985) *Small States in World Markets. Industrial Policy in Europe*. Ithaca, N.Y., London: Cornell University Press.

Keller, Berndt (1988) 'Olson's "Logik des kollektiven Handelns". Entwicklung, Kritik - und eine Alternative', *Politische Vierteljahresschrift* 29: 388 - 406 .

Kuran, Timur (1989) 'Sparks and Prairie Fires. A Theory of Unanticipated Political Revolution', *Public Choice* 61: 41-74

Kuran, Timur (1990) 'Private and Public Preferences', *Economics and Philosophy* 6: 1-26

Lange, Peter (1984) 'Unions, Workers, and Wage Regulation: The Rational Bases of Consent', pp. 98-123 in John H. Goldthorpe (ed.) *Order and Conflict in Contemporary Capitalism. Studies in the Political Economy of Western European Nations.* Oxford, New York: Oxford University Press.

Lash, S. (1985) 'The End of Neo-Corporatism? The Breakdown of Centralised Bargaining in Sweden', *British Journal of Industrial Relations,* 23: 215-39.

Latham, Earl (1952) *The Group Basis of Politics.* Ithaca: Cornell University Press.

Lehmbruch (1984) 'Concertation and the Structure of Corporatist Networks', pp. 60 - 80 in John H. Goldthorpe (ed.) *Order and Conflict in Contemporary Capitalism. Studies in the Political Economy of Western European Nations.* Oxford, New York: Oxford University Press.

Lehner, Franz (1987) 'Interest Intermediation, Institutional Structures and public policy', pp. 54-82 in Keman, Hans, Heikki Paloheimo, and Paul F. Whiteley, *Coping with the Economic Crisis.* London, Beverly Hills: Sage.

Hollingsworth, Rogers C. and Leon Lindberg (1985) 'The Governance of the American Economy: The Role of Markets, Clans Hierarchies, and Associative Behavior', pp. 221 - 252', in Wolfgang Streeck and Philippe C. Schmitter (eds.) *Private Interest Government.* London, Beverly Hills: Sage .

March, James G. and Johan P. Olsen (1989) *Rediscovering Institutions.* New York: Free Press.

Marin, Bernd (1986) *Unternehmerorganisationen im Verbändestaat. Politik der Bauwirtschaft in Österreich,* vol I. Vienna: Internationale Publikationen.

Marin, Bernd (1990) *Generalized Political Exchange.* Frankfurt, Boulder, Col.: Campus/Westview Press.

McLean, Ian (1987) *Public Choice.* An Introduction. Oxford: Basil Blackwell.

Moe, Terry M. (1984) 'The New Economics of Organization', *American Journal of Political Science* 28: 739-777.

Mueller. Dennis C (1979) *Public Choice,* Cambridge: Cambridge Univ. Press.

Niskanen, William A. (1971) *Bureaucracy and Representative Government.* Chicago: Rand McNally.

North, Douglas C. (1981) *Structure and Change in Economic History.* New York: Norton.

Offe, Claus (1981) 'The Attribution of Public Status to Interest Groups. Observations on the West German Case', pp. 123-158 in Berger Suzanne (ed.) *Organizing Interests in Western Europe.* Cambridge: Cambridge University Press.

Offe, Claus and Helmut Wiesenthal (1980) 'Two Logics of Collective Action: Theoretical Notes on Social Class and Organizational Form', *Political Power and Social Theory* 1: 67-115.

Olson Mancur (1965) *The Logic of Collective Action.* Cambridge: Harvard University Press.

Olson, Mancur (1982) *The Rise and Decline of Nations. Economic Growth, Stagflation and Social Rigidities.* New Haven/London: Yale University Press.

Olson, Mancur (1986) 'A theory of incentives facing political organizations', *International Political Science Review* 7: 165-189.

Opp, Karl-Dieter (1983) *Die Entstehung sozialer Normen: Ein Integrationsversuch soziologischer, sozialpsychologischer und ökonomischer Erklärungen.* Tübingen: Mohr-Siebeck.

Ouchi, William G. (1980) 'Markets, bureaucracies, and clans', *Administrative Science Quarterly* 25: 129-141.

Peterson, Eric, A. 1977: *Interest Group Incorporation in Sweden. A Summary of Arguments and Findings,* ms., Washington DC: APSA-Annual Conference, 1.-4. Sept. 1977.

Rothstein, Bo (1988) 'State and Capital in Sweden: The Importance of Corporatist Arrangements', *Scandinavian Political Studies* 11: 235-260.

Scharpf, Fritz W. (1989) *Games Real Actors Could Play: The Problem of Complete Information.* Köln: Max-Planck-Institut für Gesellschaftsforschung Discussion Paper 89/9.

Schmidt, Manfred, G. (1987) 'The Politics of Labour Market Policy. Structural and Political Determinants of Rates of Unemployment in Industrial Nations', pp. 4-53 in Francis G. Castles, Franz Lehner, and Manfred G. Schmidt (eds.) *Managing Mixed Economies.* Berlin, New York: Walter de Gruyter.

Schmitter, Phillippe C. (1981) 'Interest Intermediation and Regime Governability', pp. 287-330 in Suzanne Berger (ed.) *Organizing Interests in Western Europe. Pluralism, Corporatism and the Transformation of Politics.* Cambridge: Cambridge Univ. Press.

Schwerin, Don S. (1980) 'The Limits of Organization as a Response to Wage Price Problems', pp. 71-106 in Richard Rose (ed.) *Challenge to Governance.* London, Berverly Hills: Sage.

Truman David B. (1951) *The Governmental Process. -Political Interest and Public Opinion.* New York: Alfred E. Knopf.

Vanberg, Viktor (1982) *Markt und Organisation. Individualistische Sozialtheortie und des Problem korporativen Handelns.* Tübingen: Mohr-Siebeck.

Weber, Max (1972) *Wirtschaft und Gesellschaft. Grundriss der verstehenden Soziologie.* 5th. ed., Tübingen: Mohr-Siebeck.

Weber, Max (1968) *Economy and Society. An Outline of Interpretive Sociology.* Berkeley, London: Univ. of California Press.

Weber, Max (1965) *Politics as a Vocation.* Philadelphia: Fortress Press (first published in German 1919).

Weir, Margaret and Theda Skocpol (1985) 'State Structures and the Possibilities for "Keynesian" Responses to the Great Depression in Sweden, Britain, and the United States', pp. 107 - 168 in Evans, Peter B., Dietrich Rueschemeyer and Theda Skocpol (eds.) *Bringing the State Back In.* Cambridge, New York: Cambridge University Press.

Williamson, Oliver E. (1975) *Markets and Hierarchies. Analysis and Antitrust Implications. A Study in the Economics of Internal Organisation.* New York: Free Press.

Williamson, Oliver E. (1985) *The Economic Institutions of Capitalism. Firms, Markets, Relational Contracting.* New York: Free Press.

Name Index

Subject Index

AUTONOMY

associational 204, 247, 250; individual 32; institutional 43, 102, 123 pp.; bureaucratic 123 pp., 148, 151; political 176, 262; power and 262; state 34, 36, 103 pp.

BARGAINING 41, 45, 58, 60, 63, 69, 70, 71, 99, 100, 106, 163, 202, 243, 244, 247, 252

"BATTLE OF THE SEXES" 12, 16

BEHAVIOR

appropriate 91; associative 27, 224; bureaucratic 27; competitive of interest groups 281; of decision makers 94; solutions, problems and 90; electoral 35; environment and 34; established patterns of 139; ethical 97; human 32; individual preferences and 46; of interest groups 247; normative approriate 91; norms governing market 203; organization and 96; organizational 89, 90, 91; of organizational members 92; organizing 181; political 28, 31, 35, 36; rational purposive 170; routinized 90; social 32; social rules and 41, 18; strategic 219, 223; style of decision-making 69; traditional 32; of transaction partners 209; value-oriented 32

BELGIUM

medium corporatism 247

BOUNDED RATIONALITY 17, 90, 215, 216, 223

information problems 89 pp.; and opportunism 215, 223

BUREAUCRACY

autonomy of 124; centralized 142; costs of 271; discretion of 124; ethos of 19, 151; formative phases of 18, 135 pp.; general interest and 150; Hegels notion of 150; hierarchy and 131; interest intermediation and 123; "iron cage" of;. 257; organization 91, 170, 174; parliamentary control of 32; policy networks and 135, 148; poltitical dialog of 59; powerful groups and 107; professional 138; social organization and 124; social organizations and 144; strategic codes of 18, 148 pp.; strategies of 131; unitary 18, 54

BUREAUCRATIC STATE 146

BUREAUCRATIZATION 262

BUSINESS ASSOCIATIONS

class interests vs. production interests 188; optimal size 173

CANADA 141

business associations & unions 178; collective bargaining 185; trade associations 204

CAPTURE

executive agency and 284; of bureaucracies 151

FISCAL POLICY 238
FLEXIBLE SPECIALIZATION 59
FRANCE 142, 144, 145
banking regulation 244; bureaucratic elite 123; bureaucratic tradition 144; cartels 221; illegitimatcy of corporatism 145; industrial policy 244; public financing 241

GAME THEORY 6, 63, 260
Assurance Game 64 pp., 70; Battle of the Sexes 64, 65, 69, 70, 71, 266; Chicken Game 64, 65, 70; equality of actors 261; Prisoner's Dilemma 64, 65, 70, 71, 260; rule systems 261
GENERAL INTEREST 150
GERMANY 140, 142, 146, 147, 273
anti-trust policies 221; business associations 177; cartels 206, 221; construction policy 45; de-facto unanimity 75; federalism 59; health policy 36, 41; medium corporatism 247; public financing 241; rules governing federalism 73; trade associations 207, 211; tripartism 35
GOALS
choice of 55; normative 54
GOVERNABILITY
and distributional conflict 265; of western democracies 233
GOVERNANCE
associational 202, 278; bargaining and 58; bureaucratic 200; of competitive relations 207; economic

GOVERNANCE (CONT.)
122, 201; emergence of 261; equilibrium and 110; forms 218; and interest intermediation 6; levels of 19; market 204; through networks 200; non-market 205, 208; problems of 289; state and 224; structures of 201, 216; theory of 199, 211; transaction-costs and 21; change of 20, 200, 209; unanimous agreement 58 and welfare 21, 289;
GOVERNMENT 9, 96, 112, 233 pp.
benefits of 261; intervention 53, 105, 125 pp., 235 pp. organized interests and 18, 121 pp., 163 pp., 272, 277 pp.; regulatory function 58 pp., 244, 276
GREAT BRITAIN 122, 133, 136, 142
cartels 221; collective bargaining 185; health policy 36; Keynesianism 35; public financing 241; sectarian unionism 275
GROUP POLITICS
costs of 270 pp.
GROUP-POWER
ordering potential of 268

HEALTH POLICY 36, 41, 125, 127, 132
HETEROGENEITY
of interests 171 pp., 178, 182 pp., 186, 195, 280n, 286; of interest systems 128 pp., 161 pp., 167, 217, 282
INFORMATIONAL PROBLEMS 11, 29 pp., 89, 123 pp., 130, 216, 270, 273, 286
INSTITUTE OF NUCLEAR POWER OPERATIONS 282, 285 pp.

INSTITUTIONAL
autonomy 43, 102, 123 pp.; development 101; equilibrium 43
INSTITUTIONAL ECONOMICS 6, 270
INSTITUTIONALIZATION
of class conflict 140; collective choices and 259; game theory and 260; governance and 6, 101, 199, 284; national paths of 12, 139 pp.; policy networks and 125, 127, 139, 148; of political action 257 pp., 288, 289; public goods problem 258; time-horizont of action and 269
INSTITUTIONS
advantages of 257; as constraints 29, 54; authoritative 261; choice-genesis of 39; definition of 57; non-intendended effects of 40; stickiness of 257 pp., 268; two faces of 41
INTEREST INTERMEDIATION 59, 123
administrative 149, 122 pp.; consociationalist 22, 243 pp.; comprehensive 238; corporatist 99, 121 pp., 164 pp., 133 pp., 237 pp. 250, 275, 277 pp.; cross-national variations of 124, 128 pp.; and economic efficiency 22, 238 pp., 270 pp.; encompassing 235, 244, 248 pp., 273 pp.; levels of 122, 129, 134; networks of 125 pp., 134+ pp., 281; patterns of 58, 128, 134, 237, 271; pluralism 126, 134 pp., 173, 184, 233, 237, 245, 270 pp., 278 pp., 285, 289, 291
INTERMINISTERIAL COORDINATION 66

INVISIBLE-HAND MECHANISM
politics as intervention in 273
ITALY 72
public financing 241

JAPAN 275
anti-trust 221; banking regulation 243; cartels 206, 211, 221 pp.; concordance 242; industrial policy 241; management style 59; neo-corporatism 251; public financing 241; trade associations 207, 211

KEYNESIANISM 42, 54, 190
Great Britain 35; Sweden 35

LEGAL ORDER
limiting competition 267
LEGITIMACY
disributional conflict and 234, 267; encompassing associations and 277; institutions providing 97; maintenance of 33; of collective decisions 234; of rules 72, 93; of standards 100; of state-society interactions 122, 124, 148; organization of 262; participation of interests and 123; problems of 234; stability, efficiency and 237; symmetry, efficiency and 163; unanimity rule and 234
LOBBYING
nuclear power interests and 283
MACRO-ECONOMIC POLICY 55
MAJORITIES
changing 234; instable 235